In the Spellmount/Nutshell Military list:

The Territorial Battalions – A pictorial history
The Yeomanry Regiments – A pictorial history
Over the Rhine – The Last Days of War in Europe
History of the Cambridge University OTC
Yeoman Service
The Fighting Troops of the Austro-Hungarian Army
Intelligence Officer in the Peninsula
The Scottish Regiments – A pictorial history
The Royal Marines – A pictorial history
The Royal Tank Regiment – A pictorial history
The Irish Regiments – A pictorial history
British Sieges of the Peninsular War
Victoria's Victories
Heaven and Hell – German paratroop war diary
Rorke's Drift
Came the Dawn – Fifty years an Army Officer
Kitchener's Army – A pictorial history
Marlborough – As Military Commander
On the Word of Command – A pictorial history of the RSM
Scandinavian Misadventure
Epilogue in Burma 1945-48
Blitz over Britain
Napoleon's Military Machine
Wellington's Military Machine
Falklands Military Machine
The Art of Warfare in the Age of Marlborough
The Indian Army of the Empress 1861-1903
The Fall of France
The First Victory – O'Connor's Triumph in the Desert Dec 1940-Feb 1941
Deceivers Ever – Memoirs of a Camouflage Officer

In the Nautical list:

Sea of Memories
Evolution of Engineering in the Royal Navy Vol I 1827-1939
In Perilous Seas

In the Aviation list:

Diary of a Bomb Aimer
Operation 'Bograt' – From France to Burma – Memoirs of a Fighter Pilot
A Medal for Life – Capt Leefe Robinson VC

C.A. Form 24

PILOT'S LOG BOOK

The Third Generation
(1936 To 1965)

WILFRED EMM

First published in the UK in 1990 by
Spellmount Ltd
12 Dene Way, Speldhurst
Tunbridge Wells, Kent TN3 0NX

British Library Cataloguing in Publication Data
Emm, Wilfred
    Three Decades a pilot.
    1. Aeroplanes. Flying – Biographies
    Rn; W. T. Mellor I. Title
    629.13092
    ISBN 0-946771-97-9

Typesetting by The KPC Group, Ashford, Kent
Printed in Great Britain

ACKNOWLEDGEMENTS

Special thanks to Mrs Jessie Coates and her family for their agreement to the dedication of this book to the memory of her husband Charles. Also to Mrs Ly Bennett for her approval of passages directly concerning her husband who was at the time Captain (later Air Vice Marshal) D C T Bennett.

To the many friends (too numerous to mention individually without creating a special booklet) whose solicited criticism has humbled the original text into something more acceptable, corrected grammar and expressions, suggested change in format, edited, typed, proofread, debunked some arrant nonsense and injected shots of sound common sense, lending their long-suffering ears the while to my grizzles – I can only say 'thank-you' and trust you will know how very deeply that is meant, for (without all that) the project would have ended in a ripped-up heap at the local garbage dump.

AUTHOR'S NOTE

This book is not a work of fiction. The incidents, and circumstances under which they happened, relate directly to the personal flying log books of the main character and form the factual basis of the story. Apart from the names of some well known people, companies and their managers, and those of some personnel involved with the 1940/41 ATFERO (Atlantic Bomber Ferry Organisation), all others are fictitious and any similarity to persons living or dead is purely coincidental.

The sketches and maps and Dust Cover design are very much the amateur work of the author. They serve to impress atmosphere, geography, and aircraft configurations to assist in following the text. The aircraft registrations (civil and military) are correct in every detail, and refer to those described in the text.

CONTENTS

REMEMBERING CAPTAIN C E COATES
(1924 to 1987)

Charles, firm friend, relentless taskmaster,
epitome of all that is best in my
generation – a truly humble great achiever.

ILLUSTRATIONS

FOREWORD

A 'generation' is defined in the Oxford Dictionary as being a period of about 30 years for persons born at about the same time. It has a bearing on the purpose of this book which is to do with a 'generation of commercial air pilots', unique in the annals of civil aviation, and covers a period in which technical developments for both personnel and machines were themselves unique.

In every aspect of life each generation influences the next, especially where learning and character development is concerned. When each generation reached around 30 years of age their knowledge will begin to be passed on to the next, and so on.

In most countries commercial pilots retire at the age of 55, but are unlikely to have gained enough training and experience to be employed as co-pilots until the age of 25 years. Therefore, with a working life of a further 30 years, perhaps only half will influence the next generation.

The first two generations, covering the between-wars period, learned the hard way with little help available from past experience. The second, having benefited from the first in terms of rule of thumb 'dos and don'ts', had to absorb and apply rapidly developing technical innovations. Thanks to those two the third generation began their careers with a great deal of common sense know how on which to build their own experience. They were also able to draw on generously given advice for quite a few more years during a challenging period of major development in aircraft design, engines, navigation, radio and radio aids.

From 'stick and string' biplanes through prop-jets to the early pure jet aircraft; from 'nil' radio facilities – (other than radio officer operated morse code communications) – to VHF and UHF pilot operated systems; from no radio navigational facilities to computerised inertial systems, and through a war period often without any basic navigational or uncoded communications at all.

It is no denigration in the least to the incredible feats and innovative exploits of those first two generations to say that their pupils had a uniquely challenging period for personal initiative. There were constant adaptations to changes in aircraft and engine design, equipment, navigation and communication facilities and procedures, not the least of the latter being international regulatory introductions to cover improved safety in flight, maintenance, and design parameters in all major – (and many minor) – areas. There were no heroes, just ordinary people doing an everyday job.

This book is in effect a biography, all events being taken strictly from a pilot's log books over a third generation period from 1936 to 1965. It is mainly concerned with small air charter and independent airline operations, including wartime BOAC when conditions were similar, rather than scheduled airline work as known today which could, arguably, cover a lesser variation of experiences. Work loads, problems, and satisfaction would however have been very similar for both types of operation during that period. A great deal of personal initiative was required, additional to the absolute command by captains allied to acceptance of absolute responsibility and self-confidence which remains a pre-requisite of the job today. That confidence has to be tempered with genuine humility to admit the possibility of making a mistake, to take every precaution against that, ever mindful (to quote Don Bennett) that 'Eternal Vigilance is the Price of Safety' – the day-to-day basic criteria observed by all commercial pilots, no matter which generation.

In this narrative the pilot concerned is named simply 'Jim'. Although the events are taken directly from his very detailed log books the book is not about him personally, nor is it a novel. It is intended to illustrate a career common in the main to most third generation pilots. Anyone who was there in any of the recorded occasions will recognise his real name, but for the readers for whom the book has really been written (the non-flying citizen), the intention is to describe an era unique in British Civil Aviation history, not the story of a single personality. It deliberately avoids real or hearsay details of any individual's personal life except, very broadly, Jim's own.

It is hoped that the many people to this day nervous of flying, in particular those who have no other alternative yet must travel, will find comfort and interest in following through the 30 year sequence of events leading up to the supremely safe and efficient conditions enjoyed by all sectors of commercial flight in the 1980s and beyond. Even in the early days civil aviation was (statistically) the safest, if not always the most comfortable or reliable, form of travel.

PART I – (1936 to 1946)
Fledgling, through war, to the chaos of peace

1 Fledgling 1936-1939

It was 29 June 1927, very early on a warm, hazy summer's morning in the seaside town of Southport, Lancashire, England. Huge crowds equipped with heavily smoked glasses waited expectantly, chattering excitedly, to observe a total eclipse of the sun.

It was 6.15am BST, totally silent except for the distant drone of an aircraft engine. A nearly 9 year old lad gazed upwards to spot the tiny dot high in the sky and yearned to be up there, his fertile imagination enthralled with certain conviction he would become a pilot.

Since 1919 the French Canadian-born Giraux brothers, one a World War I pilot and the other an engineer, had been running a summer joyriding business from the seashore landing ground close to the town's fairground. On this occasion the pilot, S N (Norman) Giraux, had as passengers a scientist and a photographer in the tandem front seating open cockpit of his De Havilland DH 6 to observe the phenomenon from on high. Three years later that lad thrilled to his first ever flight in the same open cockpit. Six years later still, in May 1936 aged 17 going on 18, he gained his 'A', or private pilot's licence number 9603, a number retained for all subsequent grades of flying licence issued to him in Britain.

His instructor was that same Norman Giraux, a short olive-skinned man whose brilliant hazel eyes were permanently crinkled with a smile, the sharp clarity and directness of look masked by his habit of blinking rapidly. When annoyed the blinking stopped and the fire burning behind those eyes bored right into those of the transgressor, an uncomfortable moment which Jim experienced only once during the many years they were friends. It was enough!

A different aircraft, an Avro Avian with 80 Bhp Blackburn Cirrus II engine, was used for instruction. It's registration, G-EBZM, indicated a construction date before 1926. Thereafter registration started G-AAAA, progressing alphabetically to G-AAAB and so on.

That particular aircraft, a delightful machine to handle, had a disconcerting habit of shedding push rods whenever out of gliding distance from a landing ground. In consequence she was not used for cross country training, though Giraux would occasionally take her

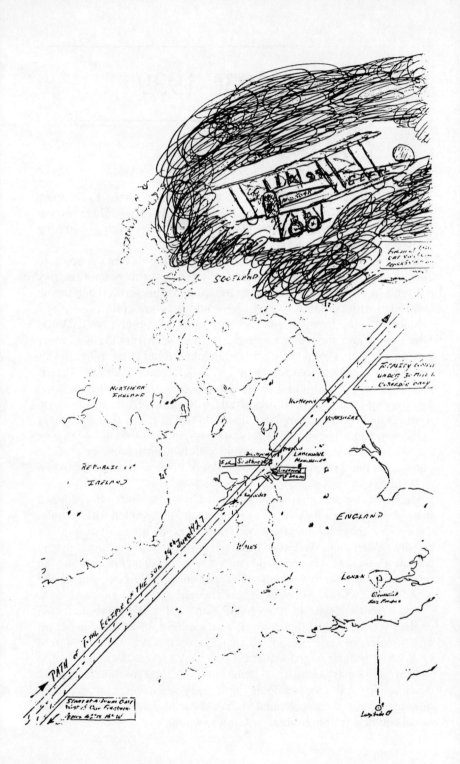

SCOTLAND

NORTHERN
IRELAND

Hartlepool

YORKSHIRE

REPUBLIC OF
IRELAND

Southport   Preston
              LANCASHIRE
              MANCHESTER

Anglesey

ENGLAND

WALES

LONDON

Greenwich
Zero Meridian

PATH OF TOTAL ECLIPSE OF THE SUN 29th June 1927

Start of a Total Belt
West of the Eastern
Approx 42°N 18°W

Longitude 0°

himself for short trips. On one, on 27 November 1936 to Speke, Liverpool, a distance of 20 miles, he rang to ask Jim if he would care to go with him to experience practice following a railway line in the strong gusty wind and low cloud prevailing that day. That promised to be the best of all Christmas presents for Jim, who was on holiday from the De Havilland Technical School. It was to be a typical example of that Avian's unusual habit.

Giraux flew to Speke demonstrating the effect of drift angles as the railway line was followed, with the wind blowing strongly from the sea across the direction of flight, and pointing out various landmarks. They arrived without incident and Jim was to fly the return leg, Giraux of course with dual controls in the front (instructor's) cockpit.

Not 200 feet up on take off from Speke, heading straight for the large gasometer rising close to the western boundary of the aerodrome, the engine stopped dead – no splutter. Giraux showed lightning reactions as he took over control, swung the machine back down the strong wind in a steep continuous turn to land with a very short run into wind, rolling to a stop a few yards short of the tarmac area.

The old, wise and well tried rule – (**NEVER** turn back after engine failure on take off) – had been broken, as Giraux emphasised to Jim, but the alternative would have been a crash straight into that gasometer rather than a possible one onto the airfield. As it happened the very strong wind actually made the manouevre marginally safe that day, creating a very rapid drift back over the field as the 360 degree gliding turn was made. The split second decision in choosing the lesser of two evils was proved right because of those World War I, first generation reactions, learned the hard way.

The engine failure was due to four assorted push rods missing, never found, possibly falling in the river Mersey which parallels the take off direction, flowing close to the boundary. G-EBZM, after repair, was flown back to Southport and was not used again for any cross country flights. During some 80 hours Jim flew in her, all from the Southport sands landing ground, and as far as he knows during the years following, she never had another engine failure. So are superstitions born, not so irrational when considered in the light of tempting fate for (Ernest K Gann) 'Fate is the Hunter'.

Eleven months after obtaining his 'A' licence, having had just under 10 hours dual instruction and three hrs 50 mins solo time Jim had increased the latter to 10 hours solo, at which stage he was allowed to take passengers – should anyone be brave enough to volunteer!

His first one, on 26 April 1937, was his 47 year old Mother who, wrapped up in a borrowed sheepskin jacket, helmeted and begoggled, occupied the front cockpit of the Avian for a 20 minute trip within gliding distance of the landing ground, sitting on two extra cushions so that her tiny under 5ft frame was just able to peep over the side. She had paid for his training and wanted to be sure she had got her money's worth!

In those days propellers on the smaller aircraft were hand swung to start the engine and most of them were left hand tractor, viewed from the cockpit turning anti-clockwise. On a few aircraft the propeller was mounted to the rear of the engine, becoming thus a pusher, but still left hand if rotating anti-clockwise when viewed from the rear. The Avian's Cirrus engine was different, it's propeller turning clockwise and thus a right hand tractor. The word airscrew later more commonly used, would really have been a better name than propeller. Part of elementary flying training was learning how to swing a propeller safely which, in the Avian's case, was an exercise requiring even more care than for the left hand tractor case.

With the engine warm the prop could be swung facing it and with the left hand, unless a right handed person was unable to use the left with reasonable dexterity. With the engine cold the job just had to be done from behind the prop back jammed against the lower wing, using the right hand to swing whilst the left held a petrol soaked rag over the carburettor intake as the prop was pulled down to rotate for starting. The blade edge, being its trailing edge, was quite sharp and the grip could not be helped by using the flat of the hand as for a position facing it. Therefore care had to be taken not to hang on with the fingers as the blade came down towards the bottom of the stroke, and also not to lean forward with a downward arm movement in order to avoid being decapitated as the engine started.

When that had been achieved, the prop swinger had to sidle crabwise along the leading edge of the wing until well clear of that whirling blade and its battering slipstream. If nothing else, that procedure certainly rammed home a great care and respect for the lethal capabilities of airscrews.

After completing 75 hours of circuits & bumps in the Avian Jim was allowed to fly the De Havilland DH83 Fox Moth, which Giro Aviation used for joyriding, and to start cross country flying practice. There were two of them, both fitted with DH Gipsy Major engines of 130 bhp, which allowed for the carriage of four passengers in an enclosed cabin behind the engine. The pilot sat behind in an open cockpit with a circular glass window, which could open for communication with the passengers, top centre of the instrument panel. They were registered G-ACCB and G-ACEJ, both with, respectively, red and blue lettering.

It was a delightful aircraft to fly and quite comfortable for the passengers, if a little noisy and vibratory, but normal conversation was

Southport Sandlemaring Ground (Summer 1937)

possible in the cabin. It was also a very cleverly designed machine in that the fuselage was aerodynamically shaped in a sort of deep aerfoil cross section which provided a good deal of lift to assist the biplane wings. These were exactly the same as those fitted to the DH82 Tiger Moth two seater trainer. The cruising speed was, at 125/130 mph, some 20 mph faster than the two seater open cockpit Tiger, yet with the same 130 bhp Gipsy Major engine.

It was August 1937 before Jim started a series of cross country practices which amounted to 27 hours by October. It was also time for his first lesson in discipline – resulting from over confidence. Those 75 hours of circuits and bumps round the shore aerodrome, weaving around the fairground towers on the approach (as had to be done by all the aircraft in order to get down into the very small roped off landing area) while sideslipping to lose height quickly for the last 100 ft or so of the approach, had become a great 'show off' thing. He would descend from the cockpit in white overalls and helmet, goggles high on forehead, to chat up the crowd on the excuse of getting them to take a five shilling joyride – incidentally geting a few dates with some of the lovely North Country lasses enjoying their 'Wakes Week' holidays. One day he went too far, sideslipping very low before flare out and making the crowd by the ropes duck. Giraux saw it and Jim was promptly grounded from local flying, though allowed to continue cross country practice in the Fox Moths, until the finish of the season at the end of September.

That short break did two things – taught him an early lesson, much needed, and caused delay by over six months of the date where he obtained the minimum of 200 hours needed before qualifying for 'B' licence, commercial pilot, tests. Over confidence is a disease which, at various stages in a career can creep up on a pilot. There would be a few, if any, immune from it or not honest enough to admit it. That realisation is the best prevention for a cure is very must harder. Fortunately the mandatory six monthly flying checks for commercial pilots keep them pretty much in line should any cocky nonsense tend to arise but, particularly in the early stages, it does happen and no doubt always will. Occasionally a lesson is learned by giving oneself a fright but it is much better to be brought up sharp, as was Jim, for he never forgot the lesson and was able throughout his career to recognise and check himself whenever the tendency arose. It did happen from time to time, and usually when the job happened to be one of dull routine on a day-to-day basis without much challenge involved.

There was a limit to the training facilities with Norman Giraux, and blind flying was one of them, so Jim transferred to the Redhill Flying Club where that, and up to the minute licence training, was available. This was mostly carried out on De Havilland DH60g aircraft fitted with

DH Gipsy I engines but was supplemented by cross country practice in DH80a Puss Moths, DH85 Leopard Moths, a 120 bhp Gipsy III engined Fox Moth (three passenger type). It was a bonus when allowed to nip around in a privately owned Miles Martlett single seater, with 80 bhp Armstrong Siddeley Genet II five cylinder radial engine.

Perhaps it should be noted here that it had been agreed that he could leave the De Havilland Technical School, where he had started a four year course in aircraft engineering and design after leaving Oundle School in the summer of 1936. The daytime instruction there involved very interesting practical work on aircraft and engines, including helping to build the school's third design for the King's Cup race, the TK3, but he just could not settle down and apply himself to evening study classes as his interest was solely in flying.

It was July 1938 before he was able to join the Redhill Club and progress with flying training. Instrument flying was conducted with the pupil in the rear cockpit of a DH60m, Metal Moth (a metal fuselage frame instead of all wood box frame for the 60g), the open cockpit being enclosed by a canvas hood, the pupil being unable to see outside. The instructor was in the clear in the front cockpit. It took seven hours of training before he was considered good enough to attempt the test for the 'B' (commercial) pilot licence, plus some 80 hours of general practice on cross country, forced landings, short field landings and spins.

On 2 September at Hendon aerodrome north of London, scene of the famous annual Hendon Air Show and headquarters of the RAF 'B' Flight testing unit which carried out both Air Force and civilian flight testing, Jim's ego was dealt a useful blow – when he failed the tests. The examiners were very, very good and extremely fair but candidates had to be absolutely spot on in every aspect, instrument, cross country, general and emergency handling, and he was just not good enough. Tail between legs and mentally prepared to buckle down to it instead of playing around and having great fun, he put in another 50 hours of hard practice before again, presenting himself at Hendon where this time on 17 October, he passed his tests.

After an obligatory solo night flight, from Lympne in Kent to Croydon, where the landing was made with ground fog wisping fairly thickly over the field, resulting in a bit of a pancake through holding off too high though nothing was damaged except his own self-esteem – the Department of Civil Aviation issued Jim his commercial licence on 22 October 1938. The number, 9603, remained unchanged from that of his 'A' private pilot's licence and indeed for subsequent grades of flying licence issued by Britain, such as the post-war Airline Transport Pilot's licence, ATPL, which for some reason, doubtless due to alliteration, was commonly called the ALTP. Examinations on meteorology, form of the earth, maps and charts, and air legislation had been passed previously.

In some strange way holding that little green book had a humbling effect, as though he was now charged with enormous responsibility about which he had not really thought much before. It was a feeling which remained to the day he finished flying, nearly 27 years later, whenever he handled his licences.

Now to find work! On Monday, 31 October, he found it with the De Havilland Aircraft Company at Hatfield. It was not a flying job but maintenance under a licenced engineer on the experimental DH94 Moth Minor, registered with the experimental aircraft number E8. It was fitted with a new type of De Havilland engine, the 90 bhp Gipsy Minor inverted four cylinder air cooled type. It had several novel features, in particular a single magneto which had a dual function instead of the more normal fitting of two separate ones. It proved to be just as reliable over the years as every other De Havilland engine.

It was interesting and fun at the same time, his boss being John Cunningham, the test pilot in charge of the project, who was to become known during the war as Group Captain 'Cat's Eyes' Cunningham for his heroic exploits in night fighters. After the war he became the company's chief test pilot responsible for the initial testing and introduction into BOAC service of the World's first true jet airliner, the Comet I. John, always the thorough gentleman, was friendly, good humoured, considerate and helpful and, as might be expected, an exceptionally smooth pilot. During the four months there Jim was actually allowed to fly that lively little low-winged monoplane, his first experience on one (the Puss and Leopard Moths both being high-winged).

Just before Christmas that year he witnessed the first flight of a new all metal airliner, De Havilland's first, the DH95 Flamingo, a high-winged monoplane fitted with two Bristol Perseus sleeve valve engines. She looked sleek and fast as she rose from the snow-covered airfield with those marvellous engines making very little noise, tucking her wheels up quickly as she climbed away upwards glittering silver in the weak winter sunshine.

The DH91 Albatross, yet another sleek beautiful machine, low-winged with four DH Gipsy King engines, was much in evidence, the type already in service with Imperial Airways. Top secret at the time was the Mosquito, being constructed like the Albatross of wood (balsa sandwiched in birch ply) and which was to become one of the most famous light fighter/bomber/reconnaissance aircraft during the war. There was an experimental night fighter, the Don, which was not to see service. Periodically, from the engine testing area, a strange high pitched noise screamed; but it was not until after the war that the first De Havilland Jet engine, the Goblin powering the DH Vampire jet fighter, was fully developed.

It was a far from dull time, and he was paid, his first ever earnings being £3 8s 4d per week, at a time when his full board and lodging for seven days, with three square and one light meal a day, cost a mere £1 10s!

By the end of January 1939 Redhill Flying Club were needing more flying instructors to help with the Government pilot training scheme known as the Civil Air Guard – (CAG). This was set up to train a pool of elementary trained pilots who, in the event of war, could go on to advanced training with the RAF and so save precious time and the wasteful procedure of sorting out unsuitable candidates. The cost to the pupil was 5 shillings an hour, the Government making up the difference from the normal dual rate of £2 10s or solo £2 for private tuition, though probably there was a contract rate rather less for the Club trainees.

Naturally Jim wished to use his new licence to fly for a living so, with some regret, he left De Havilland to train for an instructor's licence with the Redhill Club. Qualifying as an assistant instructor on 12 March, which allowed him to give instruction up to the solo stage – (when a full instructor took over) – he gave 83 CAG and 22 club members their initial training in the subsequent four months and 23 days to 4 August. That involved 203 hours instructional flying, plus 16 hours on other duties such as joyriding.

Instructional flights were normally 30 minutes or so. In an average of two hours per pupil, each would have had around four flights with him before being passed on or passed over. There were quite a few of the latter so the individual who made it would have had rather more time and flights. Many of the several hundred CAG trainees – (most flying clubs joined in the scheme) – did very well with the RAF or RNAS during the war, and two of Jim's lady pupils went to Air Transport Auxiliary – (ATA) – for the duration.

Having really only just become competent as a pilot himself, with 280 hours total when he began instructing, he found it a strain and had had enough by the end of July, by which time his total hours were 480 and just sufficient to get him work with a small charter company, Air Commerce, based at Heston Airport west of London. It was associated with the long established and successful company run and owned by Captain Gordon P Olley, of Olley Air Services based at Croydon, who was a first world war pilot. He was a fair, but fiery, little man though his staff remained loyal to him, several returning to work for him when the company restarted after the end of the second world war.

Capt Olley's friend Mr Stace ran Air Commerce which had a DH90 Dragonfly, two DH89 Rapides which were seconded from Olley, a Percival Vega Gull, and two DH85 Leopard Moths. Jim flew the three latter on joyriding, Army Co-operation by day and night giving gunnery laying and searchlight practice to anti-aircraft units, and a few charter flights. The other machines were twin-engined and Jim had not enough experience yet to fly them.

The pay was £350 per year plus flying pay of 10s per hour or per 100 miles, whichever was best for the pilot, but only the Vega Gull at 135 mph paid by the mile when on charter flights; Army Co-op and joyriding could not be measured by the mile. It was good pay and interestingly varied work which lasted until 1 September 1939 when the Government posted the whole of Air Commerce and much of Olley's to Ronaldsway on the Isle of Man. That was part of the grouping of all civilian charter companies into what was called National Air Communications – (NAC) – putting them on a War footing as a supplementary to the RAF's Communications Flight.

War was declared on 3 September but it was to be 11 October before the first movement order came. In the meantime Jim was married to his fiancée of six months. He was just 21 and she a little younger. They had met at Redhill where her Father, a first war RFC fighter pilot and later test pilot was ground instructor for the ERFTS school. The Elementary Reserve Flying Training schools was created as separate sections of the civilian flying schools to provide RAF Reserve pilots with training up to the advanced stage and annual practice, the flying instructors being all qualified RAF Reserve pilots through operating in a civilian capacity. Those schools were quite different from the CAG scheme.

After enjoying a month's honeymoon Jim was sent off on 12 October in the Vega Gull, a low-wing monoplane seater with a Series I DH Gipsy Six engine of 200 bhp, to operate from Heston to Rheims in France, returning via Douai, with despatches, various kinds of freight, and the occasional passengers. That winter the weather was really foul, cold, snowy, and constantly foggy. The only form of navigation was to keep low under cloud and follow railway lines mapped as having no tunnels along them. The average height above ground and rail lines was of the order of 200 to 300 feet, and when coming to a rail junction it was prudent to check the compass heading of whichever branch line was to be followed – to ensure it was indeed the one selected without tunnels.

From Beauvais to Rheims the extra distance compared to the direct route was around 50 miles, but it was the only safe way (as there were no radio facilities). It was quite a challenge keeping those lines in sight

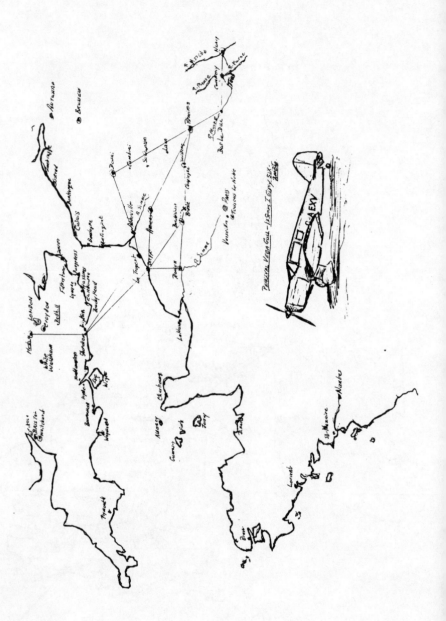

in visibilities of 500 yards or less, with the side window open and temperature below or not much above freezing. Unless the visibility was nil, or not much more, no flights were cancelled though the odd night at Rheims, a lovely city full of life and fun in those phoney war days, happened when return loads to Heston were not ready or when delays made it impossible to arrive there before dark. Only Service aircraft were permitted to operate between sunset and sunrise.

Orders came to return to the Isle of Man on 28 October, from where a series of special charters took place. Homing pigeon trainers from Liverpool to Belfast, and an Air Marshal accompanied by a warrant officer from Ronaldsway to Belfast being two examples. Training to obtain the twin engined DH90 Dragonfly on his licence was carried out at Ronaldsway before, on 12 December, Jim was again on his way in the Vega Gull for what was to be a most interesting trip, in which Lady Luck played a big part. All those flights that winter verged on the 'dicey', mainly because of the weather, but this one is worth describing in detail.

The night of 12 December was spent at Dieppe after being forced by weather to land there. It was a small grass field, very uneven, with a parking area on a distinct slope, which was indirectly responsible for the events of the following day. The Vega Gull had fuel tanks in each wing root, the engine being fed from one to the other through a selector cock in the cockpit. This was set to OFF, the normal procedure when parked. The right tank was normally selected to be used first in flight, changing to the left before the right read empty on the gauge (which was not always reliable) so the change was made on a time run basis at 10 gallons per hour consumption rate. One hour and 40 minutes had been flown to Dieppe so there should have been at least another half an hour in the right tank, both having been full when leaving Heston. The aircraft was left parked overnight with the left wing high on the slope and fuel selector to OFF. It is important that that situation is noted.

The next morning the left tank, unused the day before and presumably full, was selected for take off and for the whole one and a half hour flight time to Rheims, so as not to have to change tanks in the air at the very low height the weather dictated. Correct pre-flight procedure would have been for the fuel tanks to be dipped and exact contents thus checked, but Jim had been exhausted after sweeping heavy snow off wings and tailplane and anxious to get going before there was more build up from the sleet driving across the field in a strong wind.

Becoming airborne it was necessary to fly at 200 feet just under and occasionally in and out of the bottom of a thick layer of cloud to follow the railway line. The forward visibility through the clotted windscreen was virtually nil, and through the open side window less than 500 yards in sleet. Soon after passing Beauvais, and settled down to a change in railway line, there was an ear-splitting silence. No time to think, just duck under high tension wires running parallel to the railway, pull up over telephone wires on the edge of a partly snow covered field, apply full flap and, with a steep sideslip, manage to plonk firmly into that field, with the engine of course dead.

The load was cardboard boxes of meteorological balloons for Nancy, the last three of which were loaded after the pilot was seated so had to be removed before Jim could climb out. They were quite heavy, but with his instinctive urge to clear himself after opening the cockpit canopy, the time taken was very little indeed! However, no box broke open. The surface of the field was ridged from last year's ploughing and frozen hard. Amazingly the only damage was a broken tail wheel fork, and fortunately that sturdy aircraft had not turned over and caught fire.

Jim dipped the fuel tanks to find the left one (which should have been almost full after only 40 minutes flying from Dieppe) empty and the right one overflowing. Obviously the left tank, high on the slope overnight, had drained through the cock OFF position into the right tank. Later checks proved that it was not only possible but was not isolated to that particular aircraft's fuel selection cock, so the tank selection drill was changed to leaving one or other ON when parked and never in the OFF position. No doubt modifications were incorporated in those cocks later on. Never again did Jim fail to check fuel contents before take off!

It was not long before some men from the local sugar factory at Bresle near Laversines arrived. They examined the broken tail wheel fork, treating Jim with obvious suspicion – his dark blue uniform may have had the same colour as that of the French Air Force but in no other way resembled it. The Vega though was in full camouflage with RAF roundels on wings and fuselage yet displaying her civilian registration letters. They had in fact telephoned the police to report the stranger and his landing. Happily Jim spoke French fairly well so soon there were handshakes all round as they promised to mend the steel fork at their factory – 'but that would take at least a day'.

At that moment, bouncing over the field on a motor bike, a policeman turned up, very important and officious as he demanded papers and an explanation of the unauthorised landing. Satisfied, he agreed that the factory could mend the tail wheel. He then became very friendly and indicated that Jim seat himself on the pillion as he had to be taken in for questioning. It was an exhilarating ride – that is if a high speed gale after reaching the main road, and the adrenalin of sheer fright for someone who hated motor bikes and pillions in particular, can be so described.

A stop was made at an inn, the gendarme saying it was time for morning refreshment. He ordered two café filtres, which appeared accompanied by glasses of cognac and brioches, and proceeded to introduce his passenger to the ritual of dipping sugar cubes into the cognac until fully soaked before dropping them – as many as desired – into the thick black coffee. The butter-larded brioches were eaten whilst the hot strong brew was sipped, any remaining cognac being tipped in one shot down the throat by way of grand finale. The deep seated coldness of his damp uniform whipped in the slipstream of that terrifying ride had begun to thaw out, a slow glow running through the veins and hands ceased shaking as, on quite a high, the journey to the police station was completed.

Formalities over, Jim offered to pay for the café-cognacs, receiving a big smile from the now friendly gendarme, hands thrown out wide to accompany his . . 'But Monsieur, I am the police, it was on the house' . . with a shrug of the shoulders! It was gathered that they had been the guests of the unfortunate innkeeper, who had nevertheless been most hospitable!

The French Air Force at Beauvais was telephoned and arrived very soon in a black Citroen front-wheel drive, of the type so beloved by the French police for the chase – (magnificent road holding and enormous acceleration) – in the person of a Lieutenant Thierry of the elite Guynemar squadron, famous for their exploits during the first world war. He drove Jim back to their officers mess for lunch, telling him that he must speak only French whilst a guest of the French Air Force. Although Jim's French was good enough to get served and make himself understood basically, it was certainly a great deal more fluent after a fantastic night with those friendly fellows. Not long after he spent almost a week with them, his French almost native by the time he left. Sadly none of those fourteen officers survived long enough even to see the evacuation of Dunkirk the next June, their Morane Saulnier 460 fighters being no match for the German Messerschmidt 109s, despite their incredible manoeuverability.

Early the next day the sugar factory telephoned to say that the tail wheel repair was finished. Roger Thierry collected two mechanics and with Jim sped to the field, stopping on the way to advise the policeman who followed on his motor bike. Jim and the Air Force team watched the mechanics fit the repaired fork and re-assemble the tail wheel to the aircraft, admiring the welding job as they did so. It was also admired later on by the British Air Inspection Department (AID) officer at Heston who allowed it to remain fitted instead of insisting on a new part.

The field was small so all the cartons were offloaded and trundled over to the Citroen whilst willing hands lifted the tail and wheeled the Vega Gull backwards tight up to the boundary fence, lining her up facing along the hard furrows which, happily, were into a wind blowing 10-12 mph. Needless to say, Jim check-dipped the fuel tanks before starting the engine, the now full right tank being selected. After a thorough warm-up and magneto check he opened the throttle fully before releasing the brakes.

The Vega gathered speed slowly at first on the sleet covered ground, the undercarriage taking a bit of a beating on the hard uneven surface, but take off speed was achieved about 100 yards before the deep ditch separating the field from the next one. The flaps were then lowered to the first position causing her to leap into the air to clear that ditch by a good margin. After the customary 'shoot up' of the crowd, wings waggling in thanks, Jim headed for Beauvais to land eight minutes later, refuelled both tanks to full, reloaded the freight (the last three cartons after him), thanked his new friends for their wonderful hospitality, and headed off for a 50 minute flight to Rheims. This time, as fate would have it, he was able to climb to 1200 feet under thinning cloud with an occasional glimpse of weak sunshine, but too late to go on to Nancy before dark.

That state did not continue into the next day, 15 December, when again it was 200 feet along the railway line and river Marne to Bar le Duc; then a branch line to Commercy, (only one so no need to check heading), for a short distance before reaching the river Meuse and another main line; heading south to a junction at Toul, before turning along another branch line eastwards towards Nancy. That one disappears into a tunnel through hills rising to 800 feet before the river Moselle is reached, with Nancy aerodrome snuggled in two thirds of a circle bend in the river. It had been snowing heavily all the way.

Normally when going to Nancy the flight would not be attempted unless those hills could be flown over in clear air, but those Met. balloons were urgent freight, due two days earlier, and were needed to provide vital weather information for the Spitfire reconnaissance squadron based at Nancy. A calculated risk had to be taken, pulling up into the clouds to 1200 feet for five and a half minutes to cover an estimated 11 miles before letting down at 800 feet per minute to break cloud just short of the airfield at a little over 400 feet for a half circuit to land. The time taken from Rheims had been little over one and a half hours.

After half an hour to refuel, and a smoke or two while chatting to the huge New Zealander squadron leader of the reconnaissance squadron – (how he managed to squeeze that tall strong frame into a

Spitfire cockpit defies imagination) – a timed climb out over those hills in cloud, then let down on direct course to Bar le Duc, breaking cloud there at 500 feet in clearing weather without snow, and it was back to following the railway to Rheims to refuel again. The trip time had taken only one hour, due to less wriggling along the railway and valleys, and using normal cruising speed instead of the reduced one employed for low level crawling.

Another night stop had been looked forward to as continuing back to England that day would have meant arriving very close to dark, even if the weather was reasonably clear. It was not to be! A bulky heavily sealed package was handed to Jim for immediate despatch to Heston, or at least to Shoreham on the coast if darkness prevented continuing to the restricted London area. Twenty two minutes to refuel and try to get some weather information along the route, and the flight to Heston was under way. The weather towards the Channel and over England was forecast to be clearing with broken strato cumulus cloud base higher than 1000 feet over the Channel and skies over England clearing, but fog likely to form during late evening in the London area.

Course was set direct for Le Treport, where visual contact had to be made before crossing the Channel to Shoreham, with the trusty Gipsy Six engine opened up to maximum permitted continuous power. It was going to be tight to reach Heston before dark. The first part of the trip was in cloud at 2500 feet, the height corresponding to the 500 foot separation rules of those days for aircraft flying blind – (odd thousands of feet heading between North and East, odds plus 500 feet between east and south, even thousands between south and west, and, as for this trip, evens plus 500 feet). Some miles before Le Treport the cloud broke up and it was possible to descend gradually, thus increasing airspeed, to cross the French coast at 1500 feet, continuing down over the Channel to cross Shoreham at 800 feet just as the sun was setting in a watery but clear sky to the west.

A green light signal from the Shoreham control tower, so Jim carried on towards Heston with time to spare before darkness fell. He felt relaxed and happy in the pleasant winter's evening weather, having experienced so little of it for weeks. He noticed some mist curling round the hills as Hazelmere was passed, and smoke from homes or garden fires rising lazily upwards, and thought what a pleasant place England was. A drink by the fire in the Rising Sun after landing was a pleasant prospect too. But where was the Staines Reservoir with the Great West Road and Heston close beyond. Fog – thickening rapidly and well before forecast. Down to 500 feet he found the Great West Road and turned to follow it towards the cross roads where a left turn to head west would bring him into line with Heston's main runway.

Total darkness set in rapidly, no lights being visible from the wartime blacked-out ground, and Jim came as close to panic as he had ever been as he retraced the heading hoping, unsuccessfully, to catch glimpses of the main road. He planned to make two minute runs each way whilst trying to decide what to do. It was beginning to seem like a return to the coast to attempt landing on the shore in the dark, despite the anti-landing obstructions placed all along the coast – at least he might survive that even if the Vega did not. At that point (and it could only have been less than two minutes though it seemed a lot longer) he was about to turn back south towards the coast when a line of yellow sodium lights flicked on for a second over to the left, repeated twice more. Heston had those lights buried into the centre line of the grass main runway, for use in conditions of bad visibility to assist pre-war night landings.

Heart in mouth he turned in the direction the lights had shown, switched on his landing lights and started to lose height on the runway heading. Flaps down (the fog swirling in the glare of his lights, so he turned them off) at which moment those beautiful warm yellow sodiums were turned on when he was almost over the boundary fence. As soon as the wheels touched down the lights went off, the compass having to be used to give direction for a slow taxi-in in the thickening fog to the parking area.

An Army corporal, flanked by two MPs, took charge of the sealed despatch packet, signing a receipt before rushing off. Renewed thoughts of that drink, a much stronger one, in the Rising Sun down the road were soon dashed by a message from the Control Tower before he had left the cockpit. He was required to report there as soon as possible.

On arrival he was faced with the senior air traffic control officer, the airport manager and two other officials not known to him, and a sergeant of the police, all with very serious faces. It seemed that a crime had been committed (by the attitude of the interrogators probably punishable by incarceration in the Tower of London, if not summary execution) – in that he had disobeyed the order to land at Shoreham, which was what that green light had meant . . 'Land here, it is clear to land'. That special signal of the day was supposed to have been on the chit detailing the various Very cartridge colours and light signal codes for that day given to him before leaving Rheims, which was supposed to have been destroyed as soon as the details were memorised. In fact the chit had not had any detail about signals from Shoreham, which Jim was able to prove by producing it, not having destroyed it as ordered. From one crime to another, and which was the worst? Exonerated from the first, the disapproval, and lectures, increased in seriousness.

During a small amount of silence Jim made his apologies for causing the break in the blackout which had probably saved his life and certainly the aircraft, if not some innocent people had it ended up in a row of houses on the airport boundary. He expressed sincere thanks for the air traffic control's initiative in switching on the sodium contact lights. At that moment the telephone buzzed.

The controller listened then acknowledged the message with . . 'Certainly sir, I shall do that. Do you wish to speak with him, he is here now?' . . – the phone was handed to Jim. . . 'Jolly good show! Just received those despatches; can't tell you how important they are. Thank you! . .

The atmosphere relaxed, plus smiles and handshakes, with admonishments from the policeman not to repeat the offence in future, and dispersal. The pub was closed by then but the controller, who was friendly with all the pilots using Heston, brought out a bottle of Scotch whilst Jim related the somewhat harassing events of the last four days. They drank to his luck holding out for many years, and perhaps that was why it did – who knows?

There were five more trips to France before returning to the Isle of Man base for major servicing of the Vega on 22 December, followed by a happy reunion with his wife and a Christmas which was to be the last one for six years with her. In fact really seven as, in Cairo 1945 where they were based at that time, Jim was away on a trip to India which did not return until 28 December that year, but at least in time for the New Year.

Off again to Heston and France 28 December 1939, the weather continuing as unpleasant as before, allowing only 11 days flying up to 25 January 1940. It was becoming sadly obvious that the RAF Fairey Battle light bombers, and even the more agile and faster Bristol Blenheim Is recently based at Rheims, were being very badly mauled and crew losses were appallingly high. The war was no longer describable as 'phoney', and the British were certainly not going to be hanging out their washing on the Siegfried line soon or ever. At that stage the civilian flights to France were halted, NAC discontinued, and the RAF communications aircraft and pilots took over all that work until the end of June and Dunkirk.

Occasionally, perhaps unfairly for so many passengers are interesting or specially noteworthy, there is one who makes an indelible impression. Looking back to those NAC days one (Sir Philip Gibbs, the well known World War I correspondent, and again in World War II, historian of both) Jim remembers for his gentle manner, extremely strong character, wit and intelligence, allied with real interest in and consideration for all around him. A great man, whose many publications reveal that character and make great reading.

It was a peculiarity of the system at that time that civilians not already enrolled in the armed services or their reserves were issued with cards listing their particular qualifications, capacities and possible functions as to what the war effort might require of them. A few, who the authorities considered in their wisdom to warrant a category designated 'RX' (standing for 'reserved occupation') were restricted to working as the Government might ordain from time to time. Jim was one of those and, since NAC ceased operations, was without job or income until he was repositioned. Fortunately he and his wife were able to live with her parents in Croydon until seven weeks later when on 18 March 1940, he was posted to BOAC whose headquarters were in the Grand Spa Hotel at Bristol. Actually the posting was to Imperial Airways, the two major British pre-war airlines being officially merged into BOAC only from 1 April 1940.

Jim's rank was second officer, salary £450 per annum, flat with no flying pay or extras, and all uniforms provided. Accommodation and meals away from base were also provided – (a great change from all his previous jobs where such expenses were met from his own pocket).

So, with five others in the same category, began six years of extraordinarily varied flying taking him to Canada, the USA (both neutral and at war), neutral Portugal and Turkey, the Middle East and Western Desert, West, South, and East Africa, Iraq and Iran, the Persian Gulf and India, the Yemen and Oman, Ethiopia and British occupied Eritrea.

2 BOAC – Training, ATA, and ATFERO.

Second officer Jim, with 602 flying hours in his log book, reported to the Knowle, Bristol, school on 18 March 1940.

The Handley Page 42, Hannibal class, four-engined biplane was the subject of lectures and study for the usual technical examinations before undergoing flying training on the type. It had been used on the London-Paris services before the war, slow in flight taking over two hours in which passengers had enjoyed silver service meals en-route. By comparison the city-centre time to city-centre in those days was much the same as fifty years later, in 1988, with jet aircraft flight times around 45 minutes between airports but congested surface transport to the city terminals at both ends each often longer than the flight itself.

The HP42, in a different passenger/freight configuration had been, and still was, used on the Middle East through India and Burma to Singapore route. It was to that service that the new recruits were to be posted after the Bristol training was completed.

In the class there were four very senior captains of the second generation who provided great entertainment for the new boys in the ribbing they gave to an instructor whose sense of humour was sadly lacking, albeit he knew his stuff as far as the technical details of aircraft and engines were concerned. They also gave great encouragement to their much younger class-mates giving practical advice on how best to fulfill the role of airline co-pilots if they were to progress in their new careers. It was good to find that those august persons were very human, nothing like the arrogant stuffed shirts heard about whilst working with the small charter companies.

The night before the day scheduled for start of flying training an unforecast gale blew both the aircraft to be used backwards over a hedge. They had not been tethered in expectancy of the gale, the windspeed of which was considerably more than the low stalling speed of those huge biplane wings. They were wrecked, which put paid to them joining the Middle East/Far East fleet and the necessity for pilots to fly them.

Plans were changed immediately, the new recruits being posted to Hythe, across the water from Southampton, to start training on the 'C'

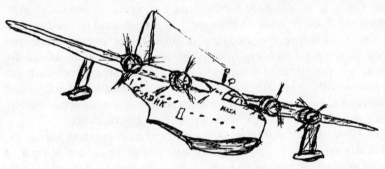

Handley Page HP-42 - 4 x Bristol Jupiter 7 Cyl. Radials.

Short S.23 Empire Flying Boat - 4 x Bristol Pegasus XC

Short S.20 (Mercury) Seaplane + Short S.21 (Modified S.23) = Short/Mayo Composite aircraft

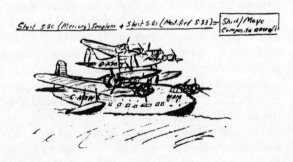

class Short S23 and S30 Empire Flying Boats for which new co-pilots were needed to supplement the crews based in Durban, South Africa, on what was known at the 'Horseshoe' route up through Africa to Cairo then eastwards over to Calcutta in India. Those senior captains from the class were posted to augment the newly formed Air Transport Auxiliary (ATA) civilian organisation crews ferrying service aircraft from factories to RAF operational bases of which more is told later. It seemed that the flying boat captain complement in Durban had been filled from the ranks of senior first officers already based out there, and the new co-pilots now to be trained needed to take their place in the right hand seats.

The ground courses to qualify for licence endorsement on the type, engines and airframe, were supplemented by addition of morse code aural and light signalling, semaphore, and knowledge of tides Then there was a two-week sailing course on a Bermuda rigged 40 foot sloop named Salome, which was absolutely superb. That course was run by a tough, no-nonsense retired Navy commander who turned out to be a terrific fellow once he became convinced his trainees were doing their best to learn. When cold and wet after a choppy sail in a stiff breeze what magic is a mug of steaming hot very strong tea, sweetened with condensed milk and extra sugar way above ration card allowance! Sailing dinghies in the narrow Hamble river, quite a tricky exercise, was part of the course and, as was found out later, of great help in manoeuvring of flying boats on the water in confined spaces.

Technical exams passed, flying training started in the second week of May 1940. Initially an old Saro Cutty Sark, with twin 150 bhp engines, was used. It was clumsy and seemed to have a one only speed of 70 knots, whether take off, climb, cruise, or descent was involved but gave a basic idea of flying boat handling techniques. Then a Short S23 called Maia, the type for which Jim's licence was to be endorsed, was employed. This was a very special aircraft having been the lower component of the 'pick-a-back' Mayo/Short combination, a seaplane called Mercury forming the top component. The combination allowed for the Mercury to be so heavily loaded that, unless helped by the power of a relatively lightly loaded Maia, it could not have taken off on it's own. The result was an exceptionally long range with which Mercury, piloted by Captain D C T Bennett, generation two's brightest star, established several long distance flying records, the first from Foynes in Ireland direct to Montreal in Canada being made on 21 July 1938 and one, still standing, 28 September the same year from Dundee in Scotland to South Africa.

A plaque marking the 50th anniversary of that flight was dedicated in Dundee in 1988. The lower component, Maia, was flown by Captain

A S Wilcockson, a first generation legend, particularly concerning flying boat operations.

To train in such a hallowed cockpit was as humbling as it was thrilling. Even more so as the instructor was Captain Frank Bailey, another of the first generation, who was one of the most experienced of all flying boat pilots. Incidentally, reverting to lessons about propellers, he had a badly damaged hand through accidental contact with one, which goes to prove that even the most experiened person can have drastic lapses of caution.

That course was not completed either for, by 4 June the streets of Southampton were choked with weary beyond description, disillusioned troops from all of the allied nations following the evacuation of Dunkirk which had started on 26 May. The phoney war was very much over and there would be no postings overseas for some time.

The trainees were posted forthwith to where they could be of immediate use; ferrying service aircraft from factories to maintenance units and to RAF operational units as fast as possible for the anticipated next phase of the war – the attempted invasion of Britain.

Jim's new base was at White Waltham, a small grass airfield near Reading, where Air Transport Auxiliary (ATA) No 3 Pool (later No 1) was based. After a day being checked out by the chief pilot, a World War I veteran, on a Tiger Moth and then a high wing monoplane (Stinson Reliant, a luxury four seater American single engined type), and studying the regulations for flying the restricted corridors to avoid prohibited areas, barrage balloons and the like, he was cleared to fly the ferry pilot passenger service which transported them to and from the various places aircraft had to be picked up and delivered.

Initially the type used was the Airspeed Courier powered by a single Armstrong Whitworth Lynx 4C radial engine of 240 bhp. It was a low-wing monoplane with a very low-wing loading and thus a low landing speed and relatively high load factor of six (five passengers and one pilot), yet had a fairly good cruising speed of 130/135 mph due to having a retractable undercarriage, an unusual feature in a pre-war aircraft of that small size. During the first eight days of that duty, before he was qualified to operate on ferrying Service aircraft, there was one somewhat embarassing situation when five of his passengers turned out to be senior BOAC captains, three of them those from the Knowle training school. He suggested that one of them might prefer to fly the aircraft to their destination but they declined very firmly.

A very nervous young man with just over 600 hours, and very much on tenterhooks with all that gold braid and each with thousands of hours experience sitting behind him, managed to deliver them apparently unshaken to their destination. There Jim learned that they were going

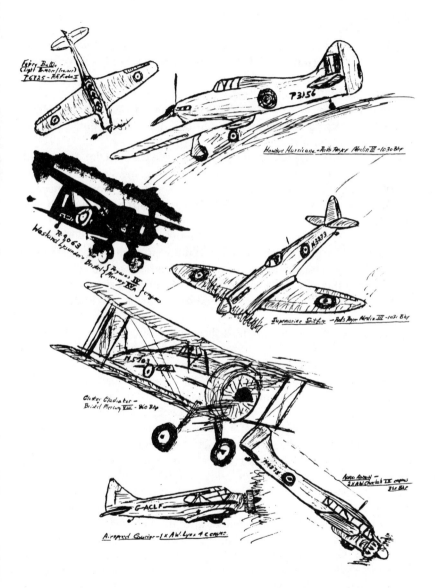

Fairy Battle
(Light Bomber/trainer)
P6725 - R.A.F Mark I

Hawker Hurricane - Rolls Royce Merlin III - 1030 BHP
P3156

R.9063
Westland Lysander - Bristol Perseus XII
engines

Supermarine Spitfire - Rolls Royce Merlin III - 1030 BHP
N.3283

Gloster Gladiator -
Bristol Mercury VIII - 840 BHP
N5703

Avro Anson -
2 x A.W. Cheetah IX engines
350 BHP

Airspeed Courier - 1 x A.W. Lynx 4 C engine.
G-ACLF

to collect Boulton and Paul Defiant night fighters, none having seen or flown that type before which was quite a normal thing for ATA pilots, but he did admire them for their obvious excitement as they trooped off to examine the new 'toy' as much as for the kind remarks to him about the flight in the Courier.

On 20 June, having meanwhile been converted to flying the twin engined Avro Anson on passenger work, Jim took a Tiger Moth to Upavon, headquarters of the RAF Central Flying school (a 'World elite' corps of instructors and check pilots) to be given a short instruction on a Miles Master, 715 bhp Rolls Royce Kestral engine, low-wing trainer before being sent off solo to perform the various tests required to pass the RAF's official acceptance permitting him to fly single-engined Service aircraft with ATA.

Late that afternoon he returned to White Waltham in the Tiger Moth to find himself rostered to ferry a Hawker Hurricane single-seat fighter first duty next day. It seemed huge, with it's 1030 bhp roaring monster of a Rolls Royce Merlin engine, or so it seemed to someone with very little flying experience and that on machines with no more than 200 bhp engines. To be honest he was terrified but, once airborne with wheels tucked up and zipping along at a speed noticeably much faster than he had ever been before, tearing around fair weather cumulus clouds on a bright sunny day, he was thrilled and soon feeling very much at home in that solid cockpit. He did remember to lower the undercarriage before landing!

The thrill continued for the next three months, for almost daily there was a change of aircraft type to ferry. In all there were fifteen different types in a total flight time of 82 hours covering 129 flights, the average trip time being 38 minutes. The RAF had issued to each pilot a small handbook detailing the main handling and control features of each type in service, so a few minutes sitting in the cockpit with that enabled the basic functions and features of a newly seen machine to be absorbed. There would always be, whether factory, maintenance unit or RAF station, someone on the ground staff only too willing to explain anything not clearly understood from the pilot's notes.

Perhaps the most helpful check list of all applied equally to any type of aircraft flying at that time, indeed to many modern machines of the less complicated airliners and smaller aircraft. The initials HTMPFGG, remembered easily by the phrase . . 'Hot Tempered Members of Parliament Fancy Giggling Girls' . ., or perhaps some other version according to the whim of the individual pilot, covered all items essential before starting up and take off, in flight, and descent for landing. Once the switches/levers/gauges had been found relating to hydraulics, trimmers (control), mixture (carburettor), pitch (propeller), flaps, fuel, gills/gyros/general, (such as checking that control movements were properly matched with movement of the control surfaces), and their operation mastered, everything would have been covered. It was simple, safe, and effective.

Jim experienced one incident which had nothing to do with an ignored check list. It was the shortest flight of his lucky life, one minute give or take a few scary seconds, from Hamble aerodrome into Southampton Water in a Spitfire. The engine stopped dead immediately after take off, Netley Hospital lay straight ahead, the building higher than the aircraft and was narrowly avoided by a sharp left turn which brought the machine, now descending rapidly, over the foreshore for another sharp turn, to the right, as petrol cocks and switches were cut off, flaps lowered, and cockpit canopy slid back, the aircraft lined up for a belly landing into the shallow water lapping the high tide mark. Then all hell broke loose, sky, water, and an indelible impression of the oil refinery over the water by Calshot upside down (as indeed was the aircraft) with a totally disorientated pilot's head submerged in water. That was the day, Saturday 13 July, he learned that to die was not such a hassle – just a deep breath, expecting water to fill his lungs, but amazingly air entered instead because small waves had receded (away from a split in the fuselage side) before lapping in again.

With the return of hope came back common sense. He wasn't going to die and, once he had managed to release the safety harness (which had become very tight due to the fact that the radio mast to which it was attached had collapsed after hitting the sand) he was able gradually to wriggle out from under the fuselage side in short struggles, whilst holding his breath as each little wavelet flowed back over him. He was soaked and was so confused he had not thought of releasing his parachute harness (so making getting out much easier) the whole clumsy caboodle still attached to his backside – the buff envelope containing the aircraft's papers quite dry between the 'chute and his bottom!

After a medical check, revealing no damage other than expected bruises, during which his uniform had been partially dried and parcelled up and some other clothes found and very kindly lent to him by the medical officer in the hospital. His shoes had not got as wet as the rest, so he was able to wear those again, without socks, for the miserable three hour train journey back to Bristol (his base at that time) shivering with fright as much as cold for the summer temperature was fairly warm that day. It was good to get home to the warm welcome of a sympathetic and loving wife! So ended Jim's first acquaintance with a Spitfire.

Like the next day's official enquiry the reader will no doubt wish to know why the intended simple belly landing ended upside down (and an aircraft totally written off instead of 'damage repairable'). It was a

Mark I Spitfire, the undercarriage being raised or lowered using a hydraulic hand pump. The procedure after take off was to move a lock/unlock lever, then select up on another before wobbling the hand pump in its fore and aft direction. In that Spitfire type (very sensitive to movement of any of its controls) it was deemed wise to wait until a little height had been gained before oscillating that pump, to avoid the possibility of moving the joystick a little in unison and possibly rocking the aircraft into the ground. On this occasion the locking lever and up-selection actions had been taken before the engine cut out. In the rapid sequence of events thereafter the pumping had been forgotten, the wheels (still down) caught in one of the groynes stretching at intervals out from land to sea, and over she went.

After the early morning enquiry Jim was sent off to Southampton (Eastleigh) to collect another Spitfire – a newer Mark with normal hydraulic undercarriage operation. It will surprise nobody that he was apprehensive to say the least. That it was a hot day was by a long chalk not the only reason why, having levelled out at 1000 ft after take off, he could literally wring the sweat out of his uniform, but it was the start of a love relationship with that superbly beautiful flying machine.

Every type flown with ATA had its own special characteristics, as of course have most aircraft, many of them their own particular character as individuals of the same type, but some do stand out from others as a bit special to an individual pilot. Of the Boulton and Paul two-seat night fighter, Fairey Battle, Henley Target Tower, Hawker Hurricane, Airspeed Courier and Oxford, Avro Anson, Westland Lysander, Miles Master, three stand out in Jim's personal selection – the Fairey Swordfish ('Stringbag' to the RNAS), Gloster Gladiator, and, very specially, the Supermarine Spitfire.

In his thoughts, too, remain many happy memories of the wonderful band of men and women he was privileged to meet in that short time with ATA. They came from all walks of life. One had only one arm, another one hand, both superb pilots, and there was a smattering of Americans who had come over to help the British war effort any way they could. There was Amy Mollison, that quiet gentle lady who, when very young, was the first woman to fly solo from England to Australia in a Gipsy Moth called Jason in May 1931, when still Miss Johnson. She was so sadly to be killed whilst still serving with ATA.

Another tiny lady, who later delivered four engined bombers (Stirlings, Halifaxes, and Lancasters), her husband another ATA pilot (a much larger size) the two of them inseparable, and many others, including Jim's lifetime friend Pat with whom he had trained for their commercial licences were all fondly remembered for their unfailing enthusiasm and universal camaradie.

On 10 September 1940 he received orders to proceed to Liverpool to embark for Montreal, Canada, with five BOAC captains and four other co-pilots, of which he and another who had joined BOAC the same date were the only second officers. Lease-Lend bombers from America, initially Lockheed Hudsons, were to be flown over the North Atlantic rather than crated for sea transport – safer, faster, and no need for assembly time on reaching Britain where they would be fitted with armaments of British make, including gun turrets.

A joint Canadian Pacific Airways and BOAC organisation had been set up in July 1940, in Montreal for that purpose and was named ATFERO – (Atlantic Ferry Organisation). Freelance American pilots were to be used alongside the British and Canadians, the technical and flying operations being controlled by a flight superintendent who, in the beginning, was Captain D C T Bennett of BOAC – of whom more a little later on. He and Captain Humphrey Page had been responsible for consulting with Lockheed at Burbank in California concerning the Hudson performance, and modifications necessary to fit it for the Atlantic deliveries. Their immense technical knowledge had made an enormous impression down there.

On 14 September 1940 the first of what were to be three Atlantic crossings by sea began, in the Duchess of Athol though her name was not known until after setting sail. There had been all sorts of plan changes and an aura of unusual secrecy about the whole embarkation procedure which (it turned out) was due to the ship carrying 1500 Naval personnel going out to neutral USA to collect a large number of mothballed four stack destroyers lease-loaned to Britain.

What was not known was that, due to a believed leak in security, those crews had been re-assigned passage in the Duchess instead of the City of Benares to which a large group of evacuee children were switched from the Athol, the Benares sailing in a different convoy. It was a long time before the torpedoing of the Benares, with the tragic loss of a majority of those children and other passengers and crew became known to Jim and his colleagues. There had been that suspected leak, and a terrible price paid for the defence of the sea lanes against the U-boats.

That had been referred to as Hitler's greatest war crime but (and as the radio officer on that U-boat stated many years later) the U-boat crew had no idea until after the torpedoing that the ship was carrying mainly women and children. Whether in fact the act of firing torpedos would have been any different (for obviously at war the non-selective sinking of the enemy's shipping and as much of it as possible would have had to be a top priority) is doubtful. In this instance, there is little doubt that the U-boat captain believed that his intelligence service had provided a prime target for him to deal a heavy blow against the British Navy.

The Duchess of Athol was a fast ship and had sailed most of the way out of convoy to reach the mouth of the St. Lawrence river by 24 September, arriving two days later in Montreal. The two-day journey up that huge river was fascinating, the scenery fantastic. There was a sharp coldness in the air, a cold that would soon cause the river to freeze over until spring allowing cars to cross over its half mile width at Montreal.

The BOAC crews were accommodated at the Ford Hotel, a tall skyscraper building but only about 18 stories high. It was no luxury place and as uncomfortably super-heated as most North American establishments seem to be in the winter, at least to those used to the relative austerity of British hotels of that period, but it was comfortable. The rooms were small and unimaginatively decorated but self-contained and homely in atmosphere. It had a drug store where almost any food could be obtained to eat from stools surrounding the servery at almost any hour of the day or night, a hairdresser/barber shop, not dear, which included a shoe shine if wanted, and a very good plain food restaurant.

It was not long before the crews learned to strip off their extra heavy outdoor clothing immediately on entering the place. Coon coats, fur hats and earmuffs which kept out the freezing (sometimes below zero Fahrenheit) temperature out on the streets – and to enjoy that indoor heat in shirtsleeves. Breakfast in the restaurant would consist of a heap of buckwheat cakes, liberally smeared with butter and soused with maple syrup, eggs and bacon, toast and jam, as many cups of fine coffee as desired (no extra charge), before braving the fierce cold on a ten-minute walk to the office situated in the Windsor station block. There they would strip off again before spending the day in the classroom studying technical details of the Hudson and the route planning for the Atlantic crossing.

Jim and his colleagues did find the North American male, (in both Canada and America, at least on the eastern sides of both countries), seemingly inseparable from their trilby hats which were worn, pushed back a little from the forehead, to meals and at most times – (not, it was believed, actually in bed). Trousers appeared not to have got to the self-suspending state, braces (suspenders to the locals), many-hued and quite eyecatching in some cases, performing that service, and an interesting pattern over some equally startling shirt designs – jackets naturally not donned until about to dress for the street, but always in attendance. No matter, they were friendly and helpful as were their ladies.

To the British it was luxury, and hard not to feel guilty enjoying such plenty in comparison to the heavily rationed people at home being bombed nightly in their blacked out, often unheated, homes.

Flying (from St. Hubert airport south of the city and river, home of the Canadair factory which provided hangar-age and some maintenance facilities), started on 28 September, with Don Bennett's number two Captain Humphrey Page, in the training type Hudson II fitted with 1100 bhp Wright Cyclone engines, twin radials, and later in Hudson IIIs (1200 bhp Wright Cyclones) which were the Mark to be delivered to the RAF. The Hudson was a militarised version of the Lockheed 14, which the pre-war British Airways operated in competition with Imperial Airways on the European routes, and was designated the Lockheed 414 model.

After five days of intensive flying, in snow and icing conditions most of the time, Captain Bennett checked out Jim and his colleagues for solo practice. That was on 2 October and there followed three weeks of shared pilot/co-pilot flying which included experience on the Hudson III and final check outs, interspersed with ground courses when the weather was too bad to fly. Then came the final briefing for the crews of the first seven aircraft to be ferried in formation across the Atlantic. Jim was crewed with Captain Alan Andrew, (a late second generation pilot previously with Imperial Airways), and radio officer Jimmy Gray, a Canadian.

It was typical of Captain Bennett, who was to lead the formation, that he personally made the selection for radio officer positions for the first four formations of seven aircraft. For months a training school had been in operation for Canadian and British volunteers already experienced as radio operators from various backgrounds. It was run by two very experienced ex-Imperial Airways R/Os (H. Jubb and G. C. Cunningham). One day early in November Don Bennett walked into the school, sat himself down at a morse key, and conducted the final selection exam in person. Such was the immense breadth of his knowledge, skills and experience – first class navigator, qualified engineer in both engines and airframes, author of a still standard work on Air Navigation (the *Compleat Air Navigator,* published whilst still a very young man before the war) and of course a fully qualified radio operator. It was also an example of how he always 'led from the front', never expecting anyone to do anything he was not himself able, or willing, to do.

Born in Queensland 10 September 1910 he was, at the age of thirty, not only the technical organiser and leader of the first-ever winter crossing of the North Atlantic by air (a truly historic achievement at the time) but the inspiration behind the success of the bomber ferry organisation. That is in no way to denigrate the efforts of his colleagues Captains Page and Ian Ross, nor those of Squadron Leader GJ (Taffy)

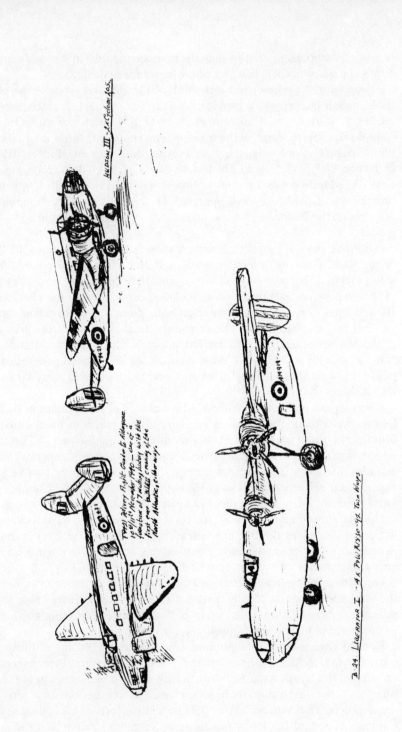

HUDSON III — AX Cyclone GAS.

TWA's Delivery Flight Crews to Prestwick
19 th/21 th November 1940 — one of a
series of Trans Atlantic flights with the
first over, made in crossing of the
North Atlantic other ways.

B-24 LIBERATOR I — AX P&W Alt/sic-92 Twin Wasps

Powell on loan from the Royal Canadian Air Force, (previously a captain on Imperial Airways flying boats and later Air Commodore), whose organisation of the aircraft despatch complexities, from Gander in particular, were outstanding.

The first of the seven Hudsons to be delivered were positioned from Montreal to Gander Airport (also known as 'Hatties Camp') in Newfoundland at the beginning of November 1940, the others arriving at intervals until, on 10 November, Captain Bennett came in with the last one. In the meantime the crews had lived in steam-heated railway carriages, two sleeping and one dining car, provided by the Newfoundland Railway Company and positioned in a siding on the airport boundary. The predominant smell was of American tobacco, Camel cigarettes and honey/rum/molasses pipe tobacco, for four of the crews were from the USA. Volunteers, all characters much of the barnstorming type, but with lots of tough experience behind them. One of them, Smith, had been a senior captain with the China National Airline (C.N.A.C.) before the war; another, Rogers, a relative of Will the comedian and a look-a-like. Adams, Clausewitz, Gentry, Lyons, and Hutchinson, a flying grandfather who had flown a Sikorsky amphibian with his family to or over the North Pole, and one other whose name is not recorded.

There were five Canadian radio officers, and two British from BOAC who flew with Captains Bennett and S T B Cripps ('Crippo') who was to be Bennett's left-wing man. The latter had been a World War I pilot with DFC, yet looked young enough to have been in the cradle then – brilliant blue eyes, snow white curly hair, tall and forever smiling; an exceptionally kind man, especially to the younger and less experienced, and a non-smoking very fit batchelor.

It so happened that the American Presidential election occurred, Friday 8 November, and it was the Civil War all over again as the various American factions took sides in fierce argument. The British and Canadians wisely kept quiet, or there might have been another War of Independence! Franklin D Roosevelt was elected, perhaps fortunately for Britain.

Immediately after his arrival on 10 November Captain Bennett went to discuss the weather situation over the Atlantic with PD McTaggert-Cowan, the brilliant forecaster who remained throughout the war in charge of the Gander weather unit. After some time the crews were called to a briefing to cover all aspects of the crossing which Bennett had decided would be that very night. He had worked out flight plans for each aircraft and some time was spent in a crystal clear covering of every aspect of the flight, which included the forecaster's interpretation of the weather to be expected en-route. To this Bennett added his detailed summation of how the flight plans would be affected if (and he explained why it could) the forecast situation were to change. No details were left out and he clearly and patiently answered all the several questions asked by both pilots and radio men.

Jim was not the only crew member to feel butterflies in the stomach now that the curtain was about to rise on that grey-green heaving waste of water (2025 miles of it to cross) the clearly remembered scene from the deck of the Duchess of Athol less than two months ago.

Snow and some ice had to be cleared from wings, tailplanes and fuselages before the engines were started to be warmed up gradually in the intense cold before being checked for full power, the various systems functions being checked at the same time. The fuel tanks were then topped up before, at 6.30pm local time, the six other Hudsons followed Captain Bennett's lead aircraft out for take off, forming up in loose formation behind him as course was set climbing eastwards out over the ocean.

It was almost a clear sky as they settled down at 12,000 feet, a moon nearly full casting its cold light over a watery scene below. During the third hour rapidly thickening cloud was encountered and the formation had to disperse for, even if navigation lights had been displayed none of the crews was experienced enough to fly in close formation. Icing became so heavy (as what was a warm front which had developed more than expected had to be flown through) that climbs to over 20,000 feet in Bennett's case (18,000 in that of Captain Andrew with whom Jim was co-pilot) had to be made to get into air so cold that only light icing occurred. Nevertheless, all seven aircraft landed at Aldergrove in Northern Ireland within 50 minutes of each other on Monday 11 November 1940, flight times being between 10 and 11 hours, Jim's taking 10 hours 52 minutes.

The forecaster, McTaggert-Cowan, had done a wonderful job calculating wind conditions enabling flight plans to be made (remaining unaltered) which had proved so accurate. He continued to provide forecasts for the whole ferry operation out of Gander which were of almost unbelievable accuracy.

With the Battle of Britain and much other intense and stirring RAF action going on, not to mention the Lufwaffe's continuous air raids on Britain, that historic 'first' in what was in effect a civil operation did not (at the time) seem to be of much note, even to the aircrew involved. In retrospect Jim feels proud and privileged to have been part of it. Two publications, both titled *Atlantic Bridge* – (Warren Armstrong/Muller: and a 1945 HMSO pamphlet) – describe the concept and operation in detail, 1940 to 1945, of the whole air ferry action from the America's to Britain and Africa.

The ex-factory Hudsons were not fitted with oxygen equipment for the crews. The Atlantic crossing necessitated very high altitudes above the 10,000 feet mark to be flown, so oxygen was essential. Initially a small single bottle of it was provided and this was fitted with a 'T' piece having three outlets, each with a rubber tube running to individual crew members position. There were no masks, oxygen intake was by sucking the tubes – primitive but there was urgency to get those aircraft to Britain, and later proper masks and regulators were fitted. If proof was needed of the essential necessity for that, the following story will illustrate it.

One of the co-pilot's duties was to take half hourly readings of all instruments and enter them in the technical log. This was done diligently and not one entry was missing from Jim's log, but the 11 entries for the last five and a half hours of the flight above 10,000 feet were totally unreadable on inspection after landing, due to anoxia from insufficient oxygen intake. Alan Andrew, a keen mountaineer and alpine skier being superbly fit fared much better, remarking to Jim rather rudely how peculiar he had looked with his face turned purple. Perhaps though after all the skipper had also missed out on the oxygen for, as Jim was able to tell him, his face too had been the same hue but he had not wished to seem cheeky by commenting at the time! Jimmy Gray had managed to keep his radio contact going but even his meticulous script had wobbled a lot in places.

After delivery the next day of the Hudson to Liverpool (Speke) where the aircraft was to be fitted with its war equipment before going on to Coastal Command, there was a blacked out train journey to Ayr in Scotland where Jim's wife was staying. They had a month together before he received sailing orders to return to Canada. On 14 December he sailed from Gourock on the Clyde in a Dutch freighter, the Leerdam, for New York. There were eight passengers incuding a family of five, and the crew helped the rest of them to make a real Christmas Day for the three children, just two days before docking in New York.

Sailing past the Statue of Liberty for the first time is an experience Jim remembers with some emotion, and a realisation of just what that experience must have meant to the thousands of migrants from the Old World as they were about to arrive in that promised land – and perhaps why 'God bless America' stirs such patriotic fervour in the breasts of the citizens of the USA.

A short wait in the circular bar at La Guardia airport, with a marvellous view of the city and harbour lights, and the runway lights (all so bright after blacked out Britain) then came the unique experience of a sleeper flight to Montreal in a DC3 of North West Airlines and back to work.

From 6 January to 25 April, 82 flights were made with various captains, interspersed with practice flights with other co-pilots, alternating the pilot/co-pilot roles, to keep their hands in. Most of the flights were part of a pre-Atlantic delivery test of performance, equipment operation, and an airborne compass swing allied with a Loop swing for the radio direction finder.

The compass swing was very accurate, being airborne with all normal flight equipment switched on as it would be for the delivery flight. To describe in detail how railway lines with known magnetic direction were used to check compass headings is not necessary and would take lengthy explanation. Suffice to say that the deviations on the easterly headings used for the Atlantic crossing were able to be reduced to negligible amounts. The process did however take some time, and with climb to 20,000 feet to check through the full range of altitude performance, which included correct functioning of a hand wobble pump fuel transfer system, the flights averaged between three and a half and four and a half hours.

The fuel transfer system pumped fuel from a 200 gallon tank fitted in the bomb bay up to a 100 gallon one in the forward fuselage – (both required to give the Hudson enough range for the crossing) – from which fuel was fed by gravity to the normal wing tanks as they emptied.

Winter flying from St. Hubert could be very beautiful, but also provided plenty of really bad weather flying practice – ice, snow and rapid changes of weather systems, not always forecast, taking place during those long flight times away from base.

Late that April of 1941 the first deliveries of the Hudson Mark V arrived. Their engines were a different type from the Mark IIIs, Pratt & Whitney Twin Wasp R1830-92 S1-3CG double rown 14 cylinder radial engines. They had the same 1200 bhp rating but a small frontal area which should have given the aircraft a small speed advantage. They did not, but there was no loss either. The main difference in performance between the two Marks was in single engine performance.

The Mark V was fitted with non-feathering airscrews so, in the event of engine failure, the blades could not be moved past the fully coarse position to a fully feathered one streamlined with the airflow. The extra drag made single engine operation a deal more difficult than with the Mark III, not only with failure after take off or for approach to land, but to the cruising condition when both forward speed and ability to hold optimum altitudes were affected. Fortunately those engines were extremely reliable and failures few and far between. By the time the Mark VI Hudson became available later in the year the shortage of fully feathering airscrews had been overcome and all Hudsons thereafter retained the Pratt and Whitney Twin Wasp engines.

May 1941 saw Captains Cripps and Andrew, with newly promoted to Captain Ken Garden from South Australia, in New York to take delivery of some Consolidated B24 Liberator I bombers, also to assist two RAF crews with airborne compass swings for the Boeing B17 Flying Fortress bombers they were collecting from Floyd Bennet Field. Jim was lucky enough to go with them as he was to be co-pilot to Ken Garden on a Liberator ferry to Britain.

Ten days, mainly nights, in that dirty, brash, noisy city (none the less very exciting) was really great, living in a hotel in Brooklyn just over the bridge from downtown Manhatten. Highlights were a Radio City show, with the world's most highly trained chorus girls adding a spectacular sparkle to an already typically snap-snap polished American variety show, and a night out at the Stork Club marked by two significant happenings.

Watching the dancers on the crowded small floor there was obviously a commonly used technique of tapping a male dancer on the shoulder, his lady partner then politely coming into the arms of the stranger until reclaimed, or some other strange male repeated the performance. Jim, greatly daring, collected in his arms for a short dance a very beautiful redhead.

It was not until he returned to his British and American friends in the bar, all aircrew, that he learned the charming lady had been Rita Hayworth! They met again in 1950 when she was married to the Ali Khan and about to fly to Cannes in an aircraft chartered from Morton Air Services at Croydon, and she had not forgotten the exuberant young man who had trodden on her toes nine years previously!

The other happening was becoming a member of the 'Short Snorter Club', exclusive to aircrew who had crossed the Atlantic by air during the war. An American dollar note, signed by all other members present was the card of membership, the only rule being that any member unable to produce his card when challenged had to buy drinks all round for all other members present in possession of theirs. Jim still has his and will present a copy of this book, or refund the purchase price if already bought, to any Short Snorter able to produce the appropriate Greenback, or to any near relative in possession of it should the original member be deceased.

On 13 to 14 May 1941, Ken Garden in command, Jim his co-pilot and a crew of radio officer and engineer, both RAF sergeants, with three top ranking officers as passengers, ferried Liberator Am 919 to Prestwick, Scotland, via Gander. On landing at Prestwick the nose wheel collapsed, fortunately causing little damage and no injuries, due no doubt to a very muddy runway.

Jim had permission from Don Bennett to return to Montreal with his wife, provided they could find passage for her as a private citizen, for BOAC could not sponsor or claim priority passage for other than essential personnel, and provided also that his return was in no way delayed. His return passage had been booked on the liner Georgic by the company, due to sail from Gourock 20 May so there was six days in which to find passage for her if possible. Incidentally the Return Air Ferry Service, using roughly converted Liberators and BOAC crews, was not in service until the July of 1941 or he would have had to travel on that and there would not then have been any opportunity for his wife to be with or even to follow him.

The Georgic was solidly booked for service and a few essential civilians such as Jim, so some other ship had to be found with space for the two of them, and by 20 May latest. After many enquiries, few gaining answers in view of the 'Careless Talk Costs Lives' syndrome, they finally found out that one of J. G. Salveson's whaling ships was scheduled to sail in the same convoy as the Georgic on 20 May and might have room for a few private passengers – (she was not an official passenger transport, being used as an oil/petrol tanker sailing outbound in ballast).

Leaving their baggage in the care of a very pleasant NCO in charge of small boat departures at Gourock they took a train to Salveson's Glasgow offices and were accepted for passage in the Southern Princess at a cost of one pound per day each for an expected 17 days at sea, all at their own risk. A cheque for £34 was accepted by a trusting manager (no rebate if the trip was shorter but please pay the Captain if longer) and they were advised to hurry as the ship's sailing time was expected to be some time that afternoon. It was almost 1 pm before they found a train leaving for Gourock, arriving there fifty minutes later. The NCO with whom they had left their baggage examined their tickets and letter to the captain from the owner's Glasgow office, got a couple of lads to load the bags into a small motor boat and sent them off with a cheery safe voyage, and the advice that they could be lucky to get aboard before the anchor was raised. So it proved, for she was under way within the hour.

The Southern Princess was large, a whaling factory ship whose huge tanks normally for whale oil were to be filled with aviation fuel on reaching her destination, Halifax in Nova Scotia. Her captain came from Aberdeen, a dour Scot with ancestry going back to Norwegian and a tremendous sense of humour. Jim and his wife had been given a cabin with a double bunk bed, an unusual facility, but captains on such ships were allowed to take their wives with them and this cabin was his own. During those wartime Atlantic crossings the Captain did not use the cabin, having a day cabin aft of the chartroom on the bridge which he could not leave whilst at sea. It had a huge desk on one wall, deep armchairs and a table, with a small wash basin on another wall. Toilet facilities, showers and baths were not far down the open deck. The other passengers, an authoress and an actor, had separate cabins on the other side of the ablution centre. They met the actor again in New York at a party given for Gertrude Lawrence in 1941, and again much later, in 1945, in Cairo where he was with ENSA. The saloon, where meals were taken and cards or social activities happened, was down one deck.

Darkness fell soon after seeing land fade behind the convoy of some 25 ships escorted by busy little Corvettes, jumping like spring lambs through quite a brisk sea, and one Destroyer (though probably there may have been more out of sight ahead sweeping the convoy's path for U-boats).

The next morning, having donned life jackets after breakfast to go out on deck, there was no sign of any other vessel. The bow wave creamed high in a long swell sea and it was obvious from that, and the throbbing vibration of powerful engines, that the speed was around 18 to 20 knots. The first mate joined them for a few moments to say that they had been ordered to leave the convoy, along with other vessels capable of more than 15 knots, and proceed on their own. This was not so much for the menace of U-boats but because the pocket battleship Bismark had managed to escape from the Baltic and was headed out into the Atlantic. The grey sky suddenly seemed much greyer, the sea much greener and colder to look at. The air was whipping along the deck, almost freezing on their faces. A sober foreboding rather than immediate fear ran through the four passengers, and it was not long before they went below to play cards until lunchtime.

Two days later (the air was noticeably warmer, indicating that they had probably moved further south during the many zig-zag courses the ship had steered) the captain joined them for the evening meal. His face was very solemn for him as he told them that HMS Hood had been sunk by the Bismark with the loss of almost all on board, some 1500 souls, and that he had new sailing orders intended to keep them away from the possible track of the Bismark.

Passengers were to wear their life jackets at all times from now on, keeping them close and spread out ready to put on quickly at night, preferably sleeping in their clothes with warm pullovers handy near the life jackets. He was sorry, but they must remain below at night in case someone might stumble on the totally blacked-out deck and get hurt. As that blacked-out condition had applied since leaving port it was taken that his orders included ensuring that noboby on board would be in a position to make signals or sneak a quick smoke on deck, but he did not wish to say so directly to the passengers.

The next night, 27 May, they were playing cards in the saloon when the captain came down to ask them up on deck, which was brilliantly illuminated by searchlights and then suddenly switched off. A signal lamp flickered from close on the port side as he left them in the care of one of his officers to go up on the bridge, from where there soon came answering signalling. Just discernable was the black outline of a large ship in the faint phosphorescent glow from the sea, her signalling lamp snapping out a short reply, then moving away rapidly, the wake of the propellers visible for a short time. A smiling captain rejoined them to announce that the Bismark had been sunk, this being the last message from the British battleship once it had made sure of their identity.

It was learned later that it had been the Rodney – in a farewell chat to that marvellous man just before his ship dropped anchor in Halifax harbour, 17 days less four hours since leaving Gourock. Returning from America in 1943 Jim's wife was sailing in the same convoy as the Southern Princess, then loaded with aviation fuel, and saw her torpedoed and blown to pieces. The horror and deep sadness of that moment never left her.

Mr and Mrs Jim stayed overnight in the Lord Nelson hotel in Halifax boarding the next day, 7 June, a Canadian National train for Montreal. It was a slow but marvellously scenic trip, taking 38 hours, through Nova Scotia, through Quebec, and along the St Lawrence river. The stateroom accommodation was warm and comfortable, luxurious compared to the austerity of the British railways. They were met by Geoff Panes, a co-pilot colleague soon to become a very close friend. He had been sent by Don Bennett, who was unable to come himself, to welcome them formally with delight that they had managed to come over together – typical of his caring attitude to his staff.

There followed two months of intensive pre-delivery testing of Hudson Vs for which Jim was promoted to command, though remaining a second officer in rank and pay. The honour of that promotion was the main thing and typical of the rapid advancement brought about by wartime conditions. There were now no co-pilots as such for the test flying, but observers fresh from Empire Training school, RAF and RCAF personnel recently passed out as navigators. They operated the drift sight (which was used in the airborne compass swing procedure) and took down in the technical log the many recordings of instruments, some of them special equipment, needed to check engine and performance figures. In that way they gained a little practical airborne experience before crewing in ferry aircraft as navigators for the Atlantic deliveries, and then posting to active service squadrons. Mainly corporals or LACs, with the AC1, they were a fine bunch of keen fresh young men.

For some unexplained reason Jim's eyesight quite suddenly became faulty (loss of depth perception) which grounded him from 6 August to 2 November 1941. Exercises and prescribed glasses finally corrected the problem which never returned during the remaining 24 years of his flying career. For those non-flying three months he had the good fortune to be set to work, initially for Don Bennett as assistant to his position of flight superintendent for ATFERO. After he had returned to Britain, he worked under Group Captain (later Air Commodore) G J (Taffy) Powell who, as mentioned before, had been a senior captain with Imperial Airways on Empire flying boats based in Bermuda, joining the RCAF as a squadron leader on outbreak of war and having been in at the start of the Atlantic Ferry operation.

In those three months Jim learned a great deal about operations control, produced a route manual for use of ferry aircraft and, under Don Bennett, prepared cruise control charts for both Hudson and Liberator types. He learned at the same time how to work 16 hour days and coming more and more to admire the man – not for his incredible energy so much as for his patient teaching, for he never showed irritation when it took ages to grasp what to him would be a simple matter. He just made it clear that, when Jim finally said he understood, he was expected to have done just that and then get on with the job. Also he would never leave the office after normal office hours to go out for a snack without insisting that Jim go too. To get on with him it was necessary to work hard and to the best of one's ability. Given that, his kindness, interest in and understanding of his staff, their problems and their joys must be as much the reason as his outstanding technical abilities, why he was so successful in establishing the famous Pathfinder Force.

In the August Captain D C T Bennett, BOAC, was recalled to the RAF, soon to be promoted to group captain and form that special Pathfinder arm of the Bomber Command. He retired from the RAF at the end of the war an Air Vice Marshal (at 35 very much the youngest to have held that rank) became the Director General of the Government airline, British South American Airways, then later formed his own independent airline.

Taffy Powell took over the position of flight superintendent and at the same time the operating base moved from St. Hubert to a new international airport, Dorval, north west of the city. Flight operations and offices were then located together for the first time, and the RCAF took over officially what was renamed the North Atlantic Ferry Command. However, the personnel, both flight and ground staff, continued to be a perfect mix of service and civilian people from Canada, Britain and the USA, and included were Norwegian, French, and other nationalities – a happy association which lasted throughout the war.

Jim continued working as an assistant to the flight superintendent, his new boss proving very pleasant to work under though he was an entirely different character from Don Bennett. Formerly a Welsh international rugby union player he was physically rugged, shortish and solidly square in proportion and when annoyed (which could happen quite easily) inclined to the sort of natural aggression one might expect from devotees of that particular sport. The signs were pretty obvious so it was not all that difficult to steer a clear course.

Not long after the move to Dorval there were three fatal accidents with the Liberators in the space of two weeks. At the time Group Captain Powell was away, so the 23 year old Jim was faced with a learning experience of a more difficult nature than being left in charge of the operational organisation for a few days. Writing letters to bereaved relatives and dealing with all the other unhappy details which accrue at such times has a maturing effect.

The first one was on delivery to Prestwick, flying into the Mull of Kintyre in very bad weather – Jim's friends Ken Garden and Geoff Panes were killed. Then a return ferry Liberator flew into the top of the Isle of Arran shortly after leaving Prestwick – Captain E R B White and navigator F D Bradbrooke (the first Commander of ATA) and all others on board died. Another return ferry Liberator crashed on take-off from a muddy subsidiary airfield (Ayr by Prestwick) with the loss of all on board – the captain was R C Stafford with whom Jim had shared a cabin on the Duchess of Athol in September 1940.

Up until the time he was given two weeks leave (late October) there were no more accidents and in that time he made many friends, mainly Canadian men and women, in the operations department. When Jim went back to flying they presented him with a waterproof wash bag, on which they had signed their names. Nothing can have more sentimental value that such gifts and the loss of it (later in the war) was a very sad event.

Another co-pilot, though more senior as he had flown with Imperial Airways before the war, had become a close friend. He was a batchelor and had acquired a beautiful Chrysler limousine whilst in Montreal which he very kindly lent to Jim and his wife for them to drive down into the USA on holiday. He was about to go away on a special flight expected to take a week or two so did not need the car himself. That 10 day trip in the fall, with the reds of maples and yellows of oaks bright in their autumn livery, and magnificent other scenery through the White Mountains to New York, then back through New England and the Anorondaks to Montreal was one of the most memorable in Jim's life.

It was overshadowed by the sad news on their return to Montreal that Jack Hunter, owner of the car, and his Captain, Humphrey Page had been killed in another Liberator which, returning from that special VIP flight to Gibraltar, had been shot down over Eddystone Lighthouse by an RAF Spitfire flown by a Polish pilot.

The weather at the time had been very bad and the Liberator was a type of aircraft new in the skies of Britain and to that unfortunate pilot who, coming on it suddenly in the murk, mistook Aldis lamp recognition signals coming from it for gunfire. A tragedy for which understanding of a very difficult situation, rather than blame, must apply.

On 2 November Jim was declared fit to fly again, eyes perfectly normal, and was checked out on a Hudson to regain flight qualification. Two days later he was given instruction on a Liberator to qualify as a co-pilot for a delivery flight with Captain S W A Scott to Prestwick, and re-posting to Bristol for navigation training for an unspecified reason. On 12 November a year and a day since his first trans Atlantic flight, he landed at Prestwick after an uneventful trip. His wife was left behind in Montreal, booked to travel to Portland in Maine to stay with friends made on the holiday trip in October.

By 14 November he was behind a desk starting a crash course in navigation for the second class licence, plus learning the use of sextant and astro navigation. The licence exam was passed on 22 December 1941, and he was given two weeks leave during which he visited his wife's parents in Grangemouth, Scotland, where his father-in-law had reverted to ground instruction with the RAF of pilots training on Spitfires, many from Poland and Czeckoslovakia. Then on to see his own family in Southport before reporting back to BOAC headquarters in Bristol.

On 22 January 1942 orders were received to report to the Whitchurch airfield with all possessions for take off at 11 am in one of those beautiful De Havilland DH91 Albatross four engined airliners operated just pre-war by Imperial Airways – as a passenger of course. Apart from being unable to see out (the windows in all passenger aircraft flying in Britain were blanked out as a security measure) the trip over to Dublin in Ireland, as it turned out to be, was smooth and quiet as though the engines were sewing machines. A car was waiting to drive over to Adare, in County Limerick, where he met the crew of one of the three Boeing A314 Clipper flying boats he was to join as second navigator. This one had just brought Winston Churchill back from meeting with President Roosevelt, the USA having been at war since 7 December after the Japanese raid on Pearl Harbour.

The home base of the Boeing Flight was Baltimore in Maryland USA, so Jim and his wife would be reunited again periodically between the six week average round trips made by the flight, so their parting had not been so permanent as feared. The captain gave Jim a note which advised that he had been promoted to the rank of first officer with salary increased by £75 per annum to £525, and that on arrival in Baltimore he would be measured for a new uniform, custom made to conform with the very high standards required of the Boeing Flight crews. It was explained that there was no rank less than first officer on that flight, so Jim had got promotion a good deal sooner than he would have expected!

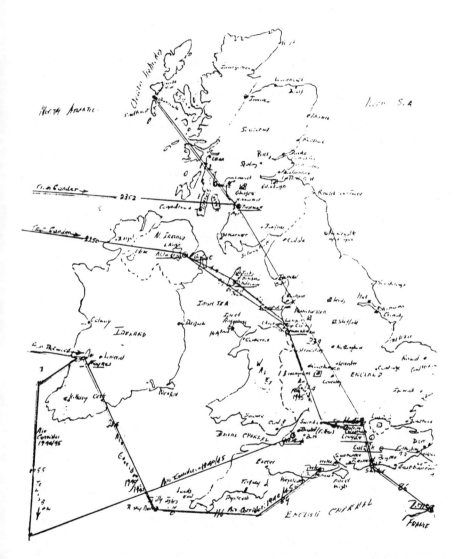

Distances in Statute Miles.

3 BOAC – The Boeing Flight 1942.

Named Berwick, Bangor, and Bristol the Boeings were very much a VIP Flight. Royal Mail and Diplomatic Mail, members of the Diplomatic Corps and King's Messengers, with senior service officers were the main passengers. Occasionally a group of ferry pilots required urgently back in the USA or Canada were carried. When stopping in Portugal at Lisbon, or in Brazil at Belem at the mouth of the river Amazon, the only uniforms in evidence in those neutral countries were the civilian ones of the crew. One of the reasons why special ones were issued was to give the best impression of a Britain far from down and out in those days when the neutrals were sensitive to all signs of how things might be going, on either side.

White shirts and shorts with white cap cover were worn for summer, the usual dark blue double breasted uniform for winter but cut like Saville Row. There was also a white duck dress uniform in the event of possible special occasions, but Jim only wore his once – when visiting an old friend in Trinidad who had attained senior rank in the Royal Navy, only to find his host very comfortable thank you in the sticky climate wearing shorts and sandals! The company even supplied the shirts, Van Heusen naturally, which would normally have been the individual's responsibility.

Perhaps it would be as well to note here that those august sounding passengers were not travelling on anything else but Government authorised business, not luxury fare paying or expense account champagne popping jaunts. The food served on board, though able in some cases to be cooked in the ovens which were part of the basic equipment on the type, was no silver service despite the fact that the two stewards carried would have been providing such a service on the pre-war Imperial Airways craft. It was none-the-less a cut above the dull lunch boxes provided on less spacious aircraft operated by BOAC on behalf of the Government. Furthermore the large crew carried was necessary due to the very long non-stop distances flown and the fact that round trips involved lasted several weeks away from base.

The crews, four all told in order for reasonable rest periods and occasional sickness to be covered, consisted of a senior captain (commander), a junior captain (chief officer) who was the co-pilot – both very experienced flying boat captains – and two other pilots (first officers). These two acted as navigators and could also carry out some of the minor co-pilot duties if necessary (such as taking over the controls in flight for an hour or so whilst the pilots themselves ate or rested a little). Then there were two very senior flight engineer officers, two equally senior radio officers. a purser (with office and typewriter who did all but the flight deck paper work and assisted the stewards when necessary), and the two senior stewards – eleven all told.

The atmosphere amongst the crews was superb, whether it be the team of eleven on board or mixtures of all the forty four flight crew members under the overall command of Captain J C Kelly Rogers who was one of the earlier second generation pilots and who had had a notable career on the Empire flying boats before the war. Anyone could be swapped into another crew and find harmony and a strong sense of self-discipline and loyalty to their commanders and other crew members. The 'bull', the special uniforms etc., were for the benefit of the public particularly in neutral countries. On the longest route, Bermuda to Lisbon averaging around 20 hours non-stop flight, only thirtyseven passengers and some freight could be carried. A rare maximum load could be over sixty or so on, say a 7 hour flight from Lisbon to Foynes in Ireland.

The aircraft itself was huge, even by modern standards, with a wing span of 158 feet. Like it's modern big sister, the Boeing 747 Jumbo jet, there was a circular carpeted staircase (not a ladder) leading up to the flight deck where the space was much larger than that of the 747. The two pilots sat forward with a space between them amply wide enough for a navigator to stand full height to take astro sights through the flat plate glass windscreen. Throttle controls were duplicated, each pilot having a full set of four situated on the outside of his seat. There was no central control pedestal, the flight engineers handling all engine and systems controls from their very complicated panels on the right hand wall of the flight deck behind the pilots and forward of the radio control panels. The pilots used the throttles only for take off, approach and landing, and for manoeuvering on the water.

On the left hand side of the flight deck, behind the screened off pilots' control cabin, was a 6 ft by 4 ft 6 in chart table for the navigators. This had four deep drawers underneath for the Admiralty charts and maps needed to cover navigation from Canada over the North Atlantic to Europe, down to West Africa, over the South Atlantic to Brazil, then up through the Caribbean to Bermuda and to the eastern seaboard of North America, and of course the Mid Atlantic covering Bermuda, the Azores, and to Portugal. Astro sights were provided for by an astro dome further aft in which was a plate for a bearing compass (or

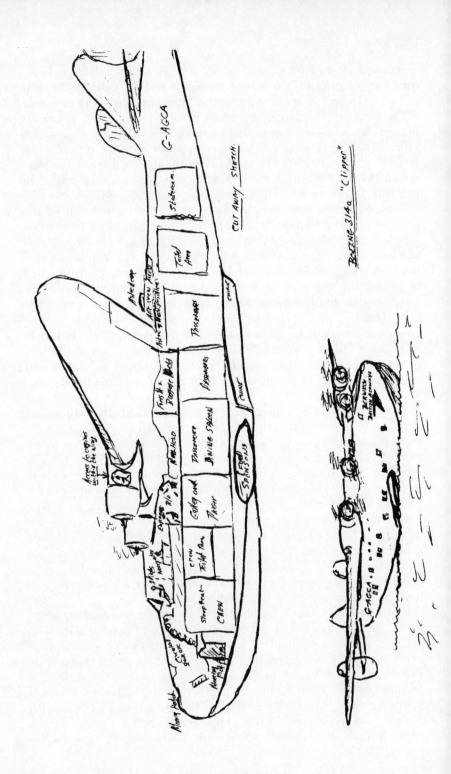

CUT AWAY SKETCH.

BOEING 314a "Clipper"

G-AGCA

Pelorus). A hatch below and just aft of that provided fittings for an optical drift sight allowing either vertical or back bearing readings to be taken on the surface below or smoke/flame floats to the rear. There was a Star Chart projector in the roof over the chart table which could superimpose a picture of the night sky directly onto the navigation chart. Everything a navigator could possibly wish for. And that was Jim's new domain.

The aircraft was powered by four Wright Double Cyclone radial engines each of 1800 bhp. An amazing, and unique, feature was the facility for an engineer to move out inside the wings in flight to reach an even outer engine where the nacelles were amply big enough for him to get at most of the engine parts (from a platform inside the nacelle) to change a magneto for instance, which had in fact been done. However, those engines proved as reliable as their smaller brothers fitted to the Hudsons so there was little drama of that sort necessary when airborne, but the built-in platforms in those nacelles were of tremendous use when servicing the engines on the water.

To describe the whole internal layout would take pages, but a cut-away sketch has been provided which will give a pretty clear idea of that incredible machine. Mention should be made of the high-ceilinged dining area in the centre under the huge high wing, into which passengers and crew made their entry from outside when boarding the aircraft from the walkway on top of the huge 'sponsons'. (The short-wing shaped fuel tanks which doubled as stabilisers on the water instead of the more usual wing tip floats on most flying boats). Another unusual feature was the stateroom cabin lying athwartships aft and almost under the massive tailplane, which had its own facilities. When not in use by special VIPS like Winston Churchill, the two pilots, commander and chief officer, would use it when off watch on the longer flights.

She was a slow aircraft, indicating 107 knots (123 mph) in long range cruise condition, such as for the 2730 nautical mile (3140 statute miles) flight from Bermuda to Lisbon. In so called 'High speed' cruise, which might be used on short routes such as Baltimore to Bermuda or Lisbon to Foynes, the indicated speed was 125 knots (144 mph). She was unpressurised so operated at 10,000 feet or below, down to 500 or 600 feet on occasions such as when battling head winds over the North Atlantic, – a route used during summer months only.

Her official maximum range when fully loaded with fuel and a take off weight of around 42 tons was 3000 nautical miles (3450 statute), but with the long range cruise condition used by BOAC that could be bettered. The take off run at maximum take off weight was between three and four nautical miles, depending on the sea state. When moored there was a single cylinder auxiliary power unit, situated on the right

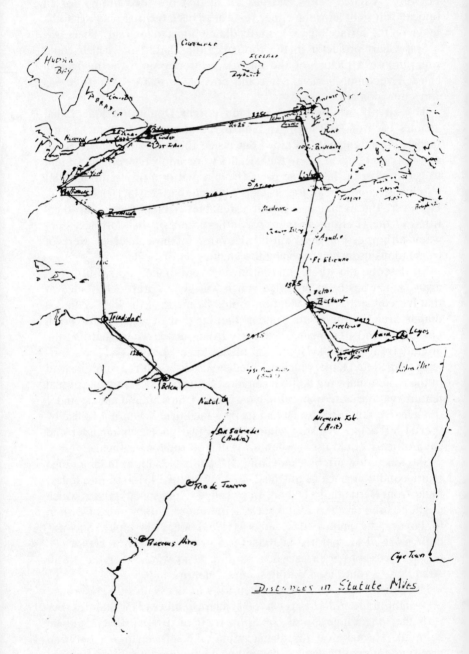

Distances in Statute Miles

side to the rear of the flight deck, which could be started to provide internal power though air conditioning was not part of the scene – moored or airborne.

The commanders were not just competent, and all first class navigators, but superb at handling her on the water for, with only the sponsons to assist with lateral stability, she was very tricky taxiing in strong winds – it was quite easy for her to tip over in gusty cross winds to a point where a wing tip could become submerged, especially if rough water prevented keeping her 'up on the step' like a speed boat and so fast enough for the aileron controls to hold the wing up. They were also, to a man, friendly and ever ready to give advice to any crew member asking for it. Apart from the older Kelly Rogers they were all second generation, much in same mould as Don Bennett.

Jim's first route experience was from Foynes on the river Shannon leaving at midnight to cross the Bay of Biscay at night to avoid the possibility of interception by German Ju88 fighter/bomber versions operating from France. Altitude was kept low so that exhaust fumes were less likely to be seen, and a crew member was always up in the astrodome keeping look out for enemy planes. Landing on the river Tagus seven hours later, mooring to the jetty at the flying boat base Cabo Ruivo, there was 10 hours of daylight rest in Lisbon in a hotel smelling strongly of cedar wood and associated polish (seemingly Lisbon's overiding and very pleasant smell) before continuing on to Bathurst, close to the mouth of the river Gambia in West Africa. That leg was for 13½ hours, mostly at night and keeping well clear of the coast and Dakar where both German and French air forces were stationed, and when astro navigation provided accurate positioning well out to sea.

Fifteen hours was spent resting at Bathurst, that is as well as possible in the sticky heat of the daytime there. A 10 hour leg from there to Lagos in Nigeria, landing at 8am on the lagoon to moor to a vessel named the Lady Bourdillon, a servicing vessel, completed the first stint.

That was on the third day out from Ireland and now there was to be three days stay in the BOAC Ikoyi mess, a delightful place despite the humidity, and some wonderful food. Jim came to like the West African curries better than any he had tasted before. The native 'boys' were a happy lot, full of almost childish fun and always ready to laugh.

At 10pm local time on the sixth day it was airborne again for a 10 hour flight back to Bathurst, arriving 7am local time. There was a full day's delay there (reason not specified in Jim's log book) until take off for Belem at the mouth of the river Amazon which was reached at dawn after a 15 hour flight. The heat and humidity were unbelievable, worse than the Persian Gulf at its worst. Until the Brazilian customs and port officials came on board it was forbidden to open up the aircraft to get at least some fresh, if thick, air into it. The 12 minutes or so until their arrival seemed like hours. As soon as they boarded the doors were quickly shut again whilst anti-bug spray was spread all over in clouds of what smelled like pure paraffin – (it was before the days of the DDT aerosol spray which came into international use some two years later). Everyone was choking and coughing for a good 10 minutes before permission was given to open up. At least the officials shared the misery!

Breakfast, after a boat ride to the docks, was a very pleasant meal despite the awful heat and humidity. That was a 2½ hour break before returning to the aircraft to take off for an 8 hour daylight flight up to Trinidad, Port of Spain – a very pleasant trip up the tropical coast of Brazil in perfect weather to arrive, relaxed and surprisingly not very tired.

The early evening drive from the flying boat base, through most attractive scenery, to the old town and the Queen's Park Hotel was superb. Then it was a long bath followed by Jim's first Planter's Punch, a marvellously cool fresh mint in local rum and ice drink, enjoyed in the balmy open air with calypso sounds drifting over from the town. It was not quite dinner time and he was about to order another one when the Skipper advised against it, at least until food had been eaten, as the drink had a delayed action punch in it unsuspected from its taste.

The stopover was scheduled 24 hours which gave time the next day to drive out, through coffee plantations, to one of the many lovely beaches for a picnic lunch, preceeded by another Planter's Punch bought from a tiny beach-hut stall. A lazy swim in the warm waters of the bay, then back to the hotel for a short sleep before take off for an 11½ hour trip up past the Windward and Leeward Islands, Barbados, St Lucia, Martinique, Guadeloupe, and Antigua to Bermuda for a night landing early on the eleventh day. There were two hours for refuelling and breakfast before the final leg to the base at Baltimore, Maryland, landing on the Chesapeake at midday. In those 11 days 10,780 nautical miles (12,400 Statute) had been covered in 81 flying hours, of which 55 had been at night and 26 hours by day.

There were then two weeks leave (during which the new uniforms would be made for which measurements were taken the same afternoon of arrival). Jim travelled by train to New York then on to Boston, where he was met by car for a drive up to Portland, Maine, where his wife had been staying with friends. After a most pleasant week there the two of them travelled down to Baltimore to find a flat and get settled in before he went off on the next trip. There had not seemed to be much change in America since he was last there, but the attitude of people seemed even more friendly than before. Conversation with casual acquaintances was noticeably more matey, if that can describe a feeling that (since Pearl Harbour) American and Britain had a joint concern being in, and to win, the war.

Leaving on 19 February 1942 for his next trip he was to experience the very long Bermuda to Lisbon flight for the first time, one which relied entirely on pure navigation without any landmarks, in an area where weather conditions could change rapidly and unpredictably. On this one, which was fairly quick at 17 hours 18 minutes, nothing very strange happened, but the very experienced first navigator was able to give Jim a very thorough briefing, and some special exercises to practice, on most of the things which could crop up and how to recognise and deal with them before they became too serious. That was to prove more than valuable later on when Jim had been promoted to first navigator.

The round trip, returning via the South Atlantic and Belem again, took 24 days. There were 10 days off, then another one returning to Baltimore the same way but lasting 53 days due to a double shuttle having to be made between Foynes and Lagos. 11 days off were rostered, by which time it was mid-May and the North Atlantic weather had become good enough to allow the out and return trip to Europe and Africa by that route. The first of three round trips via North Atlantic started on 23 May.

Baltimore to Botwood, Newfoundland, (1255 statute miles – nautical miles will no longer be used in the text to save confusion for the average reader. Conversion factors to nautical miles and kilometers are provided in the glossary for use if required) was the first leg of seven and a half hours. Then over to Foynes (2025 miles) taking 12¼ hours. Return trips westwards would average 16-17 hours over the Atlantic then 9-9½ down to Baltimore, the differences being winds from the west helping to Europe and hindering on the return.

Overall the North Atlantic route saved 1620 miles compared with the mid/south Atlantic one per round trip, and avoided the extra long Bermuda to Lisbon leg which not only involved some navigational problems due to temperamental weather conditions (as explained before) but was close to critical as far as range was concerned.

After 14 days off, the second North Atlantic trip of 25 days started, with then only 6 days off before the third one. That one took 35 days due to an 11 day period in Lough Erne, Northern Ireland, whilst the aircraft was serviced at the RAF flying boat base there. This gave the crew members opportunity to visit relatives and friends in Britain for a few days, or remain in the lovely little village of Baleek where their hotel accommodation was provided, and where the world famous Baleek China is made.

On return to Baltimore there were 13 days off before, 29 September 1942, the fourth trip outbound over the North Atlantic returning by the South Atlantic route as the weather, particularly head winds, going into November made the northern route impractical. Return to Baltimore was 2 November for another 13 day rest period, which was to be Jim's last one there, for he had been posted back to Bristol for more schooling, (and this time there was no secret about it), before going on to Cairo. There, after flight training on Lockheed Lodestars – (Lockheed 18, a longer version of the Lockheed 14 and similar 414 Hudson) – he was to be promoted to junior captain. An unbelievable rate of promotion, particularly as his total flying hours had only just topped 2000 with half that as a navigator on the Boeings. It was exhilarating but much tempered with the realisation he would be saying goodbye to his wife almost certainly for the last time before the end of the war, as no way would transport be available to her in any form out to the Middle East until then.

She had obtained work in Baltimore with the British Consulate and had made many friends, so at least she would not be at a loose end. He would miss those marvellous crew members too, very much. They had had some memorable trips and interesting experiences together and Jim had come to feel part of a very special family. He has not recorded innumerable happy and amusing tales, en-route as well as home in Baltimore, for there were so many which occurred all the time – there is no memory of any unpleasantness or disagreeable relationships, though of course individuals were ribbing each other unmercifully even in moments of operational stress. However, and enough time has elapsed not to cause embarassment by the telling of it, there is one story which caused the 'ribbing' game to go on for a long time.

One of the commanders, with his wife and Jim and wife together with another couple, were dining together in one of Baltimore's more up-market restaurants (the Chesapeake – 'If you can't cut your steak with a fork, no charge'), the occasion the Skipper's birthday, when in walked one of his crew members with a stunning young beauty expensively dressed. They had to stop as they passed close by the table to acknowledge the diners, the girl all social gush . . . 'Oh how nice to meet you. Captain xxxxxxx has told me so much about his crew' . . .

Face glowing red with embarassment the ship's steward declined his Skipper's offer for the newcomers to join his party and managed to find a table on the other side of the room. Well, why not? Such was the real friendship amongst all the crew members that the commander not in the least offended, was just highly amused but for some time after the unfortunate steward had to put up with being addressed, good naturedly, as 'captain' when off duty. He had been a senior steward with Imperial Airways, was a master at his job and, when out of uniform, looked every bit the part he was playing – more dignified perhaps than many captains! He did have the last word though, when the crews met another from a different flight down the route whose somewhat supercillious captain greeted him sarcastically thus his reply . . 'Some people, sir, are so easily impressed' . . . was very neat, at least his own Skipper thought so. As is said so often – it takes all sorts to make a world!

There were several operational incidents of interest which happened during those 10 months on the Boeing Flight, and perhaps the most unusual occurred on the last one, leaving Baltimore 16 November, Jim completing acquaintance with all three of the boats by navigating on Bristol, appropriately en-route for the city of the same name. The first leg was as usual to Bermuda, incident free. Then, for some reason not recorded nor explained but probably due to some expected transport for a Very VIP – (Churchill again?) – 10 days was spent there. Whatever, it was a very pleasant little holiday on that peaceful and beautiful island (no cars in those days allowed), transport by horse and carriage, on foot or bicycle, and a magnificent golf course close by the hotel. It was the first time Jim, and most of the crew, had had a chance to see the island properly for, during the normal stop, it was eat/sleep/eat and go, with the sleeping bit during the daytime.

On 25 November, landing in Lisbon 26, the flight took 20 hours 40 minutes, the longest yet experienced and the most interesting, for a totally unexpected and unforecast change occurred in the weather pattern en-route.

After five hours flying the cloud formations did not match at all the forecast situation, and drift readings and roughening state of the sea confirmed that things were not right. Fortunately a break in the cloud cover during the sixth hour gave the opportunity for the first time to take star sights. A good three-star 'fix' gave a position almost 120 miles south of where the flight plan and dead reckoning, corrected by drift readings, had been calculated. Course was altered immediately and considerably to start an initial correction until an amended synoptic chart had been drawn based on assumptions – ('intelligent guesstima-tion' as Don Bennett's maxim states in his *Compleat Navigator*) – from the newly confirmed position and reasons for it.

The two captains, equal in rank but taking it in turn to command, were the most junior on the Boeing Flight, both with tremendous senses of humour and never missing a chance to rib each other. Needless to say Jim got his full share of that in snide remarks about his ability to find the way, but got a 'well done Nithead' as Lisbon came up on the nose 13½ hours later. He was to be replaced by another first navigator there (as the Boeing was to go down to West Africa without returning to Ireland this time due to the long stay in Bermuda) and return to Britain on the Golden Hind Short flying boat – a very much enlarged version of the 'C' class boats, though not as big as the Boeing. That had brought to Lisbon the passengers the Boeing would have picked up had it been on time in Foynes, and was to return to England, direct to Poole Harbour, with delayed Boeing passengers including Jim.

He stood out on the small platform let down on the left side by the nose of Bristol, safety belt firmly in place, ready to catch the cricket ball thrown from the Cabo Ruivo pontoon with the light line to which the main mooring rope was attached. Then he would pass it up to the radio officer standing in the bow mooring hatch, who would attach the main rope to the bollard before the boat was warped to the pontoon. While standing ready Jim found it hard to take that that would be the last time he would perform the act. It had always been his duty and, particularly in rough weather and low temperatures when the stint on the little platform could last even three quarters of an hour, it required a certain amount of skill to catch an often slippery ball first shot, a feat of which he was proud though, on reflection, it was no big deal really.

That midday scene on the Tagus on one of Lisbon's very best early winter days, balmy air with hazy blue skies, the water sparkling on the beautiful bay, the white walls and pink/blue/green roofs of the city rising up often quite steeply, added to his nostalgia. At least, as he was going on the next day as a passenger, he could have a really good night out on the town!

In the 10 months he had flown as navigator, with a few as pilot under training, 1019 hours during which 139,335 statute miles (the equivalent of a little over five times round the world) had been covered – the average speed 137 mph! His total flying hours were now up to 2,174.

4 School in Bristol, Flight out to South Africa, – Lodestar training, – Start of three and a half years based in Cairo with the BOAC Number 5 Line.

The school in Bristol lasted two very interesting weeks. First the technical details of the Lockheed 18 Lodestar were studied, needed to pass the necessary exam to get the type endorsed on his licence after flying training was completed. Apart from being six feet longer in the fuselage than the Hudson, (with the tailplane raised up from the rear fuselage instead of being flush with the top), there were few differences between the two. The engines were the same Wright Cyclone 205s and Pratt & Whitney Twin Wasps, both of 1200 bhp, that had been fitted to the Hudsons, but as well some of the Lodestars still had Pratt & Whitney Hornet engines of 875 bhp. Instead of bomb bays the space was divided into luggage/freight lockers and therefore the loading required more attention to ensure that the centre of gravity remained close to the optimum for best performance and safety. Flying training was to be done in South Africa before going on to Cairo – there were no aircraft of the type in Britain then.

The No. 5 Line route network covered over 15,000 miles, radiating from Cairo, and for the rest of that two weeks this was studied in some detail together with associated weather conditions. The Western Desert run to Tripoli (Castel Benito) was still in operation and would remain so until the Germans had been removed from Africa. The main routes otherwise stretched down through the Sudan and Kenya to Gwelo in Southern Rhodesia. To India via a northern route through Iraq, the Persian Gulf to Karachi then over to Calcutta, and via a southern route through to Port Sudan, Asmara (Eritrea – from where a short day return trip was made to Addis Ababa in Abyssinia) to Aden and then, at least projected, via the Yemen and Oman to Karachi. From Khartoum in the

Sudan there was a route to Lagos (West Africa) via El Geneina, Maidugeri, and Kano. North to Istanbul (Turkey and neutral) via Nicosia (Cyprus) and the capital Ankara, and another eastward run to Teheran (Persia/Iran) via Lydda (Palestine – now Lod/Israel) and Baghdad (Iraq), were the remaining routes, and were probably the ones most difficult operationally – certainly in winter.

Another long, cold, and pretty miserable train journey to Southampton, to report at Hythe New Year's Day 1943.

A Short S-30 'C' Class flying boat was ready to be ferried out to Durban in South Africa to join the rest of that fleet, which operated the so called 'Horseshoe Route' up to Cairo then east over to Calcutta. Jim was to act as navigator, there being a senior captain with his co-pilot a young second officer, and an old hand radio officer. They flew over to Poole in Dorset on 2 January, leaving for Foynes on 3 January, and continuing from there to Lisbon, arrivng on the fourth.

The next day was spent being given some flying practice on the aircraft from the river Tagus. The Skipper, knowing Jim had had initial training on the type, and more recently on the Boeing, said he wanted Jim capable of acting as co-pilot should the other one fall sick, and to relieve either pilot in the air as there would not be much real navigation to be done down the African coast to Lagos then overland to Durban. He was particularly nice and Jim suspected that this bit of training was a kindness rather than a planned part of the trip, but it was most welcome and what a lovely lady to handle G-AFKZ (Cathay) was. A second nightstop in exciting Lisbon was also most appreciated by all.

A twelve hour flight down to Bathurst was enjoyed, as the African coastline on that leg had always been done at night on the Boeings. To see the fascinating scenery, previously in the imagination only, was great – Dakar being given a very wide berth as usual. A night stop at Bathurst was followed by a short day flight to Freetown, Sierra Leone, for another night stop. On that leg Jim had operated as co-pilot whilst the other got in some basic navigation practice. It was obviously going to be the captain's way of keeping them from getting bored as well as giving each some practice at the other's job. The Freetown to Lagos leg of nine hours on 8 January was shared by those two, half each, with Jim being given the landing on the lagoon at Lagos. There the crew changed, that is captain, first officer and radio officer, Jim to continue to Durban with the aircraft.

Three clear days at that delightful Ikoyi Mess was very welcome, and during that time the new captain and crew arrived from South Africa. The legendary Captain Dudley Travers, no less, with a senior first officer, and Irish radio officer with an unbridled sense of humour. In view of some of the tales told about that autocratic captain, (and they were legion despite the short time Jim had been with the company), he was understandably apprehensive at departure 12 January.

Airborne, he passed the course to steer for Libreville to the captain, the navigator's normal procedure unless asked before take off. He was firmly and quickly put in his place, the chit passed back with the curt remark –

> 'You have applied magnetic variation incorrectly – kindly revise!'

Red faced and flustered (it really was a very silly mistake) the error was corrected and re-presented to the captain with a simple –

> 'Sorry Sir!'

and the addition of estimated time of arrival at Libreville. Straight faced, his rather high pitched voice loud enough for all to hear he said –

> 'Perhaps we shall arrive before we left if you have applied the speed in reverse' –

which did nothing to ease Jim's embarrassment!

Two course corrections due to drift change were handed forward during the rest of the trip, being acted upon without further comment. As Libreville came into sight ahead, Jim was motioned forward to take the co-pilot's seat from which to make the landing. Fortunately it went well, more by good luck that good judgement in view of his nervousness, but –

> 'That'll make you feel better, young feller' –

from the great man put the world to rights instantly.

Jim came to like him more and more as the trip went on. Autocratic certainly, and no sufferer of fools lightly, he was unexpectedly considerate to all crew and ground staff, and posessed a mischievous sense of humour in which sarcasm played no part at all. So much for the 'grapevine' which, as the years went by Jim learned to attend to, but always to find out for himself (with bias towards the maligned) before making judgement.

That night was spent on the river Congo at Stanleyville (now Kisangani) where it was a pleasant surprise to find that the native servants spoke excellent French, maybe Belgian accented, quite unlike the pidgin English of the areas influenced by the British. One up for the Belgians, whose colony the Congo was until independence re-named it Zaire.

A dawn start was made on 14 January for Kisumu on Lake Victoria in Kenya for a 50 minute re-fuelling stop before climbing out over the Mau escarpment, passing Nairobi before landing again at Mombassa on the coast for a slightly longer refuelling. A shorter leg was then flown to Dar-es-Salaam (one and a half hours) to refuel again for a four hour final leg of the day to Lourenço Marques, Mozambique. It had been a long day of over 17 hours, of which 13½ had been in flight, so a tasty dinner of fish Portugese style, and a few drinks in the cool of a white-walled hotel within sight and sound of the tropical sea, a big yellow moon flooding the scene with soft light, was very relaxing before early bed.

Mozambique was at the time a Portuguese Colony and (unlike in the Belgian Congo where white families would be stationed for twenty or more years before repatriation home) mixed marriages with the native population were common, as occurred often also in the French Colonies. Thus the Portuguese influence in way of life and cooking was strong, with mixed race families living out their lives in the Colony adopted as home.

There were two four hour legs to be flown on 15 January. The first to Beira, still in Mozambique and port for goods to and from Rhodesia, the capital of which, Salisbury, is at the western end of the main railway line which passes through Umtali on the border. Jim was again given the landing there, which went off well enough for him to be allowed the take off for the second leg – to Durban. By then he was convinced that the 'C' class flying boat could do the job by herself, so effortless was the handling. However, he understood there were conditions, on the water, which required considerable skill and experience, none of which had been needed for his four en-route landings and one take off (plus training at Lisbon) since leaving Britain.

He was in some ways sorry that he was not, as the captain had thought, about to join the 'Horseshoe Route' crews on those boats, a type of flying machine he had come to love and feel thoroughly identified with, especially the crews. In a not easily identifiable way flying boat crews seemed to be a different breed from their landplane brothers, quite probably because of the cross between sailing and flying inherent with their type of work. That is not to imply they are any better, or more skilled, people or for that matter any more likeable – just that the flying boat atmosphere overall tended (and now extinct with their withdrawal from the civil aviation scene) to be perhaps the more relaxed of the two. Given the choice Jim would probably have gone on as posted anyway, for an early command could not be ignored no matter what type he was to fly.

A friendly farewell after arrival in Durban and he was on his way forthwith to the railway station for a sleeper journey to Johannesburg. There he was met by the flight sergeant, part of a two-man RAF team not unlike the pair who had done his 'B' licence testing a little over four years before, who shared the training of BOAC pilots on the Lodestar aircraft with two BOAC captains. A taxi ride to Germiston, the small private aircraft field at Johannesburg, then to board a freshly serviced

Lodestar and be given a thorough briefing about the differences between that and the Hudson. Then it was the co-pilot's seat for a half hour flight to Vereeniging, a small grass airfield where the training took place close by Vaaldam, the great lake from which flying boats operated.

Accommodation was in a very comfortable separate room, four to a block, in a sort of bed-sitter arrangement. There was a Mess, with a bar and lounge area, in which everyone ate – no rank discrimination. It was cooler there than in the living blocks, having fans to keep the very hot midsummer air on the move.

Seven days of classroom study (a follow up on the Bristol preview but with actual equipment available to examine) before flying training started on 23 January. That went on for two weeks until 5 February, the BOAC and RAF instructors sharing out their trainees impartially so that all of them had four separate assessments of ability and progress, when Jim and the other four trainees passed the final exams and checks.

After another sleeper train journey to Durban, which unfortunately did not allow for much viewing of the magnificent scenery (much of which had been admired from the air during training flights) where three lazy days were spent enjoying that lovely city, despite the sticky heat. They had not heard much of the South African accented English and found it quite hard to understand at first, and in Johannesburg, Vereeniging, and Kimberley (which had been visited to play a cricket match with the RAF one weekend) the strong Dutch overtones of the Boers had been particularly difficult. In Durban, and they heard Cape Town, there was a distinct sibilant lilt to it which, especially with the ladies, came softly and pleasantly to the ears and easily understood.

On 10 February they boarded one of the flying boats as it set out on it's trip to Calcutta and back. There were nightstops at Lourenço Marques ('LM'), Kampala on Lake Victoria, and Khartoum before landing on the river Nile at Cairo on the fourth day. What comfort, space to walk around in, and outside views passengers enjoyed on those boats, and what a very pleasant change for Jim and his colleagues, none of whom had travelled far as passengers in a proper airliner before.

For some months to come the river Nile was to be their home, in single cabins on the river steamer Delta moored to the banks of Gezira Island, where meals and accommodation were all found. When individuals found their own accommodation then an annual allowance of £E 200 (two hundred Egyptian pounds) to cover the cost was made, drawn monthly with salary (or that part of it not deducted for subsistence of relatives at home in Britain) – it was quite adequate.

Jim's salary had been raised from £450 to £525 when he was promoted to first officer rank on joining the Boeings, overseas allowances being paid in Baltimore as they had been for Montreal. That would remain until promoted to junior captain after a few months route and general experience as co-pilot on the Lodestars, and on a few Hudson VIs, temporarily supplementing the fleet until more Lodestars became available. The princely sum of £600 per year would then become applicable, with annual increments of £20 a year. It was really not bad money at all, though hard to imagine in the 1980s. Uniforms (khaki shirts with epaulettes, bush jackets ditto, shorts, long trousers for night and mosquito country, and a pair of mosquito boots) were provided, expertly tailored by local Egyptians, taking only a day or two to make and fit.

Jim's first flight on the routes was on 25 February, to Castel Benito (Tripoli in Lybia) in a Hudson VI in RAF livery and colours. It was also the start of three and a half years based in Cairo with No. 5 Line. The Lodestars, and until the war ended all other types, were camouflaged but had civil registrations and no roundels or other military markings.

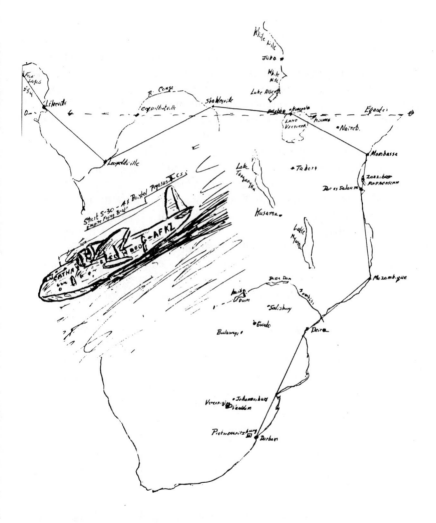

White Nile
Juba
White Nile
Lake Albert

Four Places
S54
Libreville
R. Congo
Coquilhatville
Stanleyville
Butabo Kampala
Lake Victoria
Kisumu
Nairobi
Equator

Short S-30 & Bristol Pegasus XCs;
Empire Flying Boat
G-AFKZ
CATHAY

Leopoldville

Lake Tanganyika
Tabora
Mombassa
Zanzibar
Dar es Salaam
MADAGASCAR

Kisuma

Lake Nyasa

Kariba Dam
Mozambique

Kaincy Dam
Salisbury
Zambesi
Beira

Bulawayo
Gwelo

Vereeniging
Johannesburg
Germiston

Pietermaritzburg
Durban

5 The first six months – Promotion – Lodestars.

The Hudson VI had the same Pratt & Whitney R1830-92 Twin Wasp engines of 1200 bhp as the Hudson V flown in Montreal with ATFERO, but had fully feathering Hamilton constant speed airscrews. For civilian use the gun turret was removed from the upper fuselage, the bomb bay turned into baggage compartments, and metal bench seats down each side to accommodate eight passengers a side – the toilet in the rear of the cabin retained.

The first trip, over the desert to El Adem (the airfield for Tobruk) then after refuelling passing over Benina (airfield for Benghazi) before letting down towards Castel Benito, was impressive mainly for the huge number of wrecked tanks and vehicles piled up and stretching either side of the narrow bitumen road to miles out of sight, the road itself busy with traffic – a stark black straight strip standing out against a shimmering background of endless hot, hot sand.

That must have been the greatest junk heap in history. It was as awesome as it was terrifying to think of the ghosts of the thousands of men who had died violently down there in the alternating retreat to El Alamein and the current advance back over that totally arid lifeless desert – not a tree or bush anywhere. The sight brought cold shivers down Jim's back as he sat by his captain, also quiet and thoughtful. That sight, seen each time to June 1943 when the BOAC Western Desert Service finished as the Germans were pushed out of Africa, never failed to make the same impression, until the hills and green strips of Italian cultivated fields and vineyards appeared ahead as the let-down towards Castel-Benito airfield was begun.

There the passengers (mainly army personnel, for the RAF had their own transport) the all important mail and, almost as important, fresh vegetables for the various Service Messes were offloaded. Similar off-loading had been done at El Adem, with the occasional passenger pick up.

Of all those sombre trips there was one in April 1943 which remains a horrifying memory. It was during the final push. The Germans were fighting fiercely to slow up the Allied advance to enable them to evacuate as many troops as possible to Italy. Casualties amongst the

78

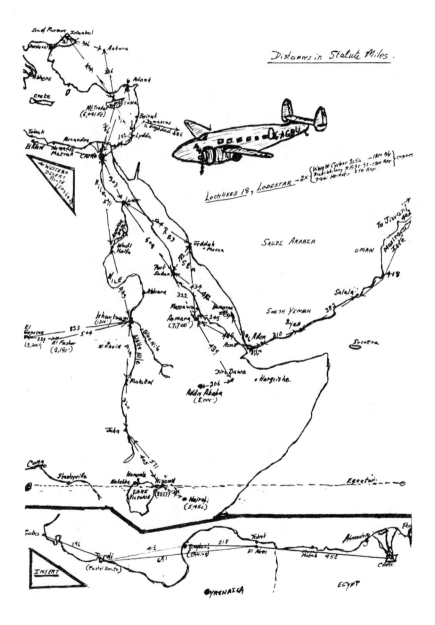

Distances in Statute Miles.

LOCKHEED 18, LODESTAR - 2X

Sea of Marmara Istanbul
306
Ankara
290
206
Adana
Athens
Crete
Mt. Taurus
(6,041 Ft.)
Beirut
Damascus
To Baghdad 486
382
Lydda
Tobruk
Alexandria
EIAan
Mersa Matruh
CAIRO

WESTERN DESERT ROUTE

Nile 393
571
Luxor
Wadi Halfa
RED SEA
Jeddah
Mecca
Port Sudan
434
NILE
Atbara
322
Messawa
El Gezeira 823
329
El Fasher
(2,190')
Khartoum
(1300')
504
El Obeid
Asmara
(7,700')
White Nile
Blue Nile
239
Asmara
Aden
310
Malakal
Dire Dawa
206
Addis Ababa
(8,000')
Hargeisa
Socotra
Juba
Coro
425
571
Stanleyville
Kampala
Kisumu
Entebbe
LAKE VICTORIA
3937
Nairobi
(5,450')
Equator

SAUDI ARABIA
OMAN
To Jiwani 482
Masira Isle
418
Salala
382
SOUTH YEMEN
Ryan

INSERT

rubes
196
Tripoli
(Castel Benito)
413
681
Benghazi
(Benina)
218
El Adem
Tobruk
Matruh
458
Alexandria
Port
CAIRO
CYRENAICA
EGYPT

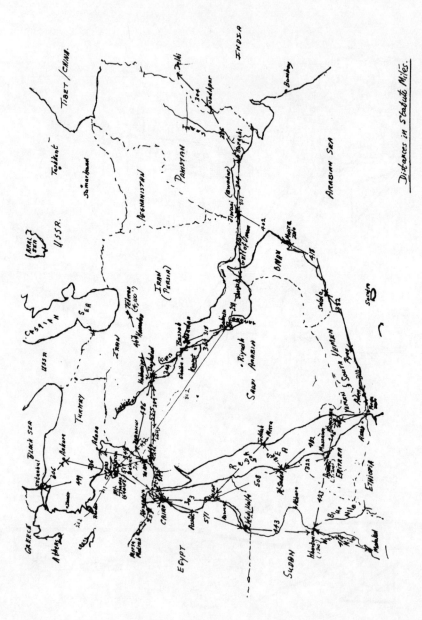

Distances in Statute Miles.

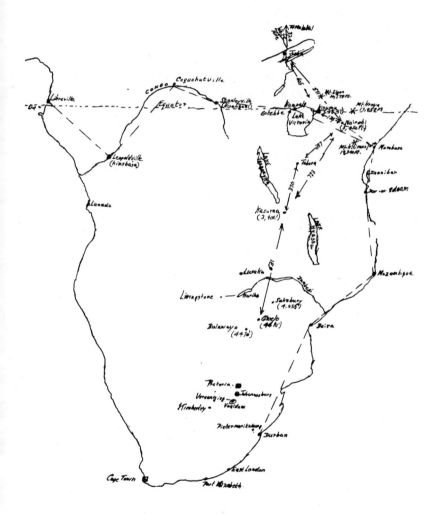

Distances in Statute Miles.

Commonwealth troops just past Gabes were so high that the RAF ambulance planes could not cope and help was asked from the BOAC aircraft, normally not allowed to fly close to the lines.

It was the afternoon of 17 April, after landing at Castel Benito from Cairo, that an emergency trip was made to Gabes. Landing there one hour 20 minutes later the sound of heavy guns, even machine gun fire, was clearly heard even before the engines were switched off. The place was a shambles of ambulances and stretcher bearers, with soldiers lying wherever their wounded bodies had found space. Eight stretcher cases, one not loaded as the very young soldier died before he could be lifted up into the Lodestar, and four 'walking wounded' (though, how anyone with an amputated arm and another with two heavily splinted legs on crutches could be so described, only wartime front lines would know) were secured in the cabin with a corporal medic urging the crew to get back to Tripoli and its forward base hospital as quickly as possible. One more stretcher case died on the way.

The worst part of that trip was the simple gratitude of those shattered men as they were taken off the aircraft. If ever 'there but for the Grace of God go I' applied it was then. Whenever looking back to the war days (certainly interesting, challenging, sometimes difficult, and occasionally sad) and to the fine people met and worked with, those three and a half hours of the smell of blood, cries of pain, and infinite courage, will live for ever in Jim's mind.

The main load was heavier than usual for the return trip to Cairo and as passengers, accompanied by two Army Medics, were three of the previous day's stretcher-cases to be taken to the main Service's hospital in Cairo for urgent surgery. There is a story about one of them in particular (as it turned out a happy one) but to relate in isolation in this book something which deserves a volume of it's own is not the purpose. Suffice to mention that there was at least one happy eventual outcome from that first, and really only, close-up Jim had of the appalling horror of war at the front.

By comparison, watching (whilst himself next in line for take off) three colleagues in a Hudson at St Hubert just become airborne, flip over on to its back when the starboard engine cut out, then being cleared for take off over the smoking wreckage (by air traffic control), Jim's reaction was simply that it was a rotten but mercifully quick demise for them – they had died instantly. Now, three years later, he had vivid confirmation that that reaction was one not without feeling – nor without personal sadness at their loss.

Promotion to captain came 1 June 1943. In the four months since arriving in Cairo Jim had flown with ten different captains, been checked out on all the Lodestar routes and the three different engine

BOAC'S WELLINGTON SQUADRON

Loading the Wellington Fleet Flagship

Captain Spooner's recent article about '5 Line' just after the war and his stories of Salalah and Masira Island brought back memories; and whilst thinking of those days it occurred to me that nobody has written of the time when BOAC operated a fleet of Wellingtons.

In 1942 the landplane fleet in Middle East consisted of a number of Lockheed 18 Lodestars, one Lockheed 14 which had flown Chamberlain to Munich, a few Ensigns and about nine Flamingoes. They were not enough to meet the commitment of the Tedder Routes and no further civil aircraft were obtainable, so the bomber squadrons in Egypt were directed to transfer four Wellingtons. One can imagine the joy with which Engineer Officers got rid of their Jonahs. (I remember Q of 38 Squadron which became, I believe, BAW 2). The aircraft were modified by the removal of front and rear turrets and the fitting of primitive seating for some 16 passengers. Entry was by ladder through the hole in the floor alongside the pilot's station. The logo was interesting — the Speedbird motif with the words "British Airways", not BOAC. Anticipating some 30 years perhaps.

The Wimpey was not a bad aircraft for its day, though with its Pegasus engines the Ic was always underpowered and the hotter and more humid the climate the more underpowered it was. Take-off run always seemed to be 95% of the available distance whilst single engine performance was downhill. With the boost and rpm advised by BOAC for cruise — which, of course, had to be different from the RAF thinking — the cruise speed out of Cairo was of the order of 125 mph. By the time we reached the Gulf the fabric would be stretching until the wings resembled eiderdowns and the speed would be barely three figures. A few cases of torn fabric in these conditions resulted in very unorthodox handling.

The early flying was done by contract captains, but there were legal problems since the aircraft were not civil registered and lacked details such as C of A. So, they were handed over to a dozen or so ex-Wellington seconded pilots, and we got commands within a year of joining — must be a record.

We operated a scheduled service Cairo – Lydda – Habbaniyeh – Shaibah – Bahrein – Sharjah – Jiwani – Karachi and back.

Supposed to be six days, and once or twice it was, though I think I held the record at three weeks. After Alamein the Wellington was also used up the desert to Matruh, El Adem, Marble Arch etc.

The fleet was in being for some nine months. Something of a 'private airforce' atmosphere developed as many of those who remembered the glories of Imperial Airways did not care to be associated with such a Fred Karno outfit. Although rough and slow the Wimpey was robust and viceless, so though there were many incidents and damn close-run things we managed not to break anything — so its BOAC safety record was 100%.

One or two funnies. At this time the airfield on Masira Island was under construction by a gang of Arabs supervised by one RAF officer and one NCO, under the command of Sharjah. One night Sharjah received a garbled radio message which was understood to say a demonstration of force was desirable. Our aircraft was commandeered to take a force of soldiery down to sort out the Arabs. We had no radio contact with Masira but on arrival overhead everything seemed to be calm so we landed and deployed the Army ready for war. The resident RAF were greatly entertained by all this and told us the story — they were a bit upset to realise that all the workers carried knives and muskets whilst all the RAF had was one 38. So one Friday they said 'Hand over your arms or you don't get paid' and to their surprise the locals gave up their ar-

moury. So to clear his position, the CO signalled Sharjah that he had carried out a desirable demonstration of force . . . There was a story later that the Navy had sent a destroyer in reply to the same signal which went flat out until it ran aground on Masira. But that *may* not be true. We flew a red-faced and disappointed task force back to the boredom of Sharjah.

I had occasion to tick off my first officer one day when the bottom hatch blew open on take off and we were subjected to a sandstorm. He got a bit excited, but as he pointed out, the cause was that my suitcase had dropped out of the hole and vanished into the Western Desert.

I remember watching a Wellington which had been grossly misleaded trying to get into Almaza. After some half dozen hairy efforts

Hand Fuelling the 'Wimpey'

including hitting the boundary wall and various bounces it eventually made it — just. The captain got out, very white and trembling, to be surprised by one of his passengers coming along and saying 'thank you captain for a delightful flight'.

And the day we landed at El Adem with an ENSA party including four young females, to be surrounded by about a thousand sex-starved 'erks.' There are times when one wonders how far one can be responsible for the safety of one's passengers.

Most of the pilots involved stayed on in BOAC or BEA to fly ever more efficient and sophisticated equipment, but I suspect that they remember the Wellington Flight as one of the most interesting — and in a perverse way — amusing episodes of their careers.

F. Tricklebank
(ex BOAC, BEA, BA, Retd.)

The ENSA Party

All Photos: F. Tricklebank

configurations, and completed 220 hours flying on them. His total experience was by then 2399 hours of which 854 had been in command, 1019 as navigator, and 526 as co-pilot which included dual instruction. It was natural that he should feel proud as he smoothed over the two and a half gold stripes on his epaulettes, a junior captain aged 24, yet with so little flying time – and so short a time with the Company. As he did so, instinct signalled a warning – 'watch it boy; don't get cocky!'

During this period the No.5 Line fleet was augmented by the addition of four Wellington bombers, converted to carry 16 passengers in the bomb bay – gun turrets removed. They retained RAF markings but had added the BOAC Speedbird Logo on the nose with BAW 1, 2, 3, and 4 identification underneath – denoting British Airways Wellington flight.

They were crewed by RAF pilots seconded to BOAC who wore RAF uniforms when flying them, and that of BOAC when flying BOAC aircraft. Their job was to supplement the so called 'Tedder' routes of supply and communication. Apart from operating up the Western Desert their main route was from Cairo to Karachi via Lydda, Habbaniyeh, Shaibah (Basrah), Sharjah and Jiwani.

The pilots soon got commands on the civil aircraft when the Wellingtons were phased out late in 1943 with the arrival of some Dakota (Douglas C47: militarised DC3) aircraft civil registered to BOAC. Most of those great chaps remained with BOAC until the end of the war, some remaining afterwards and some transferring to the newly formed British European Airways (BEA).

An article written by one of them, Captain Frank Tricklebank, appeared in the *Log* (official publication of the British Airline Pilots Association) July 1980 issue, and both the author and BALPA have kindly given permission for it to be reproduced in this book. Frank has retired, after many years with BEA during which, among other things, he was involved in the early trials and introduction into service of the first fully automatic landing systems as fitted to the DeHavilland Trident jet aircraft.

Whilst on the subject of personalities, as stated before real names, other than those of well known personalities, companies and some of their better known managerial staff, are not being used in the text of this book. So far many actual names of personalities have appeared, mainly in connection with the influence they have had on civil aviation development and on the Third Generation of pilots. From now on there will not be many new ones introduced, the majority of the subject matter being more directly concerned with Jim and his peer group.

His first trip in command was to Castel Benito, this one uneventful, and he was glad to have operated that route first off for he felt closely identified with it. As it happened it was also his last trip up there, for the Western Desert service closed down shortly afterwards with the Allied victory in North Africa.

In the 14 days following there were a series of short test flights out of the Almaza base in Cairo before the second command trip, this time to Adana (Turkey) returning via Lydda (Palestine). Then 23 June, he was scheduled to fly to Aden, night stopping at Asmara (Eritrea) out and back, returning to Cairo on the fourth day. He had been to Asmara three times before but only once to Aden, each time when getting route experience, and he was looking forward with pleasure to the refuelling stop (between Asmara and Aden) at Kamaran Island, and to the breakfast which crews enjoyed so much on the wide verandah of the Resident's bungalow.

Major Thompson was in charge of this coral and sand island close to the coast of Yemen and due east one and a half hours flying from Asmara, its highest point around ten feet above sea level. His bungalow was a thick-walled Arab building which remained cool during the summer and where the sleeping and ablution areas were situated. An extremely wide verandah had been constructed all round carpeted with Indian and Persian rugs, and furnished most beautifully and which served as lounge and dining area in the front section. In the morning two hours after sunrise, the normal arrival time, it was cool with a fresh breeze and never seemed to get hot and sticky as the Red Sea can.

The airstrip was coral sand, its line marked by white painted stones with a windsock at one corner. The Major had to clear the runway of goats and Arab children when the aircraft was heard approaching, and sometimes a small gazelle of which there were a few wild on the island. Taxiing in, the Union Jack could be seen hoisted beside a small shelter which served as the Terminal Building. A line of khaki uniformed Arabs, buttons polished and looking very smart, formed a well-drilled guard of honour, the Major towering above them straight as a ramrod. The Arabs apparently vied for the honour of being in that little group and thoroughly enjoyed the old fashioned pomp and ceremony, which of course helped with general discipline.

The major, a man of indeterminate age though clearly well mature, was employed after World War I by, it is believed, the Colonial/Indian Government on behalf of the British to whom the island had been ceded from the Turks. He and his wife, with two daughters, lived happily there between the Wars, with the children at school in Britain where they and their Mother remained throughout the second War. They were the only white people on the island, which was used mainly as a quarantine station for pilgrims going in and out of the Holy City Mecca, itself very close.

They have become loved by the few natives, to whose children the major was godfather (whether in reality or assumed Jim did not know) and they were as part of his family. He had become known as the 'King of Kamaran' over the years and that kindly man was a most benevolent 'Ruler', whilst sticking firmly in dress and manner to the best of the old British Colonial principles.

The major had a yacht in which he went fishing regularly, catching among other things the very large Red Sea salmon, a delicious fish, one of which (in ice) was loaded on the return trip to Asmara for the BOAC Mess there in return for the load of vegetables (fresh) sent down with the morning aircraft once a fortnight – later weekly. Every visit there was much looked forward to by all the crews, who enjoyed the major's hospitality and good humour as much as he seemed to enjoy their company, and the latest titbits of news or gossip coming out of Cairo – or other places visited.

Returning to Asmara from Aden and Kamaran, as scheduled, the second day out from Cairo, another crew was waiting to take the aircraft over for the return flight to base. They had brought a Lodestar, fitted with the smaller 850 bhp Pratt & Whitney Hornet engines, with instructions for Jim and crew, (plus an engineer whom they had brought from Cairo), to operate a new route from Asmara to Karachi. This would start from Cairo in future, via what was called the Hadramut, that is the coasts of South Yemen and Oman from Aden, Ryan, Salala (nightstop), Masira Island, and Jiwani. Maps and briefing, as full as possible, on facilities, aerodromes, weather conditions (as far as known) had been sent, also a bag heavy with Maria Theresa dollar coins and a small calibre Beretta rifle (with instructions not to be used other than inn dire emergency).

There was also an envelope containing 'Guli Chits', these being written in Arabic script, promising that His Britannic Majesty King George would reward (with more Maria Theresa dollars) the natives who lived along those coasts if, having captured the occupants of the aircraft should it be forced to land, they were cared for and returned (unharmed) to the British Authorities. That unharmed bit was apparently meant for males to retain their ability to reproduce. (For 'Guli' read testicles!)

Departure was scheduled for 27 June 1943, for a nightstop at Aden before proceeding further. That gave the whole of 26 June in Asmara to study the route and maps which, as far as heights of mountains were concerned, showed very few spot heights. Unless the sky was clear it was obvious that there could be no safe use of straight line tracks between places, and that the coastline would have to be followed most of the way.

At breakfast, again with Major Thompson on Kamaran en-route to Aden the following day, he gave the sound advice that the gun be kept well out of sight (should a forced landing have to be made) as the natives would certainly take it as a belligerent act, even to handle it, let alone fire it. He said that the tribes all along the coast were very wild and temperamental, with a habit of dyeing their hair with henna (not unlike a form of warpaint), would steal everything they fancied, whether parts of the aircraft or personal clothing and possessions, and could not be relied upon to understand (or even care about) the Guli Chit procedure. The only hope was to maintain a smiling face and an open, friendly manner.

It was comforting to know that all three versions of engine fitted to the Lodestars were extremely reliable and that, once airborne, the machines could fly well on one only!

Not unusually, Aden was very hot that night and nobody slept very much despite the comfortable officers' quarters provided by the RAF at Khormakser airport. Constant use was made of the tall stone jars in which fresh, very cool, drinking water was kept in each room. The dull taste of the water, being evaporated from salt water as Aden has no fresh or spring supply nor rainwater (a little rain once in several years) was not too pleasant but tasted nevertheless like nectar in those conditions.

So soon after getting his command this pioneering trip (at least it was for him, though the RAF had been flying the route for some time) laid pretty heavily on Jim's shoulders. Happily his first officer was experienced, competent and of a steady nature (also good humoured) as were the radio officer, an old hand ex-Merchant Navy man, and the engineer (who was carried because BOAC had no maintenance personnel on that route).

At dinner that night there was a flight lieutenant who flew the route fairly regularly, and he was happy to give Jim the benefit of his own experiences which, particularly at Salala in the frequent conditions there of low cloud and rain, were to prove invaluable.

Next day the first landing at Ryan, a longish sand strip parallel to the coastline just past Mukalla, was in dust haze and sunshine (very dry and dusty on the ground) after a flight of two hours and 36 minutes. Then it was off along the coast for a flight planned time of one hour 50 minutes to Salala – (or Salalah in the more Arabian version) – in Oman.

Weather was clear, with some upper cloud forming ahead, until about half way when strato cumulus over the sea and coastline below rapidly became a total cover, whilst the sun had disappeared with the thickening of upper cloud. It was obvious then that the approach to land at Salala was going to follow the lines described in Jim's fortunate meeting with the helpful flight lieutenant in Aden.

With the exception of Ryan all stations along that route had radio beacons on which the radio officer could take bearings relative to the aircraft's head, using his loop aerial. This was used to 'home' over Salala then to follow the let-down procedure the RAF pilot had described in detail. He had said that the airfield lay in a half saucer, open to the sea, surrounded landwards by mountains rising steeply to 2500 feet from close to the perimeter of the grass landing area. That meant no chance of a 'go-around' when landing (necessarily straight in from the coast) unless the surface wind was strong enough to force a very tight circuit close to the perimeter in order to land into it.

Let-down was to the south east over the sea until breaking cloud then reverse course, lowering the undercarriage and first stage of landing flaps, expecting to cross the coast (easily visible by reasons of several lines of heavy breakers) at a height of no more than 300 feet. If the runway, marked clearly by white boards, was not then in sight a steep reversal of course to the left (and LEFT ONLY) would clear the western edge of the semi-circle of mountains and a return to Ryan made or, at the pilot's discretion, another approach aiming to cross the coast at 100 feet could be made (if fuel remained sufficient to allow that) then return to Ryan if unsuccessful.

Cloud was broken (following the foregoing directions) at 200 feet over a wild looking sea, course reversed and the initial approach procedures carried out, the radio officer supplying constant bearings of so many degrees right or left of the nose. Speed was reduced to the normal safe approach figure and engine revs increased accordingly. It was raining heavily but the windscreen wipers kept the view ahead clear, with two lines of breakers appearing suddenly, then the two palm trees and radio transmitter hut (which were in line with the runway) flashed past below. The runway threshold markers were dead ahead as the flaps were lowering to landing position and throttles chopped to effect a down wind landing on the end of the runway for a slippery sliding run, (brakes not much use), to a skidding turn at the far end of the runway before taxiing back to the terminal area.

That first landing at Salala would not have been attempted, at least not until weather conditions improved, had it not been for the fortuitous meeting with a pilot who knew all about it! As it was, Jim supposed, it had been pretty dicey. However, the routine became perfectly normal and was carried out with much less strain in the future.

Only once were conditions clear in nine subsequent landings in Salala. On one of those (not the one in the clear) the wind was far too strong, near gale force, to land down wind so a half circuit just had to be made. That involved a very steep continuous turn at 100 feet in rain with visibility not more than 600 yards, wheels down and flaps in the landing position, the left wing tip kept just outside the field perimeter. Had it been a Hudson that manoeuvre could not have been attempted, for with flaps extended at all only moderate turns could be made at the fairly low flap limiting speed without a risk of stalling the inner wing and starting a spin. The raising of the tailplane combined with the extra length of the Lodestar, despite the same flap areas and limiting speeds, must surely have been the reason why the extreme manoeuvre just described was able to be done safely.

Nevertheless, it was a very exciting and adrenalin-provoking occasion that would never be attempted in normal peacetime conditions, unless in dire emergency. Should the (then) BOAC doctor whose name began with a 'C' happen to read this he, as a passenger, will no doubt find the memory pretty clear!

BOAC had established a rest house at Salala, a cosy place run by a very efficient and extremely pleasant South African-born traffic officer, so the route must have been planned and operated previously, though Jim had not heard or read about it when studying the extent of No. 5 Line routes. Anyway, it was a most welcome nightstop and provided the station manager, as the lone traffic officer was called, with a change of company about fortnightly for two nights separated by 48 hours. In between times there was a small contingent of RAF personnel based there for company, and the occasional film show. He seemed quite happy with his lot, and had a keen sense of humour with a story telling ability for which he was very popular. It is believed he became a very senior traffic manager after the war, with BOAC, and no doubt an excellent one.

There is one story worth relating about that route, though later in the year (6 September 1943) and a good justification for carrying a qualified engineer. After take off from Masira Island for Jiwani and Karachi the right engine stopped, climbing through 6000 feet – no splutter, just dead and windmilling. It was just three hours and 22 minutes engine running time since leaving Salala that morning, and lucky therefore not to have happened there. Furthermore, the propeller would not feather to reduce drag, but the load was light and a long slow descent without need of extra power from the good engine effected a return to land at Masira without any problem. Then it was the engineer's problem – to find the cause of the trouble.

Two nightstops were involved, which put a strain on the RAF as accommodation was very short, as were drinking water and food supplies. The forced visit was an embarrassment to them, but they were most helpful and did all they could to make the three crew and three passengers as comfortable as possible. The station was really quite large, a staging post for both RAF and USAF aircraft. Thanks to the latter (albeit unknown to them) the stay was very much shorter than it might have been – that is, a wait until the next aircraft from Cairo if spare parts had been needed.

The engineer was a very bright and experienced man. He found the trouble to be in the carburettor, which he dismantled. That Lodestar was fitted with Pratt & Whitney R1830-92 Twin Wasp engines having Stromberg injector carburettors, and normally such a job would be done on a special rig in a workshop authorised to overhaul them. Needs must and (as stated before) in those days regulations had to be interpreted with varying degrees of discretion according to a particular circumstance. The fault was located as a split diaphragm, one of two in that type of carburettor which separate air from fuel in the process of metering the balance to provide the correct combustable fuel to air ratio, or mixture. A replacement carburettor from Cairo was the proper requirement.

Benny (that is sufficient identification) and Jim trailed over to a large dump of crashed aircraft hoping to find one using the same type of engine, and having an intact carburettor. Permission should have been sought first but almost certainly would not have been given, so they just ambled over there trying to look like sightseers – sort of Bill and Ben the Flower Pot Men!

The midday sun was keeping most personnel indoors, and they were not seen. They found a USAF C47 Dakota, or 'Goony Bird' to the Americans, whose twin wasp engines were identical with the Lodestar'. The right engine had been on fire, but the carburettor from the left one appeared undamaged so they removed it, but decided it was too heavy and bulky to carry half a mile or so back to the parking area and invite certain discovery of what amounted to theft of USAF property. The metal bench seats inside the aircraft, well dusted off, made an ideal workbench and access through the jettisoned rear door at ground level easy.

Benny dismantled the carburettor, removing both diaphragms, which appeared to be undamaged but hardened by being in hot dry conditions (so losing some flexibility), re-assembled the unit and re-fitted it to the engine. It was hoped that if the neoprene diaphragms were soaked in petrol they would regain enough flexibility, one or other of them, to be usable instead of Lodestar's split one. They were wrapped carefully in a handkerchief, slipped easily into a side pocket of Jim's bush jacket, and the two men wandered casually back to the Lodestar to set the diaphragms soaking whilst they ate a dry sandwich, drank some warm lemonade, and had a smoke or two as Benny told a great deal about his very interesting, entertaining, and unusual background. This provided the beginning of a firm friendship which lasted for several years until he just disappeared from the scene, not seen or heard of since.

The soaking worked, the split diaphragm having been replaced by one of the sound ones, carburettor re-assembled and fitted back to the engine which started straight away, delivering normal indicated power on runup. It was possible that the mended carburettor would not perform perfectly without having had proper calibration on a test rig, so variation of fuel consumption and altitude performance could be expected, but they had two engines in working order again. The non-feathering propeller trouble was traced to a simple electrical fault, easily remedied. It was too late to test fly, as the sun was setting and it would be unwise to do it at night, so it was done satisfactorily early the next morning before take off for Jiwani and Karachi, just two days behind schedule.

As it happened there were no spare carburettors of that type available in Karachi so nothing was said and the return flight to Asmara began, this time with a slight change in schedule. A BOAC Dakota was leaving by the northern route to Cairo and agreed to take the Lodestar's cargo of fresh vegetables for Jiwani, as it had space to spare and had to land there anyway. That enabled a double quantity of the same to be loaded for Masira and, the rest of the load being small, sufficient fuel for a direct flight there without landing at Jiwani. The C.O. at Masira had given Jim a list of a few extra luxuries which would be appreciated on the return trip if possible, so those with the extra vegies made up a little for the problem the unscheduled stay had caused the RAF commissariat.

The rest of the trip went without further incident and, as a bonus, the weather at Salala was clear, being the one and only time in Jim's experience as mentioned before. A new carburettor was fitted at Asmara by the local BOAC engineer, who was a good friend of Benny's, so the affair went no further.

It has to be repeated that official regulations existed which prohibited such tinkering around. However (and no question of 'press on regardless') the top priority was to adhere as closely as possible to schedules dictated by wartime supply and communications requirements. Initiative based on common sense, practical balance of probabilities allied with natural consideration for one's own neck, and (in this case) total faith in the abilities of a very experienced engineer were considered to justify the action taken. Distance and operating time on long routes, communications with base difficult, required crucial decisions to be made by a captain on his own responsibility where any change of plan had to be considered. It is doubtful if anyone would have liked or been prepared to pass the buck for such decisions to someone in a headquarters, thousands of miles away and not intimately in touch with the circumstances or problems.

From Asmara there was also a flight to Addis Ababa, capital of Ethiopia and seat of King Solomon's relative the Emperor Haile Selassie. The payload was largely diplomatic. The route went south to Diredawa then took a westerly wriggle up a deep valley in the mountains which rise to just over 12,000 feet above sea level around Addis, one of which rose sharply out of the western edge of the single east/west runway, itself 8,000 feet up. Turning in to land eastwards was therefore a matter of a tight continuously turning circuit to level off no more than 200 yards from the runway threshold for final approach (an exaggerated Spitfire approach technique); an uncomfortable situation (in a Lodestar) which was only attempted should the surface wind be too strong for a down wind landing to the west. Take off always had to be to the east, as it was impossible to clear the rapidly rising ground to west of the not very long asphalt runway.

There were two main take off techniques employed by pilots, due to the high altitude which reduced full power availability and the rare atmosphere needing greater ground speed before flying speed was reached, and thus a longer run before becoming airborne. The atmosphere at Asmara, 7,000 feet up, was similar, but there the runway was very long so there was no problem.

Before a few experiments were made the standard take off procedure was to run up the engines to full power with the brakes applied, holding the control column forward to help raise the tail quickly as soon as the brakes were released. With that method very little runway was left before becoming airborne. A more satisfactory method was sought.

After much thought, theorising, and argument (for such matters are rarely merely discussed amongst pilots) and trials with light loads, a method was found which certainly took a lot less runway to get airborne. The engines were run up to 2000 rpm (where magneto switches were normally checked and which was also past the initial 'feed-in' throttle opening stage), but not to the 2700 rpm full power, with brakes applied. As the brakes were released full power was then fed in fairly rapidly as the aircraft accelerated, giving the propeller tips moving air on which to bite rather than threshing away at a standstill, this giving better acceleration as a result.

No matter how much the elevator was used to try to assist it the Lodestar (and Hudson) tailplane would not fly until good and ready under it's own natural lifting power. So the new technique at Addis Ababa (and similar situations) was simply to hold the control column central until the tail started to lift, rather than (with column forced forward) having a huge area of elevator like a barn door creating massive drag, fully down, and not at all assisting the tailplane to raise. The combination of that, with the better acceleration given using the revised engine power technique, resulted in having at least 400 yards of runway left at the unstick point, even with maximum permissable loading for that altitude.

Examples such as that (and there will be a few more as this story goes on) are included to show how pilots of the third generation were still faced with some trial and error situations, despite the help, advice, and experimentation results passed down by the first two generations who had, of course, much more of it to do. Over the forty years or so since 1920, those which the first three generations of pilots have mainly influenced, the gradual accrual of optimum basic techniques in all phases of the art of flight operation (resulting from similar trial and experimentation to that just related) has done much towards forming the base on which the modern 'State of the Art' (dreadful expression) has become a highly sophisticated technological miracle of operational safety.

To revert to the matter in hand! The No. 5 Line route with Lodestars from Cairo to Nairobi, via Wadi Halfa, Khartoum (nightstop), Malakal, Juba, and Kisumu, then after another nightstop on to Gwelo in Southern Rhodesia via Tabora and Kasama, involved a wide change of scenery and flight conditions. The river Nile wending its life-giving way provided a dark green strip in the glaring sand of the desert, but lies away to the east as it loops away through Luxor before returning to join the direct track at Wadi Halfa. Once, on that first leg, a line of rain showers passed over the desert, the first rain of any sort the area had experienced for 75 years, and as the aircraft flew over shortly after the rain the desert was covered with a brilliantly colourful carpet of wild flowers. A fantastic and beautiful sight that would wither and die in a few hours under the blazing sun.

After Wadi Halfa the river remains in sight until reaching Khartoum where the Blue Nile (rising somewhere in Ethiopia) joins the White Nile (rising in the Lake Albert area) the airport being situated just south of the confluence, sandwiched between the two rivers.

The Grand Hotel in Khartoum provided comfortable sleeping quarters and excellent food. A game of snooker before dinner, then a cinema show in the open air under a brilliant canopy of stars (the sound of native drums beating out Arab rhythms in the distance to accompany their distinctively high pitched form of singing) would follow. Or maybe a visit to one of the two nightclubs, only one of which was really good as far as floor shows were concerned.

Possibly the best thing to come out of Khartoum was a large thermos jug containing a hot stew, strongly flavoured with ground nuts, which was available on request for the crew rather than the same old cold lunch boxes with usually kept hunger at bay until the next nightstop. It was really outstanding, and in case the reader may wonder why anyone would want a hot meal in the middle of equa' rial Africa over which the legs to Nairobi were flown, the temperature at altitude is quite cool even at the lower levels when in flight in a non-pressurised aircraft with the windows open in the cockpit. The repast was usually enjoyed on the third leg of the day at midday, after leaving Juba for Kisumu. Breakfast at the first stop, Malakal, would be about 8.30 am, having left Khartoum about 6 am just on or a little before dawn. That too was a pleasant meal with the BOAC station manager, in their rest house close to the banks of the Nile.

After take off from Malakal the river was followed right down to Juba, great island of weed called 'Sud' to be seen floating and part clogging the first part of it. About half way, height would be lowered to a few hundred feet over the river, everywhere now dark green, for the passengers and crew to enjoy miles of wildlife. Herds of African elephant, the cows surrounding the bulls whose huge ears flapped, trunks raised towards the aircraft as though to warn against coming closer, though flight right over them was avoided. Groups of Hippos floundering around in the deep pools and muddy backwaters, crocodiles basking on the banks and sliding into the water (though none seemingly disturbed by the aircraft) and occasionally a rhinoceros would be seen pounding along on harder patches away from the banks. There were, birds galore. A good 50 minutes or so of the two and a quarter hour flight was always enjoyable, flying either way, and never seemed to pall, even with crews who flew the route regularly (as it had been before the war when the flying boats used to operate over the route).

Surprisingly perhaps that low flying was never rough, at least in Jim's experience, probably due to the air being sluggish and humid, a state noticed immediately on landing at Juba, the airfield being situated right alongside the river. Refuelling there was by use of hand pumps feeding from 44 gallon drums, the work done by the very tall Dinka natives who inhabit that part of Africa and are very dark in colour. Their women folk have necks stretched to about twice the length of most races, by addition of metal rings rising from shoulder to chin. They too are very tall, and walk extremely gracefully with long easy strides carrying loads on their heads, and are often naked to the waist. The men can be completely naked, and usually are, unless in the presence of white people, and were as friendly and smiling as the West Africans. The stop lasted 25 to 30 minutes, during which passenger and crew would enjoy long cool drinks under a small thatched roof shelter.

Leaving Juba, a climb to 9500 feet would be usual to avoid as far as possible rough air, for leaving the Nile valley on the direct route to Kisumu the terrain becomes hilly, then mountainous the highest (Mount Elgon rising to over 14,000 feet above sea level) passing on the left about half way. Heavy cumulus cloud is common in the area which made it necessary to weave around them to remain visual for, if cloud were to be entered, it would be necessary to climb much higher than the normal maximum of 10,000 feet without oxygen to ensure clearance over the mountains on the direct track.

Kisumu lies on the north eastern end of Lake Victoria, five miles south of the Equator, and the aerodrome being 3837 feet above sea level with (what seemed to be becoming a common hazard) a large hill rising close to and in line with the northern end of the singly runway. Landing towards it and taking off the other way had to be done, for it was too close to make approach over it or clear it after take off, but that was not normally a problem as wind speeds on the surface were invariably light. If the surface wind was more than six to seven mph from the Lake a downwind landing could not be made safely on the short runway, in which case Kisumu was overflown direct to Nairobi, or to Juba if flying the other way from Nairobi.

The last leg of the day to Nairobi is short, 174 miles if flown direct, which takes the flight over the Mau escarpment. A climb to 12,000 feet is necessary to clear the ground safely, but only about 30 minutes of the one hour 15 minutes trip would need to be at that level so lack of oxygen was no problem. However, from September through to December, in the afternoon, thunderstorms form rapidly and are common so the direct route is not then flown, the track keeping well to the south of the Mau and in the clear. This still meant a bit of cloud dodging which extended the flight time some 20 minutes before landing at Nairobi which lies 5,450 feet above sea level on a wide plain. Africa's two highest mountains, (one of the world's most magnificent sights in clear weather), rise majestically from the plain – Mount Kenya, 17,058 feet to the north, and Kilimanjaro, 19,340 feet to the south, both snow capped for most of the year round.

Nairobi was a superb nightstop. Crews stayed in the Norfolk Hotel, usually being allocated one of the self-contained bungalows in the hotel grounds, eating in the restaurant where meals were as good as any top class London hotel or restaurant. The East African servants, generally much lighter skinned than the West African and Central African natives, spoke very little English. Swahili was the universal tongue, and most local people of European origin spoke that fluently, but the crews seemed somehow always to get served with what they wanted without rancour.

On the third day out from Cairo the flight down to Gwelo called at

Tabora only when there was some load or mail for the area, which was not often. Otherwise the route was direct from Nairobi to Kasama to refuel after a four hour trip – a very attractive landing ground, particularly as seen from the air, as its three hard-earth runways were a deep red colour standing out against a dark green background, outlined with well maintained white runway and boundary markers. Gwelo, three hours 45 minutes on from Kasama, had an Empire Training School for the RAF, pilots training on Harvards and engineering personnel and navigators at the ground school. Twin engined Airspeed Oxfords were used for advanced pilot training and navigation exercises.

Gwelo township (roughly half way but to the south between the Capital of Southern Rhodesia, Salisbury, and the mining town of Bulawayo to the west) was small enough to be a village with one hotel (at which the crews stayed overnight) and a few shops. The hotel bar was three deep every night and very noisy, but the rooms were well away from that and sleeping presented no difficulty. The evening meal was adequate, if not exactly silver service, and the people polite enough but somehow the general atmosphere was not overly friendly. In fact it resembled that experienced in Vereeniging, where it was more understandable as the Boers openly disliked the British, but in Rhodesia it seemed surprising. However, out at the aerodrome the RAF were their usual friendly selves, and breakfast in their Mess a pleasure.

Passengers on the return trip to Nairobi were entirely RAF personnel who had completed their training. They showed great interest in the Lodestar and the routes they operated, enjoying the scenery and map reading from one sent aft for them to study. Seven years later (1950 at Croydon) one of the ground engineers working for the same charter company as Jim recalled his flight up to Cairo from Gwelo after passing out from the Empire Training School. The Captain, Jim, had put him in charge of the discipline in the passenger cabin, as he was the more senior of the twelve – (rank LAC). That, and the whole conduct of the flight and interest shown in him and his mates by the crew had made a long lasting impression on him – instant mateship of course on the reunion.

To return to the matter in hand (1943) airborne over the high plain of Southern Rhodesia, the rolling plain breaks up into small hills before crossing northwards over the river Zambesi, many miles to the east of Victoria Falls. The light greens and yellows of the terrain soon becoming dark green as Kasama is approached. About half way between Kasama and Nairobi the ground becomes light brown and dusty looking (passing over Tabora) then dark green with browns of various shades over the mountainous higher ground towards Nairobi.

Apart from the odd battle with thunderstorms and heavy clouds, some torrential tropical rain, and quite often low cloud and heavy mists at Nairobi, the route was generally incident free.

Khartoum once in a while put on a sandstorm, but the airfield lay on a bend in the Blue Nile and was quite easily found even in low visibility. On one occasion, coming up from Malakal, a huge swarm of locusts had to be flown through, for about 20 minutes before landing at Khartoum, which clogged the oil coolers but in that short time not enough to cause overheating. The Arab ground personnel (let it not be said the BOAC traffic staff) could not be persuaded to do any work on that occasion until every one of the locusts roasted on the hot engine cylinders had been picked off and eaten – obviously a delicacy.

Apart from the northern route to Karachi, which is described in the chapter concerning the Ensign type aircraft which operated over it en-route to Calcutta, there were two other routes flown by the Lodestars. Cairo to Teheran, via either Baghdad or Habbinyeh according to whether the passengers were civilians or Service personnel, with a first landing at Lydda in Palestine before crossing the desert (following the oil pipeline from Haifa to the Iraq oilfields) until reaching the river Tigris at Baghdad. There there was a semi-circular bend in the river which could be followed in poor visibility to bring the main runway on the nose for final approach, having turned left after passing a sugar factory on the river bank – much like the Blue Nile situation at Khartoum.

The second route was Cairo to Istanbul in Turkey, via Cyprus and (weather permitting) Ankara, which will be described later after finshing with Teheran.

The climb out of Baghdad had to go up to at least 15,000 feet to cross the Zagbros mountain range (with peaks to 12,000 feet running from north to south across the track to Teheran) after passing the town of Hamadan which (from above when it could be seen at all) appeared to lie squeezed tightly at the bottom of a deep hole in the precipitously surrounding mountains. In the winter a higher altitude was needed to avoid the heavier icing conditions lower down. The crew had oxygen, but not the passengers so they were not very comfortable, though as far as Jim knows there were no cases reported of anoxia despite being above 10,000 feet for at least one hour of the two and a half to three hour journey. Passengers suffering from any illness (or pregnant perhaps), had to have a doctor's certificate before being accepted on board.

Teheran was interesting at that time from 1943 to 1945, not so much for its ancient history and buildings as for being the meeting place with the Russians as they collected trucks, tanks, and other military equipment sent from USA. These were formed into huge convoys to drive northwards into Georgia and onwards. Many tales could be told, eyewitness accounts, about those movements which illustrate starkly the difference in human outlook between east and west cultures (Russian and Western), but in the interest of Glasnost better not here.

The Russians kept very much to themselves, suspicious of Americans and British alike, though some stories of officers on both sides sharing memorable parties have been told, which suggests that their general attitude was more political than personal.

Winter nightstops were notable for their intense cold, though blazing fires in the hotel and enormously thick down quilts on the beds in the unheated bedrooms made life warm and cheerful enough, and the food was excellent. A particular pleasure was the ready availability of one kilogram tins of Caspian Sea Caviar at the incredible price of £E4 per Kilo, and there was no trouble with the Egyptian Customs about bringing it into that country. Jim used to buy four tins, keep one for himself and another for a friend. The other two he sold, (at £E20), to each of two major hotels in Cairo, which was a good deal for them considering the price they charged their customers, and made a nice little profit for their suppliers.

The remaining 'different' route, Cairo to Istanbul in neutral Turkey, had its problems in the winter. Passengers were mainly diplomatic, as was the mail (King's Messenger escorted), and Sir Maurice Petersen the British Ambassador was a frequent traveller. Only one in four flights would be able to land at Ankara, the Turkish capital, due to weather conditions closing in the long narrow valley where the airport's single runway was sited. This was bounded by steep-sided mountains rising to 6000 feet above sea level, and 3-4000 feet above the airfield, the width of the valley being less than three miles at its widest point, so circuits were tight and difficult. On these occasions Ankara was overflown direct to Istanbul for nightstop in the BOAC Mess, a large old house overlooking the Bosphorous and staffed by two White Russian ex-Cossacks – a Colonel and his ex-batman, who cooked sublimely, kept the place spotless, and were great fun.

The nightstop could, and often did, become two. That is, when weather conditions at Ankara precluded landing there on the return trip to Cairo, the Diplomatic Mail and any passengers who would have boarded there that day had to travel by train to Istanbul overnight, leaving for a direct flight overflying Ankara the next day, or one behind schedule. On those occasions the crew had a clear day in Istanbul to visit the fascinating markets and historical places of that ancient city, and a second very pleasant nightstop.

Foreigners were always followed wherever they went, quite conspicuously (no cloak and dagger stuff) by shabbily dressed men reputedly drawn from the ranks of the unemployed by the police, to whom they reported daily. It was the practice, when taking coffee and brandy at the end of the day (in a cafe close to the Mess) to send the same via the waiter over to the 'tail', who would turn up only a few moments after the crew to sit at the far end of the cafe, and who would always acknowledge the smile and waves of recognition. It is that sort of local difference that makes the world such an interesting place, and it is always there if one bothers to observe – no matter where.

One flight, with the Ambassador on board, an attempt was made to land at Ankara where he resided, more as a show that an effort had been made to get him to his destination despite the inclement weather prevailing there. As luck would have it, cloud was broken over the valley as the aircraft came overhead, clearly only a short break in the overall total cloud cover, and a steep almost aerobatic approach and landing was made, rather by instinctive reaction triggered by surprise at the unexpected break – certainly not by better judgement.

His Excellency thus delivered, continuing on to Istanbul was the next problem. It had started to snow again quite heavily, but the cloud base was around 800 feet so the take off posed no difficulty, unless of course there was engine trouble when return to the airfield would have been impossible. As it was to the west, where the end of the valley was not blocked by high mountains, the Lodestar's rate of climb, even on one engine, was ample to clear the rising ground at that end and so perfectly safe.

As cloud was entered at 800 feet the airspeed indicator surged and then fell off to nil – control feel normal, engine power normal, rate of climb indicator, artificial horizon, and directional gyro instruments all indicated correctly. Under the nose and facing forward is the Pitot Head, the device which actuates the airspeed indicator and also provides static air pressure base for the altimeters. It is electrically heated to prevent the device icing up (thus becoming blocked and then preventing airflow going through it). The heater switch on, as part of the pre-take off checks, was still on. There was no going back to Ankara so the climb had to be continued without airspeed indication, using attitude to power setting guides, plus feel of the controls and their response to movement, to keep the aircraft going up and not stall. Coming out of cloud at 18,000 feet, in the clear on top, the forlorn hope that the pitot tube could have become clogged with super-cooled snow, and that in clear air the electric heater might clear it when not flying through snow and ice proved to be just that – still no airspeed indicating.

Fortunately, like many aircraft, the Lodestar was pretty predictable as regards airspeed for almost every aspect of power to attitude, undercarriage and flap setting, and with a very long runway at Istanbul using a bit more power than usual with normal flap settings ensured plenty of safe approach speed for approach and landing.

As the cloud base at Istanbul was 300 feet, Jim had been flying on instruments and by hand (he could not trust the automatic pilot to sense in time any unusual feel in the controls) for over two heavily concentrating hours. He was very glad of one of those extra days rest the next days as Ankara's weather was well below limits. It turned out that the pitot heater fuse had blown, caused by the heater element having shorted out. A most unusual fault, easily rectified by fitting a new element or a whole new pitot head.

On that occasion Jim's first officer was a Fleet Air Arm pilot, RNVR, seconded to BOAC, and the date 1 February 1946. Just in case that (now retired) senior captain of British Airways should happen to read this and jog his memory, he should know that after all these years his moral and physical support remains one of the more valued memories from Jim's log books.

The three year span of time from 1943 concludes this chapter on the Lodestar type of aircraft, its route structure in No. 5 Line, and a few of the more memorable incidents experienced in that tough, noisy, highly manoeuverable, and very reliable machine. It is worth noting that their engines were eventually standardised with Wright Cyclone G205as. The Hornet engine was discontinued by 1944 and, in 1945 the Pratt & Whitney Twin Wasps also which, despite their smaller frontal area, did not match up with the airframe configuration for some reason. There was an indicated airspeed difference around 15 mph slower than the Cyclone version using the same cruising power (a fact proven without doubt in both test and route flights) which meant a true cruising speed loss of over 25 mph at altitude, thus poor economy of fuel, range and engine/airframe hours.

November 1943 saw Douglas C47, Dakotas, added to the fleet the subject of Chapter VI.

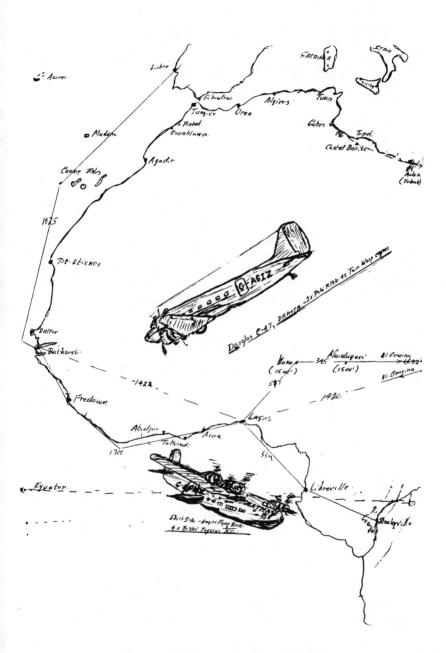

Azores

Lisbon

SARDINIA

Sicily

Gibraltar

Tangier

Oran

Algiers

Tunis

Madeira

Rabat

Casablanca

Gabes

Tripol.

Castel Benito

Agadir

Canary Isles

El Adem
(Tobruk)

1875

Pt. Etienne

Douglas C-47, DAKOTA - 2x P+W R1830 92 Twin Wasp engines

G-AGIZ

Dakar

Bathurst

Kano
(1500')

345

Maidugeri
(1500')

El Geneina
(2932')

–1422

577

El Geneina

Freetown

1426

Abidjan

Accra

Lagos

Takoradi

554

1700

Equator

Libreville

Shorts S.26 - Empire Flying Boat.
4 x Bristol Pegasus XC.

R.
Stanleyville
Congo

6 Dakotas – Ensigns – West Africa – India – 'Potpourri' November 1943 to May 1946.

The No. 5 Line routes were expanding, both in variety and increasing load factors. Capacity was increased by the addition of four Douglas C47 Dakotas, fitted with Pratt & Whitney Twin Wasp engines. There was a shortage of pilots, but this was relieved in part by the beginning of an influx of RAF pilots (tour expired from combat operations) who had volunteered to be seconded to BOAC, though it would be a while before they became fully integrated into the system.

Training on the new Dakotas started in the middle of November 1943, continuing for eight days to 24 November during which time Jim completed a total of 23 hours which included 14 as first pilot (five and a half hours night flying practice and tests) and nine hours dual and co-pilot, before passing out. There was no route checking due to the shortage of captains, so on 25 November he set out on his first trip in command on the type on the West African route to Lagos in Nigeria.

The first day, down to Khartoum via Wadi Halfa, was old ground which helped with route familiarisation of handling and performance, before embarking on the last leg of the day – westwards to El Geneina for nightstop, the first leg of an unfamilar route. The 26 passengers, seated in lightweight chairs instead of the metal benches of service versions of the type, were all RAF ferry pilots returning to West Africa after delivering Service aircraft to Cairo and the Far East, which they had collected in Takoradi or Accra after they had been flown over the South Atlantic, via Ascension Island, by the Atlantic Ferry Command group. They would be collecting more of the same after reaching Accra on this trip.

They were ravenously hungry when boarding the aircraft in Cairo and the lunch boxes disappeared (the contents and almost the cardboard containers with them) before reaching Wadi Halfa after a four hour flight. It was three hours and 10 minutes thereon to Khartoum before more food could be on-loaded to sustain them until reaching El Geneina, 823 miles and four hours 45 minutes later.

Night had fallen 40 minutes before coming overhead at El Geneina where a dust storm was blowing, which was little help to a pilot making his first approach and landing at a place not previously visited. However, the runway lights were strong and clear enough from overhead so a run out down wind, and timed turn back before descending for final approach, worked out nicely and the threshold lights duly appeared ahead. The landing was by good luck a smooth one, for it was difficult to judge height accurately in the poor visibility in the blowing dust at ground level, but the Dakota was a pilot's dream to handle, just floating down gently like a big moth to land – quite unlike the very positive cessation of flight experienced in the Lodestar and Hudson.

After almost 12 hours airborne there was another noticeable difference between the two types – there was no temporary loss of hearing which would have been the case in the Lodestar, its engine and propellers being very close to the side of the pilots' heads. One of the first impressions of the Dakota was the sewing-machine-like humming of the twin wasp engines several feet behind the cockpit.

The second day to Lagos, via Maidugeri and Kano, involved nearly ten hours flying. Scrub country passed below for four and a half hours to Maidugeri, and continued most of the way to Kano, though trees became more abundant and green against the reddish earth at Kano. Then southwards, crossing the river Niger about the half way mark where the jungle was becoming lush and darkly green, until a long line of surf appeared ahead during let down to Lagos. A feeling of returning home to a well-remembered place was to Jim very pleasant – the happily grinning native faces and unmistakable smell of the place, tinged with open drains at times, but predominantly of a fragrant wood smoke on humid air.

The next day was short, taking the passengers up to Accra then returning to Lagos for the night and two clear days off. A nice surprise was to find one of the Boeing Flight senior stewards in charge of the Ikoyi Mess, having left active flying duties, so it was a real sort of homecoming for Jim as they had become good friends during 1942. Leaving Lagos on 30 November with mail, freight, and four civilian passengers for some reason a nightstop was made at Maidugeri, which meant a second one had to be made at Khartoum, delaying the arrival in Cairo by a day to 2 December.

A week later came the second trip to Lagos. The load was light enough to permit ful petrol tanks and still be within the maximum permissable take off weight, so a direct flight to Khartoum without landing at Wadi Halfa was made; then on to El Geneina for nightstop. There was a film show on in the open air, courtesy of the RAF, about half way through which the night air became very chilly – very common with a clear sky and light breeze in the tropics, especially when nearly 2000 feet above sea level. Foolishly Jim had not brought a sweater, and even more so stayed shivering until the end of the film. A hot bath and a glass of whisky certainly helped him to sleep but didn't undo the damage.

In the morning he was very stiff, with shooting pains in the back and difficulty breathing. Obviously he would be needing hospital treatment if it didn't wear off during the day. Being able to use full tanks and finding favourable winds forecast (unlike the Atlantic, upper winds in the sub tropics are reliable to forecast and not strong, unless sandstorms for instance are expected, and that sort of weather is mainly seasonal and easy to predict) he opted to fly the direct track to Lagos, bypassing Maiduguri and Kano. The 1428 miles would take eight hours.

He dare not risk going sick in either of those normal stops and being unable to deliver the badly needed ferry pilot passengers on time – it would take at least two days to get a relief Captain from Cairo. The flight took seven hours 51 minutes, by the end of which his left side was almost paralysed. That gave the first officer the chance to do the landing at Lagos, for which he was well qualified and performed perfectly.

Jim was not hospitalised but spent five days in bed with pleurisy in the Ikoyi Mess, being treated by the relatively new drug (1943 remember) M&B sulphur-based preparation which preceded penicillin by some years. It so happened that the following weekly service from Cairo was operated by one of the Ensign aircraft (of which more later in this chapter) due to there being a greater load than usual. With it came a relief captain, arriving to take the Dakota back to Cairo only three days late, whilst Jim travelled as a passenger on the Ensign to finish convalescing in Cairo until cleared fit to fly again on 30 December.

There would be no more open air movies without proper clothing available. It had been a lesson learned, which heed of warnings could have prevented him a lot of discomfort, and would have saved the Company having to call on a pilot on leave to fill in – the shortage of aircrew had become that acute. It was of course also a black mark on his record, which it had to be admitted was more than justified.

The pilot shortage was slowly being made up by the seconded RAF pilots, and included those from the Wellington Flight as those machines were phased out with arrival of the Dakotas, to which had been added more Lodestars. The increase in aircraft establishment took care of the rapidly increasing load commitments, but personnel to fly them took time to catch up. For most of the newly joined RAF pilots, all absolutely first class flyers and most having had command of four engined bombers, the transition to civil operations was traumatic.

Before being given commands with BOAC they necessarily had to serve some time as co-pilot, not simply for route experience but to learn totally different procedures designed for safety, economy, passenger relations, and the keeping of detailed technical logs. From those the ground engineers traced faults, both reported and incipient, to keep the fleet flying with as few delays as possible, and also (as the aircraft did not return to base each day) provide engineers stationed down the routes with a technical history whilst performing servicing at nightstops.

Any immediate relief from being shot at night after night for two or more years was quite soon a non-issue as nostalgia set in. The missing of buddies with whom one had crewed as a unit (unlike the constant interchange of crew members with BOAC) homesickness for friends and families in Britain who could be seen during leaves, and the fellowship of the Station Mess. The irksome business of having to sit in the right hand (co-pilot's) seat under the command of someone who, like Jim, had never experienced Service life, let alone been at daily risk of losing it (and that of friends and comrades) in the grim business of war in the air.

Despite that, and the BOAC captains they flew with were all very much aware of their difficulty (giving take offs and landings as much as possible on a leg to leg basis to relieve the boredom and frustrations) the majority of those new recruits to the Company settled down to the task of absorbing what had to be learned if they were to be promoted to command. Gradually they were able to see ahead to when the war would end, having then a ready made career in the airline industry should they not wish to return to pre-war occupations (that is if they had not joined the RAF straight from school).

Quite soon, as the system of crew member interchange helped them to meet most of the BOAC aircrew, friendships were formed and tolerance of the rather dull routine of civil type flying changed to pride in completing whatever task given to perfection, and the beginnings of professionalism were born. It was not long before most of those fine fellows gained their own commands with the Company, many remaining with BOAC, or transferring to British European Airways (BEA) as it was formed after the war, until retirement.

Apart from a few radio beacons, most of which were positioned on or near airfields, there were no other radio facilities such as radio ranges. This did give the USAF a certain amount of trouble for, in the USA and Canada for quite some years before the war a country wide network of radio ranges gave pilots an aural method of track guidance and beam approach system. In most other countries of the world no such thing existed and simple dead reckoning navigation had to be practiced. It was quite easy, particularly on the longish legs across

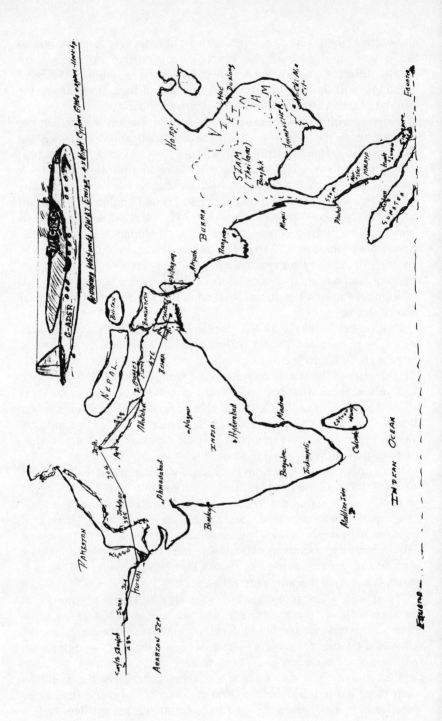

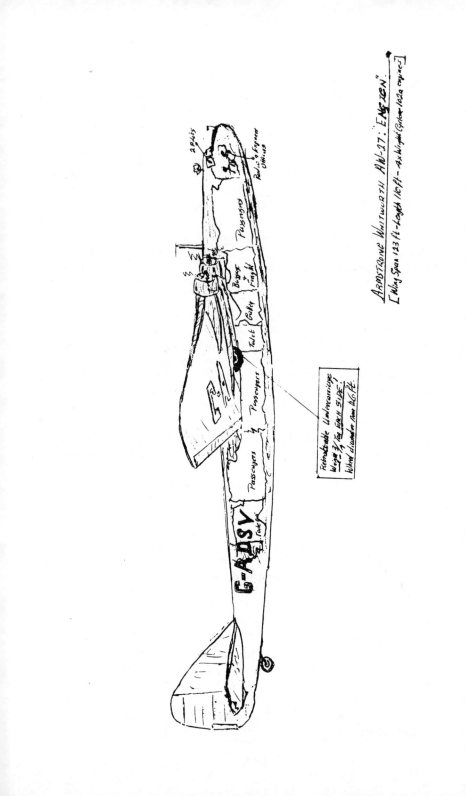

ARMSTRONG WHITWORTH AW.27. "ENSIGN".
[Wing Span 123 ft – Length 110 ft – 4x Wright (Cyclone 1020 engines)]

2 pilots

Radio & Engineer Officers

Passengers

Baggage & Freight

Toilet

Galley

Passengers

G-ADSV

Passengers

Toilet

Retractable Undercarriage.
Wings ¾ Fin EACH SIDE.
Wheel circumference from 216 Ft.

Africa, to stray from the desired track unless drift sights were taken regularly and attention paid to accurate compass headings, for landmarks that stood out clearly were few and far between and otherwise the terrain could look much the same for many miles either side of the desired track. In short, people got lost on occasion – and not just the USAF either.

Although in some ways irrelevant to the main story, Jim feels that the point is worth mentioning for, when flying long legs and long days, in weather rarely other than clear, the terrain below monotonous to look at, a slackness of attention has to be fought against. Aircraft that have had to force land, lost and out of fuel, are very difficult to find in featureless country and water and food scarce in scrubland and desert to assist in survival. Such country forms most of the terrain between Kano and Khartoum – 1800 miles, half and half scrub and desert. The moment to repeat – 'Eternal Vigilance is the Price of Safety'.

The West African flights on the Dakotas, interspersed with the occasional one via the northern route to Karachi, a couple to Aden, and a summer trip to Ankara and Istanbul, continued until April 1945. They were rotated with Lodestar operations on the routes described in chapter V, and together accounted for 1842 flying hours, which brought Jim's total to 4121 hours. He was deemed fit then to be converted to fly the Ensign type, with its four Wright Cyclone 102a engines each of 1100 bhp, designed by Armstrong Whitworth. They were introduced into service with Imperial Airways in October 1938, being powered then by the maker's own Tiger radial engines of 850 bhp, to carry 40 passengers on European routes.

When war broke out they were used initially on the NAC routes to France, where one was destroyed being shot up on the ground at Rheims, the crew being lucky to escape injury. Of the 14 built, 7 were re-engined with the Cyclones before being ferried out via West Africa to No. 5 Line in Cairo, though only 6 arrived. One was forced landed on a beach in occupied French territory just south of Dakar, an RAF Sunderland based in Bathurst making a daring and successful run to pick up the BOAC crew who were uninjured in the belly landing.

The Ensign was a high-winged aircraft, span 123 feet and length 110 feet. 107 feet of the latter lay behind the pilots' eyes when the tail was down on the ground, which had to be allowed for when manoeuvering into parking spaces. Eye level when the tail rested on the ground was 16 feet. She was certainly large, being described by some USAF personnel as the 'flying block of flats', but fly she did. As fast as a Dakota and, if a bit clumsy, docile and pleasant to handle, giving the impression of stately progress not unlike the superior feeling when driving a pre-war Rolls Royce.

Her crew of four consisted of two pilots, a radio officer, and a flight engineer – one of which had been on the 1942 Boeing flights. There were three passenger compartments (forward, mid, and aft) separated by bulkheads with central walkway connecting them, in which seating for 37 was provided in a modified arrangement using some aft space originally used for freight. The compartments were lined and sound-proofed to an extent but not to the luxurious standards of pre-war.

After two trips of route experience, initially as co-pilot the first pilot under supervision of a fully qualified line captain, and a final check out by the flight captain, Jim took his first trip in command on the type on 16 June 1945. The route was Cairo to Lydda, Baghdad, and Basrah (normally one but this time four nightstops – an engine had to be changed) then Bahrein, Sharjah, Jiwani, to Karachi (nightstop), then to Calcutta via Johdpur, Delhi, and Allahabad. The return trip landed in Cairo on 26 June, four days behind schedule.

There were six more of those trips to Calcutta in the Ensign, interspersed with Dakota and Lodestar flights, ending 28 December 1945 when it was decided to fly them back to Britain. The war was over, load requirements falling off and BOAC starting to reorganise for return to peacetime operations. Jim had flown 433 hours, 23 at night, in the Ensign and was sad to learn that they were to be broken up after arrival in Britain, as they were not really economical or suitable for post war requirements.

There were three notable occasions during that period to the end of 1945, the first being the arrival of his wife from Britain on Wednesday 23 May, preceded only by a telegram from Port Said to say she was travelling from there by train. It is not difficult to remember that it was a Wednesday as, when in Cairo, Jim lunched that day on liver topped with garlic chips (a regular precaution against 'gippy tummy' which had proved effective since arriving there). There was only time to rush to the station to meet the train, the telegram having been brought to him whilst lunching. Needless to say his fond kiss of welcome (after two and a half years of separation) was none to well received. The problem was soon rectified! She had come by sea on a troopship (the war in Europe having just ended civilian travel being again permitted, but not too many passages could have been available. As noted early in the piece, she is a remarkably resourceful lady – and he was certainly more than pleased to see her.

On the second to last trip on the Ensign, a passenger from Calcutta to Karachi on 11 December was an Army captain with DFC ribbon on his tunic, who was immediately recognisable as one of two brothers, contemporaries and in the same house as Jim at Oundle school. He had been to Burma, flying Army Observation aircraft, and was returning

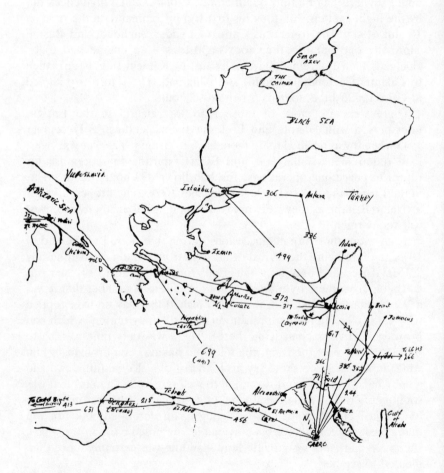

Distances in Statute Miles.

home to Britain by sea from Karachi to be demobolised. It was unfortunate that their meeting could not lead to a reunion celebration as Jim had to leave Karachi early the next day, and as he had not been back to visit the school where his school mate took over the running of the school farm after demob they have not met again.

The third occasion was on Christmas day 1945. On a direct flight of almost five hours from Delhi to Karachi (Johdpur having no load either in or out that day) a turkey dinner was served to the passengers instead of dull lunch boxes, the captain (Jim) acting as steward to serve it. Flight conditions over the desert section were rough, even at 10,000 feet, as the air was very hot and dusty with strong winds aloft and on the surface. Carving a lukewarm turkey in a tiny galley was quite a nauseous exercise! Jim has ever since felt great sympathy for stewards and air hostesses faced with dishing up food when unable to see out. Incidentally, that made him realise that passengers when flying in cloud, or otherwise unable to look outside (for orientation) must get a similar reaction towards being sick.

There was no big deal in the situation, just normal passenger relations, as no cabin staff were carried in those days out there and the day was a special one, particularly being the first Christmas after the war. He managed to complete the task without actually being sick, and assured the 34 passengers that it was all perfectly safe as the first officer was a very experienced pilot, well capable of managing on his own for the one and a half hours it took to serve their meal. His own Christmas dinner was delayed until the evening in the BOAC rest house at Karachi, and a hot curry the preferred alternative to turkey!!

Back on 2 January 1946 to alternating flights on the Dakotas and Lodestars. The last two flights on No. 5 Line were into Athens on Lodestars, passengers mainly RAF with some Army personnel. The first was from Cairo via El Adem on 25 April, nightstopping at the Grande Bretagne hotel in Athens, being used at the time as HQ for the British forces. The next day routing was via Nicosia, Beirut, then Lydda (for nightstop in Tel Aviv). On the 27 April it was to Teheran via Baghdad, two very pleasant spring days being spent the in accommodation arranged outside Teheran itself in a small village at the foot of the Demavend mountain (rising to 18,386 feet above sea level). The village, Demavan, is some 50 miles north east of the city and over 5000 feet above sea level and it was pretty cool up there, but the sun shone both days and fires burned warmly at night, those huge thick eiderdowns as welcome as they were in the winter in the hotel in town.

On 30 April a local flight was made at RAF request to help calibrate the direction-finding equipment newly installed at the Station. The rest of that day, and the following one, were again spent at Demavan in still beautiful weather. That unexpected little holiday was due to the load to be flown to Athens, mainly Service personnel, which had not been gathered together until 2 May, the schedule being to Lydda via Baghdad for nightstop Tel Aviv. That flight was in perfect weather, the first time in over three years flying over the mountains from Teheran. It was awesome to see them, stretching north to south in their rugged grandeur, and a bonus much appreciated as it turned out to be Jim's last trip there.

The next day was to Athens (nighstop) via Beirut and Nicosia. A moonlight walk up to Acropolis was a stunning and delightful experience after an excellent dinner in a Greek-style Tavern, bazouki music and dancing included. The return to Cairo, 4 May, was without any load, so full tanks enabled a direct flight of three hours 50 minutes, assisted by a strong tailwind. Again the weather was brilliantly beautiful, though even in the spring the 6041 foot peak of Mount Trudos on Cyprus was still white-capped with snow, and looking as imposing as one might suppose for a mountain also known as Olympus in ancient Greek times.

That trip also happened to be Jim's last with BOAC as well as with No. 5 Line. On 18 March 1946 his wife had given birth to their first child, a boy, in the Anglo-American hospital on Gezira Island (in Cairo). A healthy babe, but his mother had become run down in the following few weeks, to the extent that it was advised she should leave the Middle East for Britain as soon as possible. The BOAC Manager for the region very kindly gave permission for Jim to accompany his wife and child on a flight to Britain, in an Empire Flying Boat which had been chartered by the BBC whilst making a documentary in Cairo.

The leader of the BBC team was the famous Uncle Mac whose broadcasts in the Children's Hour were legendary. He agreed that the family could travel with them. So, it was goodbye to Cairo's bustle and noise, smells, mothers sitting cross-legged on pavements suckling their babes, hands out for Baksheesh, the babies eyes swarming with flies – sights so common as to seem normal, like the swarms of Gallabiyeh'd Arabs hanging on to the outside of trams like flies themselves.

The other sides of the Cairo scene have dimmed by comparison, probably because of the superficial nature of it. The King (Farouk) and the Pashas and the glitter of the Royal Club du Chase, Medina House, Gezira Club, the nightclubs (many sleezy, some less so) and their inevitable belly dancers, the gambling and the hashish, the bribery and corruption, intrigues the daily round of both social and political life in the upper strata – a 'culture' of decadence.

In between the desperately poor street Arabs (very much the majority of the population and an ever ready phalanx easily provoked into rioting) and the Upper Crust was a solid block of hard working honest family people made up of probably one of the world's most cosmopolitan race mixes – French (official first language before English or Arabic) Italian, Greek, Jew, Copt, Dutch, German, Russian (white), Spanish, Algerian, Argentinian, Portugese, Maltese, with Anglo/Egyptian variations of most. They were the clerks, small retailers, and professional men not yet tempted into the higher echelons of society and politics, their educated children at a very young age conversing together, and with their parents, in five or six different languages at the same time – selecting the most apt phrases from each the better to express their meaning. These are remembered mainly from some special friendships rather than from en masse contact.

   * Gallabiyeh:–the nightshirt type garment, basically white, worn as standard dress by the Arab in the street, the servants, the 'fellaheen' (peasants).

A nightstop at Catania (Sicily), where the female staff made a great fuss over the bambino, then the great flying boat taking them home was over France (low level flight in wet and cloudy weather, nostalgic for Jim) to land at Poole Harbour in Dorset and be met by an excited first-time grandmother who could hardly wait to take the babe from his mother's arms.

Jim had to report to the Central Medical Board in London for a compulsory examination, it being three years since his last one there. Normally the six months medical check (for commercial licence renewal) had to be done by the Board, but for pilots overseas during the war the RAF had been authorised to do them. He was found unfit and his licence suspended for three months, or until another medical passed him fit again, so there was no possibility of his returning to Cairo as had been agreed.

Looking around the post war scene in Britain whilst thus out of action he found that several new flying companies, privately run, were needing pilots. One of these, Airwork, who had operated many years before the war (mainly overseas, managing flight operations for companies such as IPC Iraq Petroleum Company) was offering captains £1000 per year and were prepared to employ Jim when fit. His pay with BOAC had started at £600 pa, with £20 pa increments, to the present £660 per annum (May 1946).

After much heart searching, admittedly greatly assisted by his desire to remain based in Britain (his wife again pregnant) he gave contractual notice to BOAC to expire 31 July and started work (pronounced fit again earlier than expected) with Airwork on 7 August 1946. By that time his total experience was 4,692 hours, of which 3,005 was in command.

PART II – (1946 to 1948)
Ups, Downs, and a Byway.

7 Independent Airways – (Charter, Tours, & Freight).

Airwork was operating a Bristol 170 Wayfarer, a high winged aircraft fitted with twin Bristol Hercules sleeve valve engines each of 1690 bhp. It is better known in the freighter form, for which it was originally designed. The nose opening doors of the freighter were not fitted to the Wayfarer, which was used as a passenger carrier with 32 seats and had a small bar at the forward end of the wide and high cabin. Those generous dimensions were due to the internal space (unlined or soundproofed) designed to accommodate up to three cars (in the freighter version) copied later in Silver City Airways cross channel car ferry services. The passenger version was of course well soundproofed and very comfortable.

Two pilots and a radio officer occupied a small 'bubble' type cockpit placed high on the top front end of the fuselage, access to which was by vertical ladder on the right side of the area where the nose opening doors were located in the freighter version. The fourth crew member was an air hostess, a pleasant innovation which was to gain rapid momentum in the next few years. On the main service – (operated for Sudan Airways between Croydon and Cairo) – an engineer was also on board to carry out maintenance en-route.

Despite the fixed undercarriage and bulky proportions the streamlining was cleverly designed so that an indicated airspeed of 155 mph (speeds in post war built aircraft were indicated in knots, in this case 135 nautical miles per hour, but as stated before all speeds will be quoted in statute miles per hour for the benefit of the average reader, and to save endless conversion figures – even into kilometres – if all variations were to be included) which at a cruising altitude of 8000 feet gave a true airspeed of 170mph.

She was a lovely aircraft to fly, agile and responsive. Even in strong cross winds her huge side area gave no problem, very similar to the Ensign in such conditions. In the forward cabin the noise level was more rumbling than roaring being close to the large four bladed propellers, but not unduly so, and further aft the level was low.

Passengers were mainly Sudan Government personnel and their families, who seemed really to enjoy their comfortable roomy accom-

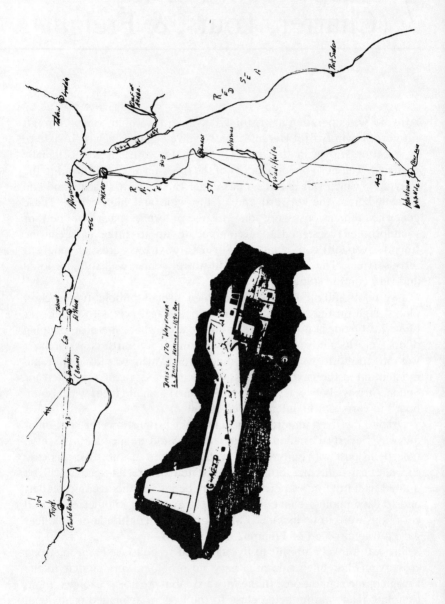

BRISTOL 170 "WAYFARER"
St Patrick Airways - 1956 Ship

modation and unobstructed downward view of an interesting and scenic route. Croydon to Lyons, Elmas (Cagliari, Sardinia), then to Malta for nightstop. The second day landings were made at Benia (Benghazi), and El Adem (Tobruk), before reaching Almaza (Cairo). On one occasion their route was extended to Khartoum via Wadi Halfa, returning to Cairo via Wadi Halfa an Luxor.

On 10 August 1946 Jim flew as co-pilot with the chief pilot (Captain Brian Davy, a veteran of the first generation – a man of vast experience and exceptionally pleasant temperament) for route and operational experience on the type to Cairo, returning to Croydon 18 August. The same day he took the empty aircraft to Bristol (Filton) the Bristol Aeroplane Company's aerodrome and works, for some modifications to be made, that being his first command flight. Five days later he flew her to Gatwick airfield (as it then was), Airwork's operational headquarters. It was at that time a grass field with one east west runway strengthened with steel matting, a wartime expedient for providing solid runway material quickly, the steel mesh sections being easily transportable and rapidly laid to take the heaviest aircraft of the day.

On 25 August, after ferrying the aircraft from Gatwick to Croydon, Jim took his first passenger trip in command (in the type, for Airwork, and for an Independent Airways Company) out for Cairo. That one returned to Croydon on the 30 August, four days off, then another starting 4 September returning six days later to Croydon and then to the Gatwick home base.

Two days later, 12 September, he began a different sort of trip – different because it was a charter, rather than a Sudan Airways service, by a firm called Peltours specialising in group travel for Jewish people going to what was soon to become Israel rather than Palestine, and who had proper authorisation from the British authorities there for entry. For instance, Jasha Heifitz, the world famous violinist, was one of the passengers on that trip.

The destination was Lydda, in Palestine (soon to be renamed Lod, in Israel) via the same stopping places as on the route to Cairo but landing after El Adem at Lydda. The return trip was scheduled differently, leaving Lydda for Alexandria, then El Adem, Benia, Malta (nightstop), Elmas, then to Geneva instead of Lyons, Le Bourget (Paris), before landing at Northolt instead of Croydon on 16 September.

Most interesting and rewarding was that the co-pilot was Captain R H MacIntosh who was on his first trip in the Wayfarer to gain the mandatory route experience before assuming command. That kindly, humorous, extraordinarily humble man was one of the first generation, having been in World War I, and had during the second World War served with the RAF on Air Sea Rescue operations. His book, *All*

Weather Mac, ghost written but great reading, covering a remarkable career in both civil and Servicing flying, was published a few years later. It was a wonderful experience for Jim to fly with such a greatly more experienced pilot, to enjoy his company listening to interesting and humorous tales, and to watch his instant identification with the aircraft as though it were an old friend of many years.

Those first trips flying with air hostesses were also rewarding. Airwork had only two of them at that time, both extremely efficient and pleasant personalities. One had flown during the war with ATA and was an experienced pilot, knowing several of those Jim had known in 1940, and enjoying an occasional unofficial turn at the control in flight where she was very competent.

It was a very enjoyable two months of introduction to working for a private company being different in many ways from BOAC, though he was still wondering whether he had made the right decision to leave. As he was to find out later, job security had been renounced by the move, as had seniority – perhaps the most important thing in the career of any civil pilot, certainly so in Britain. Such things as pensions had not even been considered in the world of the independent operators, and they had to make profit or go out of business, unlike the Government airlines.

Perhaps it was the challenge of being in at the beginning of something new and exciting, as well as challenging, that appealed to Jim – a feeling that much more depended on his personal initative and abilities, in a situation close to management, the trust given to handle the Company's money en–route in the most economical way, and to operate the aircraft similarly. With BOAC all that was done for their captains, whose duties in the main were limited to laid-down rules of operation of routes and aircraft on regular scheduled services. However, the decision had been made and what was to be would be, for better or worse in the long run.

The rightness of his decision seemed to be proved quite suddenly. He was instructed to report to the Bristol Aeroplane Company to discuss practical possibilities for continuing flight deliveries over the South Atlantic to South America, a much more economical way than to ship in parts by sea. There had been one attempt already, which had ended up ditching in the sea near the coast of Brazil, fortunately without fatality though the Radio Officer had a badly broken leg, the crew being picked up by the ship alongside which they had ditched. That had not been so economical in terms of customer relations, though insurance covered the financial loss. Here then was a task in which to get his teeth – the challenge he was looking forward to being given in the future, the use of initiative and self reliance, the confidence being entrusted to him by the Company.

8 Bristol 170 – South Atlantic Delivery Flight

The co-pilot on that first (ill-fated) delivery had been a Bristol test pilot whose job was to train the pilots of REAL (the Brazilian Airline who had ordered some freighters) after arrival in Rio de Janiro. It was with him that Jim discussed the circumstances of what went wrong with that trip. As a result it was recommended that the next deliveries should have improved navigational facilities, to which the Bristol company agreed, adding an astrodome, drift sight and flares for dropping in the sea at night to take drift measurements, and a chart table.

All would be removable after the delivery for return to Filton by sea, along with the three 300 gallon extra fuel tanks (placed in the fuselage) which were fitted to give that short range aircraft the necessary endurance for the 1862 mile crossing from Bathurst to Natal.

The test pilot was to act again as a co-pilot, with a Bristol engineer and a radio officer from Airwork to make up the crew. Between 27 September and 2 October, piloted by the test pilot, acceptance flights were made, including a three hour 45 minute night flight to check out the viability of the extra navigation equipment. On 7 October 1946 Jim took over command for the positioning flight to London Airport (Heathrow) for customs clearance and filling of the extra fuel tanks. The Air Registration Board had granted special dispensation for a maximum take off weight 2000 lbs greater than normal (just for the ferry flights) the aircraft having proved itself capable of safe single flying at that load. However, it was necessary to operate from longer runways than normal to obtain the extra speed on the ground before lifting off at the higher weight, and Heathrow was the only one convenient with customs facilities.

The seven and a half hour flight to Lisbon was made on the 8 October, for nightstop. The next day, before leaving for Rabat (Morocco), a group of Portuguese military and airline officials came to inspect the machine. A very large gentleman amongst them said something in Portuguese causing much laughter which (when translated) had likened the aircraft's generous and sturdy proportions to – 'a good woman, strong and fit for hard work' – which was not at all a bad description.

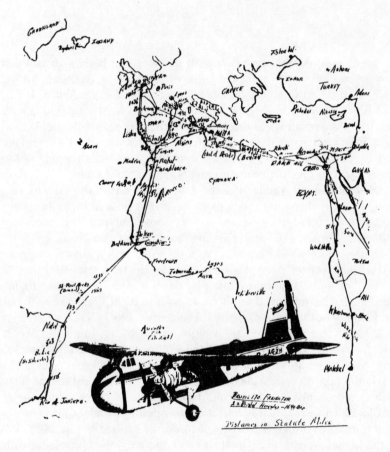

It was only a short two and a half hour flight to Rabat, but the most convenient place at which to top up all the fuel tanks for the leg to Bathurst (Gambia), a direct flight from Lisbon being too far. On arrival the following day the engineer's leg, hurt whilst refuelling at Heathrow, was showing signs of becoming septic. Although he protested, he was taken to hospital where he was detained for three days – the rest of the crew enjoying the colourful Moorish city and French cuisine.

The French Air Force were in charge of the airport and were friendly and helpful, in fact the French atmosphere had remained strong in the city throughout the war and no anti–British feeling was displayed anywhere. The hospital wanted to keep the engineer there longer but, hobbling and heavily bandaged, he insisted on joining the rest of the crew who were delighted to welcome him back.

Whilst airborne his duties were to operate the long range fuel system, switching electric immersion pumps in the fuselage tanks to uplift fuel to the main (600 gallon) tank high in the wing centre section (from which the engines fed), ensuring that quantities from each tank were kept even to maintain the aircraft's centre of gravity whithin limits. He also acted as steward with the crew refreshments. For the 11 hour flight to Bathurst overnight he was able to sit and give Jim directions about the fuel transfer system (in breaks from the navigation) with the radio officer helping out with the stewarding.

The night flight had been chosen for the crew to put in some practice simulating a similar length flight over the South Atlantic, giving Jim the chance to get back into the swing of astro navigation, and the vital accuracies necessary, which he had not practiced much in the previous four years. Everything went smoothly and the crew settled down well as a team – not very difficult as the members were experienced and had blending personalities.

They rested for two days at Bathurst in preparation for take off for Natal (Brazil) on 16 October at 1.30am. That would allow for the first five hours of the trip to be done at night, when astro navigation could be used accurately to plot positions and so check on forecast wind speeds and directions. Jim had never been ashore at Bathurst during the Boeing flying boat refuelling stops, preferring to stay on board where it was relatively cool compared to the sticky heat on land. Since the war BOAC had fixed up a pleasant rest house, which was made available for the Airwork crews in transit and, as a pleasant surprise, it was being managed by a traffic officer who had been with No.5 Line in the Middle East.

Take off was at 1.46 am, on 16 October, course being set for St Paul Rocks, a small group of rocks 1248 miles out and 633 miles from Natal (their destination). The lighthouse on a tiny islet in the group is operated by Brazil. It was a little north of the direct track, but that added only 19 miles to the total distance and it was thought that the slight deviation would be worth it to have a positive visual sighting to confirm Jim's navigational calculations.

The star position fixes during the night had indicated an upper wind to be more north westerly than the forecast north easterly trade winds, necessitating three course alterations and giving a ground speed slower than flight planned. This extended the estimated time to the Rocks by 23 minutes. Drift sights, using the flame floats and rear view facility of the sight itself, had supplemented and complemented the star fixes throughout the night. Nevertheless the hoped for visual sight of the group did not turn up on time, so a new course was calculated to take effect in five minutes time.

As Jim moved forward to pass the details on to the test pilot (who had been flying the aircraft whilst he was aft doing the navigation) there were loud shouts from the flight deck. He hurried up the ladder just in time to see St Paul Rocks lighthouse come up dead ahead, the sea foaming round the little group in a quite strong wind on the surface, just four minutes later than the revised estimate.

Suddenly no one was tired anymore and in particular the test pilot (in view of his unfortunate experience on the first delivery) admitted relief and confidence that the fairly expensive navigational modifications had proved worthwhile. A happy crew chortled their way on in perfect weather to land at Natal at 1034 am local time (after a flight lasting 11 hours 48 minutes) with three full hours of fuel left in the tanks. A REAL crew was waiting and in a hurry to get going to Rio so, after a four hour rest and a meal, the trip continued down to Bahia (or San Salvador) for nightstop, followed by a solid sleep on comfortable beds. The REAL crew had joined the flight in order to gain an insight into the general features of the machine and operating techniques, receiving their flying training from the Bristol test pilot after arriving in Rio. They were a jolly lot and interested in every little feature, studying the various manuals and asking endless (sensible) questions.

The final day of that delivery flight will remain a special memory for Jim, and probably for the rest of the crew too. The five and a half hour flight down the coastline, mountains rising to between 3000 and 6000 feet fairly close to the tropical green coastal plain, was outstandingly beautiful but, as the turn in towards Rio was made, an incredible almost eerie sight appeared ahead. Sole occupant of the scenario, rising just out of the tops of a total cover of strato cumulus cloud, stood the huge Corcovado figure of Christ, arms wide outstretched, 120 feet tall standing on the top of (invisible in the cloud) the 1279 feet high 'Sugar Loaf', 'Urca', or 'Pao de Ascucar' mountain, which is one of the wonder sights of that fascinating city. The sky above clear blue and cloudless.

Air Traffic Control advised cloud base to be 900 feet and gave permission to descend and land, at the Santos Dumont airport which lies on reclaimed land jutting out into the beautiful bay of Guanabura. Entering that dull grey swirling mass of cloud, after hours of sunshine and beautiful scenery, would normally have been an anti-climax, but that sight of Christ seemingly welcoming their arrival with open arms transcended all else. Apart from the initial gasps in which the REAL crew joined, not a word was spoken until after touch down and the aircraft (showing off her short landing capabilities) turned off at a taxiway half way down the fairly short runway without needing the use of brakes. Jim and his co-pilot exchanged conspiritorial grins, both feeling that a job had done yet knowing, nevertheless, that such a landing was the result as much of luck as skill; and maybe that the Good Lord might have had a hand in it too!

They spent one wonderful week in Rio before the next British South American Airways York (a wartime transport using Lancaster bomber wings and Rolls Royce Merlin engines (four of them) mounted high on top of a square boxlike fuselage) transported Jim and his radio officer back to Britain via Natal, Dakar, and Lisbon. There was little sound insulation on those solid workhorses and the extractor exhausts of the Merlins filled the cabin with drumming sound, more noticeable as they were the only passengers. Temporarily deafened on arrival at Heathrow they both had difficulty finding balance, and not because of the alcoholic hospitality offered!

9 More of the Wayfarer – An Israeli experience

There were three more trips on the Wayfarer, two for the Sudan Government and one for Peltours, and on each there was one hitch or another. The departure from Britain had been changed from Croydon to Heathrow, and the departure time from morning to afternoon, with only one leg to fly the first day – to Bordeaux for nightstop. Then to Marseilles and Elmas to refuel before a second nightstop at Malta, and on the third day via El Adam to Cairo, or to Lydda in the case of Peltours.

The first one started 30 October 1946 and was scheduled to go all the way down to Khartoum. One of the Airwork directors, Sir Archibald Hope, (who had been a pilot on night fighters during the war, becoming a Group captain), was travelling on the flight, and a very pleasant person he was too. He was able to see first hand that things did not always pan out as planned, and also to appreciate how his crew handled the various situations.

After landing at Bordeaux (Merignac) the brakes failed, which was not all that serious for taxiing the 170 by use of differential engine power was quite easy. However, coming up to the parking area some form of braking was needed. The engineer, having found that the single steel wire which applied the brakes from a lever on the control column had broken adrift, used his hands to apply the brake effect (as Jim directed) until safely parked and the wheels chocked. It ws a very fine effort for the wire cut through his gloves, but fortunately not the palms of his hands, though they were pretty sore for a while. He insisted on braising that wire back into position on the operating lever before leaving the airport for the hotel, and noted a suggestion for modification for the manufacturer in the technical log. It is always good when one of the management sees first hand the calibre of his crews (especially the more junior or non-pilots whose work so often goes unsung) when they pitch in with valuable help and common sense.

The next day, after landing at Marseilles (Marignane) to refuel, the weather forecast for the leg to Elmas over the Gulf of Lyons, and on to Malta, was bad. Not unusual for at that time of the year thunderstorms would cover a wide area, sometimes for days in a row, and this was one of them. It meant that the two legs would be very rough, though perfectly safe as the worst cloud could be avoided by weaving through areas of heaviest rain below cloud base and in sight of the sea. Jim decided to call the passengers together to advise the expected flight conditions, and gave them the choice of nightstopping in Marseilles or keeping to schedule and having a very unpleasant flight.

In such cases, where possible, a captain would take the responsibility of costing the Company money for food and accommodation (and transport) for passengers and crew in the interests of customer relations. Such occasions are very rare, but do serve the required purpose. There was unanimous agreement for the nightstop and the following day the weather, though by no means perfect, was much less violent – though beginning to look angry again by the time Malta was reached mid-afternoon.

It had been intended to make up for the lost day by flying on to Cairo that day, to arrive around 11 pm Cairo time, but after 40 minutes airborne from Malta a well defined line squall stretched right across the track with it's violently curling base very low to the sea. To fly through that would not only have been extremely rough but very dangerous, so there was nothing for it but to return to Malta for the night. The passengers had been given a close view of heavenly fireworks, but without being bumped about for the air up to the squall had been quite smooth.

The next day's flight to Cairo, arriving a day late, was smooth and pleasant in sunshine and blue skies, the air smelling clean and well washed even at the normally dusty El Adem. It seemed that Sir Archibald had approved Jim's decision at Marseilles (which was good and typical of him) but, had he not, the one hard and fast rule in civil aviation holds good at all times – the captain's absolute right is to decide whether to fly or not, and to conduct any flight in the manner he sees fit in the interests of safety and passenger welfare. The flight to Khartoum via Wadi Halfa and return via Wadi then Luxor was completed on 4 November. During the ensuing five day stay in Cairo before returning to Britain there was a feeling of unrest wherever they went in the city or Souk (market place) – indefinable but to Jim, even talking to old friends made whilst with No.5 Line (many of them Egyptians) there was a sense of unease, the name 'Nasser' being overheard quite often from groups of Egyptians gathered together in cafés such as the famous Groppi's. He thought quite a lot about that after returning to Britain on 12 November, but it was many months before the matter was clarified.

The following trip was to Lydda for Peltours and was itself delay and flight-incident free. However, on take off from El Adem for Lydda in the late afternoon on a Friday there was some commotion in the passenger cabin. The air hostess reported that the passengers wanted to turn back to El Adem as they had realised as the sun set that they were travelling on the Jewish Sabbath which (all the passengers were clergy) was forbidden by their faith. There was no point in turning back as the damage was already done. To continue to Lydda would take no longer than returning to El Adem where, in any case, there would be no accommodation for them.

Jim went down into the cabin to apologise that he had not realised the situation and to explain that he had to carry on to Lydda. He asked the chief Rabbi why he and the tour operator had not thought about it when the flight was scheduled, for it was in fact on schedule. It appeared that they had expected to arrive in Lydda before sunset, at five pm, which was indeed correct in Greenwich Mean Time, but in fact seven local time in Lydda – a full hour after sunset.

Nobody was happy about the situation, but it had to be accepted and goes perhaps to show that in those days passengers, and travel agents too, had not caught up with time zone variations. Nor indeed had the aircrew really thought about keeping the passengers briefed – (so used themselves to keeping flight log times in GMT wherever in the world they were, making mental adjustments to local times when not flying, unless staying any length of time in one place, adding and subtracting from personal watch time without altering the basic GMT setting).

It was another lesson learned for Jim, from then on meticulous on the matter, and the more so when he heard later that those passengers had sat on their suitcases in penance at the airport (Lydda), without moving one step from the customs hall until sunset on the Saturday. There were no untoward incidents on the return flight to Britain 29 November.

The last of the Wayfarer trips started out on 5 December and was incident free to Cairo, the passengers continuing on to Khartoum as normal on the Sudan Airways flight. There were two clear days in Cairo before flying empty to Lydda, where a load of Peltours passengers were to be picked up for return to Britain. A strong smell of petrol was noticed during the one hour 45 minute flight, which was accompanied by an indicated increase in fuel consumption. Inspection after landing found a split in the fuel tank, something which certainly could not be rectified with the tank installed, and of course precluded any further flight. It was 9 December.

The Bristol Aeroplane Company, with their usual concern and efficiency, promptly had a new tank air freighted out together with one of their engineers, but it was several days before they arrived – in fact a wonderful 12 days holiday for the crew before the new tank was fitted.

Staying in a hotel on the seafront at Tel Aviv, they enjoyed the multi-national choice of Jewish, Arab, French, and even German type food that was freely available at that time. Very close to the horrendous transition from Palestine to Israel, with the Stern Gang and other terrorist Jewish organisations already active in their efforts to force Britain to relinquish their Mandate before the Scheduled United Nations deadline.

In their innocence of that situation, travelling around the beautiful countryside in communal taxis (much like the ones Jim had experienced in Brazil, called Lotta Cheoung) sharing the trip costs with local passengers, was a wonderful experience especially as the latter seemed keen to explain about the places they were travelling through. Apart from that sightseeing the cost of food and accommodation was borne by the Company – one of the occasional perks aircrew enjoy and one that is not resented by the Companies which include in their budgets an element for unforseen expenses.

Evenings just sitting on the Mediterranean shore in the moonlight, listening in bed to the soft murmuring of the sea lapping the shore – it was a time for romance if ever there was one, unrequited other than for nostalgia for there were no partners other than thoughts of loved ones back home.

There remains to tell one more story of Jim's time with Airwork, subject of the next chapter. Suffice it to say that the Palestine adventure ended in a redistribution, (empty, without passengers), to Gatwick, with a short nightstop at Marseilles, leaving Lydda on 22 December and arriving at one pm on Christmas Eve, to the relief of crews and families. It was Jim's first Christmas with his wife since 1939.

10 A Captain's decision which didn't pay off.

A Bristol 170 Freighter delivery flight to Buenos Aires was scheduled to start from Filton on 14 February 1947, this time with an all Airwork crew plus (as supernumerary to Bathurst) a senior Marconi radio technician and positioning to Hurn (Bournemouth) took place on that date. It was to be the 39th Airwork delivery of the type since the first successful one, across the South Atlantic, four months previously.

The weather forecast to Lisbon was impossible the first day, so the flight was delayed 24 hours. It was no better the following day with a very tight low pressure system centred by the Azores giving head winds of 40–45mph, which would have meant an almost 10 hour flight instead of the normal 7½ hours – and landing in a low cloud, rain, and gusty strong winds at Lisbon. Jim decided to go round the worst weather by flying first to Marseilles (Marignane), which would take four hours with not so strong headwinds, then skirt the eastern coast of Spain, over Tangiers, and down to Casablanca to refuel before a last leg to Bathhurst.

At Marseilles, after a rough flight, the forecast for the next leg to Casablanca was very bad until after Tangiers, caused still by that strong low pressure system, and would have had to be done at night due to the late morning start from Hurn. With little chance of getting position fixes visually, star sight or radio fixes in the stormy static-laden conditions, a nightstop at Marseilles was the only answer.

Airborne over the Gulf of Lyons the following day (the low pressure system having moved north eastwards into the Bay of Biscay, taking the worst of the weather into northern France and Britain but still giving bad conditions over Portugal) the weather was cloudy with occasional rain but quite comfortable, and forecast to improve to the south and west. Jim went to the map bag to take out the area plotting chart (as he stowed away the topographical map used to that point) to discover it was not there. Admittedly there had been no original intention of taking that route but, having decided to do so he should have ensured that the bag contained the proper charts before leaving Hurn, so yet again he had been guilty of quite unpardonable carelessness.

There were at least five hours to travel before reaching the Tangiers area, after which the normal chart provision was covered. Fortunately the excellence of his BOAC navigation training came to the rescue, so he was able to construct a Mercator chart of the area (on the blank back of another one) – quite a simple process to make the grid, plot in the co-ordinates of latitude and longitude of the various radio beacons en-route from information in the radio manual, then draw in approximately the coastlines of Spain and North Africa from the topographical maps which were on board. The process took about 30 minutes and navigation proper was back in business.

Flying just beneath cloud at 2000 feet, occasionally in the lower layers in pockets of heavy rain, Ibiza in the Balearic Isles passed by in the grey murk, then Cartegena and Cape De Gata by Almeria (Spain), the weather clearing quite rapidly approaching the Straits of Gibraltar and Tangiers. By the time Rabat was overflown the skies were blue and the landing at Casablanca was made as estimated after a total of 7½ hours. After an overnight stay plus most of the next day, which gave the opportunity to look around the historic town, flight was resumed for Bathurst – once again in the evening to allow 7 hours of the 10½ hour trip to be done at night and give practice for the crew in astro navigation and other procedures in preparation for the ocean crossing to Natal.

At 3 am on the 22 February course was set from Bathurst and climb to cruising altitude fo 6000 feet in clear skies completed. As reduction of power to the cruise condition was made the lighted instruments became almost unreadable. A vibration hardly noticable from normal, which no re-setting of power levels would change, was the cause and return to Bathurst was decided upon. During the time to get back Jim believed that the vibration might be coming from the left engine but could not be sure – anyway something was not right and landing at Bathurst was made after one and a half hours from take off.

Five test flights were made in the ensuing 15 days, the Bristol engineer stationed there trying every remedy he could think of including changing over from left to right the propellers in case one might be found slightly out of balance – (if that had been the case then the delivery to Argentina would have proceeded, the minor problem of reading shimmering instruments at night a tolerable irritant). The vibration was definitely located as coming from the left engine, having got slightly worse during the test trials.

By that time it was 6 March and Jim was not game to set out on an almost 1900 mile ocean crossing, let alone deliver an aircraft to a new customer which was obviously faulty even had the crossing been made safely, so he decided the only thing to do was return to Bristol.

It was decided to do the first leg, a short one of three hours 45 minutes, at night to Port Etienne to refuel and put up with the difficulty of reading the instruments, then to have all but one hour of a six and a half hour flight to Casablanca in daylight again to refuel before a short two and a half hour leg to Lisbon. The decision to do the trip in three hops instead of one long and one short was in order not to have to carry any more fuel than necessary, just in case that engine should decide to fail.

Arriving at Lisbon 4.30 pm, the temperature was a Spring like 58 degrees Fahrenheit. On the descent there the left engine's vibration had become less noticeable which (if not an illusion due to having got used to it) suggested to Jim that there could be something wrong with the automatic mixture control in the carburettor. The trip was continued next day to Hurn, for customs clearance then, after two days waiting for heavy snowfalls to cease, on to Filton. Not long after leaving Lisbon the vibration ceased altogether, tending to confirm a possibility that the automatic mixture control might be the trouble. The sequence of events was reported in the technical log, which listed also the many measures tried out by the engineer at Bathurst, and it was assumed that the manufacturer's engineers, always so excellent, would be able to analyse the fault despite there being no longer physical evidence of the vibration. It seemed they could not, any more than their man based in Bathurst.

As the test pilots at Bristol could not reproduce the fault in the air (not surprisingly) it was assumed for some reason that Jim had been mistaken and caused huge expense and inconvenience all round by not going on with the delivery flight, so the aircraft was turned round ready for a different crew to start it all over again. It was by then getting close to the end of March, and Jim was fired, his contract terminating 30 April 1947.

He was never quite sure whether it was the vibration incident which caused his dismissal, or the fact that he had taken on as air hostess (at a nominal one shilling per day to cover insurance as a paid crew member) for the return trip from Bathurst a lady who had been stranded there without funds. A round the world yacht cruise had gone broke, the other crew members having been able to afford their air passage home and she had been a guest of BOAC for several weeks. It had seemed to Jim that this would be in the best interests of all concerned especially as her promise to pay her en-route food and accommodation costs back as soon as she reached home was faithfully kept. That was of course a risk Jim accepted personally, for he would have had to refund to the Company had she failed to keep her promise. The fact that a certain arrogance acquired whilst being a BOAC Captain had not gone down too well with the ex-Group Captain operations manager may have weighed in against him he could not deny!

However, a few days after being at home in the dismissed state he was asked to attend the firm's London head office, at his own convenience, and was advised that the aircraft concerned had had to turn back to Bathurst with the left engine totally failed. The fault had finally shown up as being the cylindrical device which controlled the degree of air heating to the carburettor, having lost a locating lug, had been slowly vibrating round to the fully closed-off position and consequent engine failure. The earlier slight vibration reported by Jim was then traced to warmer air being delivered to the carburettor (therefore richer fuel mixture than needed in the hot/humid air at Bathurst) until returning to the very cold air in Britain, where the problem had vanished and was assumed not to have existed.

Bristol had of course immediately introduced a modification to ensure there would be no recurrence of the fault, which could not have been easily traced, nor even readily guessed at, so no blame technically could be apportioned. Jim appreciated the gesture, which made it clear that he was not being blamed for having imagined a fault not there. It was typical of the Company's director concerned, but it was not practical to reverse the decision to dispense with his sevices, which he fully understood – indeed, in the circumstances where there would probably always be a strong personality clash, he would not have wanted re-instatement.

Leaving was financially and job-wise extremely inconvenient but there were no hard feelings on either side, something which in later years proved to be beneficial. It had been eight months of a very interesting job, had involved 400 hours of flying in his first job with a post war independent company, happy memories of colleagues, and especially of a great aeroplane which sold over 200 before production ended in 1954.

11 Seven months of 'bits and pieces' – March to October 1947.

It was not the last time Jim was out of work. Several of the hopeful post war independent operators had gone, or were in the process of going, broke. Ex-RAF pilots had qualified, and were still qualifying, for commercial licences in expectation of a boom for pilots, and it was particularly hard on those who had not already been seconded to BOAC or obtained contracts with the newly formed Goverment airline, British European Airways (BEA). The few charter companies needing pilots wanted civil experience if available, and there were plenty like Jim looking for work of any kind just to keep their licences valid.

He contacted his initial flying instructor, Norman Giroux of Giro Aviation at Southport, to see if he wanted a joyride pilot for the summer season flying from the sand aerodrome where Jim had learned to fly. It so happened that a second pilot was needed for the season, starting 26 June and Giroux was happy to employ his old pupil.

From 15 March, when Jim last flew for Airwork, his services were not required during the rest of the term of his contract to 30 April, though he was still paid in accordance with the contract. He had therefore over three months in which to pass technical exams on the single engined Auster type aircraft he would be flying with Giroux (a high wing monoplane with 100 bhp Cirrus Minor engine carrying a pilot and two passengers) before he started flying work again. To fill in the time he did two things, one was to enter into a correspondence course to obtain Associate Membership of the British Institute of Export, and the other an attempt to start his own air freight company.

He corresponded with contacts in the Middle East probing a possible formation of an Air Freight company to be based in Cyprus, got a few tentative contract interests, and an indication from the Governor of Cyprus that licence to operate from Nicosia could expect sympathetic consideration. A Merchant Bank was prepared to back the purchase of three Bristol 170 Freighters and the project looked like a serious possibility so a brochure and detailed proposal for company structure, routes and estimated costs of base establishment, running and maintenance costs and reserves were prepared.

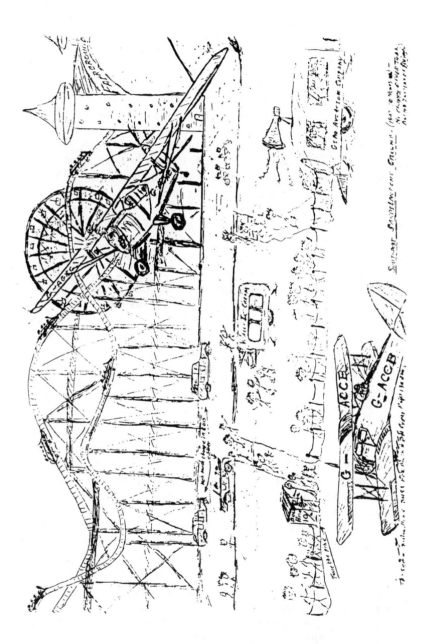

SKETCH SHOREHAM AERODROME GROUND (JUST 10 YEARS AGO)
NO CHANGE EXCEPT TREES
BIT BIGGER + ONE PETROL PUMP!

FIG. 2 — Shoreham Aerodrome. DUKE FOR THE AIRLINE. TWO-SEATER high wing mon...

By the beginning of June no progress had been made towards obtaining working capital (as distinct from the financing of aircraft and equipment) so the project was dropped, Mediterranean Air Cargoes letter heads consigned to the waste paper basket, and Jim prepared to go for a summer of joyriding. He had enjoyed the exercise, learned a lot, kept his mind busy, and completed the accountancy (basic) section of the correspondence course which came in very useful in later years, even though the rest of the course was never completed.

He discovered that flying jobs were getting more scarce so was very happy to look forward to the eight pounds per week wage (plus the usual few tips which were occasional perks on that type of flying) offered by Giroux. Accommodation was neither a problem nor expense, as his parents had a spare room at their house in Southport, though his wife and boys (the second one born in the April) remained in their Croydon home.

From 26 June to 6 September he throughly enjoyed that summer, introducing holiday folk from the mill towns of Lancashire and Yorkshire in the main, to the thrill of and joy of flight. Simple working people for the most part (some had never seen the sea before, incredible but true) those 'Wakes Week' holiday crowds were ever a happy and free spending lot, loving the fairground type of entertainment of which the joyriding was a part, the landing ground being right next door to it.

The pre-war five shillings had escalated to 10 shillings a flip, which was about the same as general wage increases, and many would come up for more during their holiday to a point where Christian names became known to all the staff. Every evening when flying back to the hangar at the north end of town Austers had two spare seats each. The boss allowed Kaz the other pilot (a Polish ex-spitfire pilot whose full name has never been mastered or written down, despite many happy evenings with him after flying) and Jim to take two passengers each (for free) on those flights. Those would be customers who had already paid for more than one joyride during their holiday. There was no shortage as the word seemed to get passed around, even to holidaymakers arriving in following weeks.

Giroux still flew his one remaining Fox Moth, with four passengers inside and he in the open cockpit, taking some of the ground staff back at night whilst the others drove the old bull-nose Morris back along the sands with the gear. That marvellous old car had been going since well before the war, still working despite being almost a museum piece.

There was the same old wooden booking hut, and a caravan from which music was relayed through speakers (the records somewhat sand scratched) and a microphone for addressing the crowds lining the roped off area officially approved as a landing ground. In those two months and two weeks the weather was rarely other than perfect, if too hot once in a while. Jim did 123 hours flying involving 1218 landings. The flights averaged three and a half minutes – up around the Marine Lake to just 1000 feet, then glide down on the edge of the attractive town with it's masses of flower gardens (the annual Flower Show being world class) to weave round the fairground towers and sideslip in to land as short as possible to avoid wasting engine time.

Passengers disembarked and the next two loaded with the engine running (a member of the ground staff assisting them and making sure they did not walk into the spinning propeller) the slipstream blowing their hair – all taken as part of the fun they always seemed to have. The most number of flights he did in one day was 43, but the average would be 28 to 30 between 10.30 am and (in the long evenings of double summer time) 10.30 pm though the normal return to the hangar would be around 9 pm. It was seven days a week, but a day off would have been sheer boredom by comparison. It was good for the soul, kept the wolf from the family door, and did wonders for keeping that seat of the pants feeling in trim.

Back in Croydon and as luck would have it, through a long standing friend since they trained together for their commercial licences and later with Air Commerce and NAC, there was a job available. This was paid by the flight, at 30 shillings an hour. The company was newly formed, operating Percival Proctor aircraft Marks I and V (differences relatively minor) for a pilot and three passengers. The Proctor was developed for the RAF, mainly for short communications work, from the Vega Gull. It had a similarly powered 200 bhp Gipsy six cylinder in-line engine, but was fitted with a constant speed variable pitch propeller, designated Gypsy Queen II.

There was some joyriding from Croydon airport, several trips to the pretty little aerodrome Toussous le Noble (just south of Versailles/ Paris) and one each to Brussels and Zurich between 13 September and 6 October, covering 36 hours flying which netted (base pay –tips, a few, on top) £54 for less than a month's work. It was not long before that firm went broke too!

It was not really surprising, for there seemed to be very little co-ordinated booking of passengers – (for instance the long trip to Zurich, which involved a nightstop, Jim's first time in Switzerland, found no passengers waiting there and no agent who knew anything about it). That sort of thing kept happening when return loads from Paris did not turn up until the point was reached when the pilots took a hand in the matter themselves, refusing to leave Paris until they had managed to rustle up a charter of some sort. That of course involved the cost of food and accommodation for them (perhaps for two or three days) so a way had to be found to cover it . The tale is worth the telling and it is doubtful if any prosecution will follow some 40 years later.

Petrol for cars was very short in Paris at the time and astronomical prices were paid to obtain any, in particular by taxi drivers. One of them had become a very good friend, giving rides into and back out of the city to the pilots without charge (the pilots being two, Jim and his friend). They were escorted round the nightspots and less expensive eating places where he had endless buddies from his days in the Resistance during the war, so the meals and entertainment were quite cheap, at least by comparison with the going rates for tourists. His name was Jacques Lautrec, believed a blood relative of the famous painter Toulouse Lautrec.

There would be plenty of petrol left in the aircraft tanks on arrival at Toussous. All but enough for a test flight the next day would be syphoned out overnight by the taxi driver or his friend for their own use. What the high octane petrol did to their engines goodness knows, but that was their problem and the cash generated more than paid for the pilots nightstops which were far more costly than the cost of the petrol to the Company. The next day a test flight of short duration would be made and the aircraft tanks then refuelled (by Carnet, the cost being the same relatively low one applicable in Britain) with sufficient fuel to return to Croydon safely to arrive there with the amount in the tanks normally to be expected after a return trip to Toussous.

That little bit of skullduggery did not involve the Company in any extra costs and got return loads instead of unproductive empty flights – and the management were not culpably involved, indeed as far as is known they never found out about it. A fine by-product was of course the fun the pilots had in the lovely city of Paris – the overtones of Edith Piaff's 'la Vieen Rose' (sung in a small restaurant on the Rue Pierre Charonne by Vicky Autier at her piano), the pavement cafés on the Champs Elysée, let alone the excitement of Montmarte and bustle of the markets. Those certainly were the days!

The next six months are remembered as perhaps the most noteworthy of Jim's career, being really an adventure rather than a serious commercial flying operation. Perhaps it should never have happened (certainly could never happen again) but circumstances demanded and it presented a distinct challenge to his initiative. Enjoy the story as he describes it but, please, do not associate it with airline practices of those days (let alone those immediately following) and of course very much not so today over forty years on.

12 The Great Adventure, or halfway round the world in 30 days.

There had always been something romantic about flying from Britain to Australia, before the advent of pressurised aircraft in which high operating altitudes prevent close sight of the ground for passengers, or for that matter the aircrew. Ross and Keith Smith in a Vickers Vimy bomber in 1919; Amy Johnson in May 1930 (first woman solo) in her tiny single engined De Havilland Gipsy Moth (registered G-AAAH, the eighth since the change from the G-E--- register); Jean Batten in a similar machine to New Zealand in April 1934, and of course Bert Hinkler (the boy from Bundaberg in Australia) in 1928, the first solo flight. The 1934 Mildenhall (UK) to Melbourne Centenary race, won on handicap by a KLM Douglas DC2 in three days 18 hours and 13 minutes (but with Scott and Black in a two seat De Havilland 88 'Comet' racer with twin Gipsy VI R engines being first in the speed section in two days and 23 hours) and many others culminating, perhaps, in 1987/ 88 with the solo flight of a tiny Microlight machine flown by a 45 year old Englishman, Brian Milton.

Passenger wise, Imperial Airways with Handley Page 42s and Atlantas down to Singapore, then Quantas operating De Havilland 86 Express Airliners (subject type of this chapter) through the Dutch East Indies (NEI, or Netherland East Indies) to Darwin and Brisbane, and finally the luxurious Empire flying boats which both Companies operated in tandem. Early post war came the pressurised cabins of Lockheed Constellations, the flying boats were phased out, and currently the huge Jumbo jets of Boeing and Douglas flying most of the time comfortably above rough weather.

It was therefore with considerable excitement that Jim heard of an Australian charter company needing a pilot and operations manager, the initial job to fly a DH 86b four-engined light Express Airliner to Australia with emigrants from Britain. At the interview he learned that the Company was operating two converted Hudsons to civil standard and two Lockheed Lodestars, one British registered, under the auspices of the Minister for Immigration (Arthur Calwell) in the Australian

Government, which was doing everything in it's power to encourage migration. Sea and Air Transport space was welcomed. As there had been a delay with one of the Hudsons somewhere down the route, this small Company had bought the DH86 to help avoid a backlog of migrant passengers. She was a twelve seater with two crew members, pilot and radio officer or two pilots, and had been relatively cheap to buy.

Jim was engaged at £1000 per year (£A 1250 in 1947), and told he would be combining the jobs of Operations Manager and pilot on reaching Sydney. The aircraft would be ready to collect from Squires Gate aerodrome (Blackpool) on 26 October, where he would be able to do the necessary three light and three fully loaded take-offs and landings to qualify for licence endorsement, after having in the meantime sat for and passed the Air Registration Board's technical exam on the type.

There were 12 days until that date, in which also he was told to work out an overall route plan with estimated costs for fuel, landing and parking fees, accommodation and food, and to engage a radio officer to accompany him, who would remain on the staff as well. It never occurred to Jim to check out the bonfides of the Company, particularly as the London agent for it was a well established reputable firm which seemed more than happy with their Australian customer, and there appeared to be no shortage of money (which bedevilled so many of the smaller British companies).

The whole prospect was simply thrilling, and of course it was a job so soon after his happy summer interlude, just seven days, with pay starting immediately – weekly into the bargain. His family were apprehensive about him going on such a long trip and then being stationed in Sydney, but his new boss had promised free passage for them once Jim was established and sure he wished to stay in Australia.

The route planning was not very difficult, in any case as far as Calcutta, for he had operated that far with BOAC. From Calcutta it would be all new ground, but the Royal Aero Club was able to provide advice and a lot of detail concerning conditions, much of it up-to-date feedback from others who had flown the route fairly recently. As maps and charts were studied, distance and landings grounds selected, flight times calculated, he read about people's customs and history of the lands through which they would pass, building a fascinating mental picture of topography, colours, smells, and habits they would encounter.

The aircraft was a biplane with strongly tapered (high aspect ratio) upper and lower wings separated by struts and braced by streamlined steel rigging wires, the four 200 bhp De Havilland Gipsy Six Series I engines with fixed pitch propellers being located on the lower wings. This particular aircraft was registered G-ADYH on 21 July 1936. It was originally a DH86a type, being converted to the considerably modified DH86b in 1937, and operated by Imperial Airways on the European routes to Paris, Vienna, and Budapest – then by Railway Air Services and NAC during the war. Shortly after that she had been used on internal British services before being sold off to an air charter company based at Liverpool (Speke), Skytravel, and now to Intercontinental Air Tours as Jim's new firm was named.

The original order for the type had come from Quantas for use on the Brisbane to Singapore section of their pre-war services. It specified larger capacity fuel tanks than the original design, two of 75 gallons each instead of the standard 57 gallon ones – the longer range being needed for that route. Although 'YH' was not one of the Quantas order somewhere along the line, and it was understood she had been used for quite a lot of experiemental work at one time or another, she did have those long range tanks fitted – a great help in this instance. It meant that maximum fuel endurance was four and a half hours, giving a safe range of three hours 45 minutes, which allowed 45 minutes to spare over destinations for diversions (in the case of bad weather for instance).

The true airspeed (that indicated by the cockpit instrument corrected for altitude and temperature) was 140 mph using the most economical cruising power setting, which gave an absolute maximum range of 623 miles and a safe range in still air of 525 miles. For forward planning of the route a built-in headwind of 10 mph was assumed, thus giving a speed over the ground (ground speed or G/S) or 130 mph and a safe range of 487 miles to use for pre-calculation of maximum distances between planned stops. Working on two such legs per day, there would be 28 stops (not all that long) therefore a minimum time to Sydney of 14 days, to which 50% was added to allow for possible delays and thus a practical estimate of 21 days overall. Without getting any more technical that was the basis on which Jim reported his estimate of trip costs.

He was provided with a fuel carnet, with which no payment is made when uplifting petrol and oil. Petrol companies all over the proposed route honoured each others' carnet, to obtain which a lump sum is paid to one of the companies (based on agreed estimate of consumption) before the start of the journey. If one or more of the other companies provides the service (due to the issuer of the carnet having no facilities at any place) they cross-bill between themselves as necessary. For landing and parking fees, food and accommodation for passengers and crew, Jim drew £1500 in Sterling travellers cheques and a small amount of French and Italian currency – as much as the very restricted amount allowed by Foreign Exchange regulations of those early days after the war. He was advised that Sydney would cable extra if needed en-route, though it seemed ample allowance had been made for a possible three weeks with a margin.

For the same aircraft crew and passengers, that sum in 1988 would need to be multiplied by at least ten times – but this was October 1947. However it is interesting to reflect that the then airline fare to Sydney was £325 or £650 return, (equivalent to $1300 at 1988 exchange rates), which means, in relative terms, that there has been very little increase in cost to passengers despite the 42 year time gap. Today air travel is faster and flies many fewer legs due to huge range capabilities, as well as carrying some 40 times the number of passengers in one unit, proving that it has become an extremely efficient operation – with the bonus of being by a long way the safest of all forms of transport. Having given the industry that little plug, which may help readers to imagine the differences about to be described as the relatively primitive journey began, let us proceed!

The next three chapters cover the three major stages of a journey which lasted a total of 30 days for the 12,434 miles from Croydon to Sydney – 28 of them to Darwin, or one more than taken by the Smith brothers in the Vimy twenty eight years previously. Reference to the route maps will show the actual route and individual distances covered (in a total of 126 hours 41 minutes, involving 40 legs compared to the minimum of the 28 planned).

13 Croydon to Bahrein – Drama in Baghdad.

On 30 October 1947, Croydon Airport was bathed in light drizzle from a low overcast of stratus could, visibility around 800 yards – cold, miserable, quite typical of the time of year.

G-ADYH had been christened Denebola partly because she had been originally one of Imperial Airways Diana (D-class) aircraft and partly because the second brightest star in the constellation of Leo bears that name. On one occasion that star had helped Jim to obtain a star fix position (once when crossing the mid Atlantic when nothing had been visible for over six hours) the momentary sighting of Denebola a guide to the identity of two other minor stars used in obtaining that fix, from which a course correction was made, saving almost an hour's flying time and valuable fuel.

A lucky star, sitting firmly now (tail down) on her fully trousered main undercarriage legs, gracefully tapered wings dripping yet not looking in the least bedraggled, her attitude purposeful (even stubborn) waiting for the moment when the deep-throated smoothly purposeful growl of her four engines would start up then urge her into flight – (the sound of Gipsy Six engines is unique, implying purpose and reliability, and certainly one of Jim's favourites of all time).

She was not alone in the swirling mist, sharing the tarmac in the light wind with a couple of Avro Ansons of a night mail and newspaper freight company, two De Havilland Doves of a small charter company, a twin engined smaller sister of Denebola (DH89, De Havilland Rapide or Domini to the RAF), three single engined light planes, and a Dakota partially stripped of its wartime camouflage in the process of conversion to civil standards. It was not hard to imagine the romance of that birthplace of British civil aviation 1919 to 1939 with Imperial Airways Hannibals, Albatross, Flamingos, Ensigns, Argosys, and Short Scyllas – Air France Bloch 220s, Farman 180s, the Golden Ray Loire et Olivers – Lufthansa Junkers 52s and G38s – KLM Fokker FVII trimotors and Douglas DC2s, all together with some of Denebola's sisters on the busy apron.

It all seemed so appropriate to Jim as he walked out towards her to make his pre-flight inspection. He was joined by Bob, a young ex-

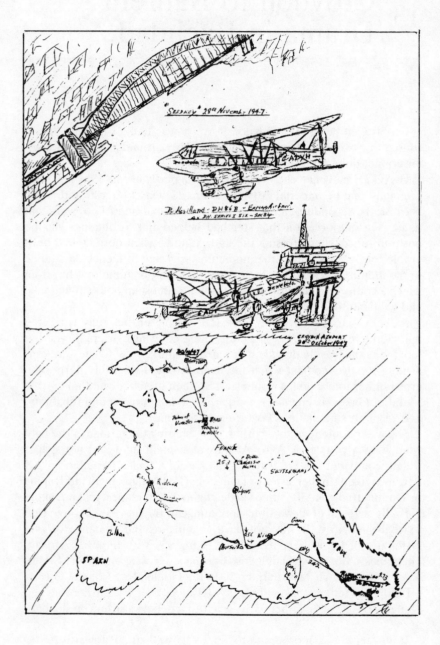

Merchant Navy radio officer, formerly employed by a local air charter company, who had volunteered to make up the two man crew for the journey to Sydney.

His radio equipment was very basic, a simple Marconi medium wave morse code only transmitter and receiver. No direction finding equipment, just communication facilities rapidly being phased out by more sophisticated equipment and VHF radio telephone systems. He was well aware that radio contact over Europe and onwards would be sketchy, with few ground stations using medium wave any more. He was coming along for the adventure and a strong desire to see Australia, and was quite prepared to be general factotum, stewared, dogsbody or whatever to help with the job of getting there. It was to be back to basics from the flying point of view, and Jim found himself once again eager to test his ability to cope and resurrect the teachings of his generation one and two masters.

There were seven passengers, six emigrating to Austrailia and the other a magnificent figure of a 'Lady', wife of a retired senior Royal Navy officer, who was going to Australia 'to see if it was worth living in'. It was never discovered why she had elected to take passage on such a relatively uncomfortable aircraft compared to the regular BOAC/Quantas services, for the fare was the same – £325. As the passengers boarded the aircraft her strong personality, and voice, made themselves felt right away for there was an intitial squabble as to who would sit where out of the 12 seats available which she settled without demur from the others, including a retired Colonel and his wife!

Seats were arranged singly, six each side of a central aisle all with large windows, the first two either side from the front looking out over the narrow lower wing but with excellent views both forward and back. They had quite good leg room and, though non-reclining, were comfortable and the aisle amply wide enough to allow easy passage back and forth to the toilet at the rear.

Jim and Bob followed the passengers in through the main, and only, entrance door, introduced themselves and pointed out the lifebelt stowage under each seat, the escape hatches in the cabin roof, and ensured seat belts were fastened. It was explained that the likelihood of forced landing was negligible (as the aircraft could maintain height on one only of the four very reliable engines) but that regulations required passengers to be fully briefed, so the method of donning a lifejacket was demonstrated by Bob before he settled in his (right hand) seat in the cockpit.

Jim advised that after take off they would have crossed the English Channel within the hour and be landing south of Paris, just after passing Versailles Palace on the left, at Toussous le Noble for lunch and refuelling after approximately two hours flight time. He had asked for the door between cabin and cockpit to be removed to avoid that shut-in-a-box claustrophobic feeling for the passengers, and at the same time avoid any mystery about what was going on up front. It also made communication simpler and, as there was no cabin staff, allowed the crew to keep an eye on events in the back. When airborne the noise level was low enough for normal speech to be heard between cockpit and cabin. He turned round in his own seat to tell the passengers that when the 'Fasten Seat Belts' sign was not on, and then only please one at a time, they would be welcome to come up to the cockpit.

The four Gipsy Six engines started with their characteristic deep throated growl and, at 8.51 am, Denebola rolled smoothly towards the south westerly take off point. There the twin magnetos on each engine were given their usual function check before lining up for take off after receiving the green light permission from the Control Tower (there being no radio communication as previously explained). Even at full power the passenger cabin was remarkably quiet, including the first two rows of seats over the wings and close to the engines. Riding between the upper and lower wings somehow gave a feeling of security. The subdued growling of those very smooth-running engines, reduced to climb and then to cruise power after a short 500 yards or so take off run to a gentle floating feeling in the mist as Denebola rose swiftly through the low stratus cloud, contributed to that feeling of comfortable security and rightness of an aircraft happy in her element.

The Channel was glimpsed occasionally through gaps in the clouds. 'There'll always be an England but it'll be a long long way behind' – came from a male voice singing from the back – so it seemed that any tensions were settling down. The white cliffs of Le Treport passed 3000 feet below as cloud began to thicken and lower, so a let down to 800 feet was made. This allowed visual contact to be kept following well-remembered landmarks flown by in similar weather (and much worse, also without radio aids) to the Paris area. As promised, and happily with cloud cover beginning to break up, Versailles came up on the left, a beautiful sight in a pool of pale sunlight, before lowering over the escarpment to the attractive little airport of Toussous Le Noble, landing two hours 13 minutes after leaving Croydon.

Lunch was taken in the very French-looking (garlic, red wine, and gaullois cigarette smelling) bistro type cellar restaurant under the terminal buildings. Four of the passengers did not smoke and found the noisy, over-warm, humid atmosphere a trial at first. However, despite remarks about the doubtful flavour and gastronomic effects of the strange sounding food, all tucked in to hors d'oeuvres, soup, the main course, chocolate mousse, and cheese.

Bob was left, as was to be his role for a lot of the trip, to play host, Jim excusing himself to sit down and chat with his old friend (the taxi driver Jacques Lautrec) for lunch. Not having finished flying duty for the day the crew could not of course drink wine, but that did not spoil the camaradie and great pleasure always experienced when the two met. A happy hour was spent reminiscing about those highly unconventional times not two months ago during Jim's Paris nightstops whilst drumming up passengers for return trips to Croydon. Sadly they were not to meet again for Jacques died, alone in his old Renault taxi, some days later before Denebola reached Australia.

After a one hour 25 minute stop at Toussous the route was direct to Dijon, flown over at 5000 feet in clear air above a half-cover of strato cumulus cloud whose tops were 1500 feet below, then following the river Saonne to Chalons sur Saonne and the Rhone valley down to Lyons for the first nightstop. The passengers, except for the magnificent 'Lady' who joined them in the cockpit shortly after take off, were snoozing in their seats, no doubt digesting their luncheon feast which, after the still very much rationed food in Britain, must have seemed too good to be true. In fact Jim was beginning to wonder how their digestions would cope and was glad the weather was fine and smooth as the peaceful countryside passed gently below.

M'Lady (as Jim and Bob had already nicknamed her) took the opportunity succinctly to sum up her fellow passengers and her view (as she saw it) of the whole operation – past and future. No compromises, even to wondering how well the two were equipped (the crew) as personalities and in technical competence to be able to cope. Tongue in cheek (for they had not yet fully appreciated the full worth of her) Jim suggested that there were regular airline flights from Lyons, and anywhere along the route for that matter, that she could take – either back to Britain or on to Australia – if her suspicions proved correct, but they would be very unhappy to lose her obvious ability to support and advise them, as well as her charming company. 'Cheeky young bugger' was the immediate response, but her eyes were smiling and he knew then that she was going to be invaluable (even a tremendous crew member) and very good value as a friend.

Typical of the time of year, after passing Dijon and entering the Rhone Valley, some heavy cumulus cloud with showers visible started to build up, but they were avoided without much trouble until arriving over Lyons where the approach and landing had to be made in a heavy shower and strong turbulence which lasted less than 10 minutes. Surprisingly nobody was sick, though faces were looking a bit grey as they disembarked two hours and 55 minutes after leaving Paris. A representative of a new French Air Charter company, Marcel, was acting as Agent and had arranged transport into the city and accommodation at an excellent hotel. Departure next day for Nice was scheduled for nine.

The family of three and the Colonel went straight to bed, feeling too ill to take dinner. M'Lady dressed Jim down for not warning them not to eat too much for lunch (about which he had had uneasy feelings during the flight) and no doubt the bumpy approach had triggered their sickness. He replied, rather curtly, that as she had eaten with them perhaps she should have offered that advice herself – clash number one, and it was not to be the last. Bob told him that she and the Colonel's lady had both enjoyed an excellent dinner, as had the single man who was a restaurateur, and that the 78 year old Colonel suffered from constant stomach problems for which his somewhat younger wife had medicines and was quite used to dealing with it. Jim did feel sorry about the family, who probably got little opportunity at home to eat out much and would have had to exist mainly on the very plain food forced by rationing, but hoped that they would have had a lesson to be more cautious with their eating for the rest of the long journey.

Marcel and his fiancée took Jim to dinner in her parent's home, where he was able to refresh his French. He learned much about the people and customs of Lyons and the Rhone valley, which were quite different in many ways from those of the North and Paris, indeed from most other places in France – especially Marseilles, about which some lurid tales were told. It seemed that in Lyons and thereabouts there was currently a strong element of dislike for the British, though why was not specified, and certainly did not temper their hospitality to him. Nine years later, when Jim next met Marcel, he was married to Janette, had two sons and daughter, and was the Lyons manager for Air France. The reunion was no less pleasant than that evening in her parent's home.

Breakfast started with a chilly response to Jim's 'good morning' to M'lady. All but the Colonel were there so he took the opportunity to apologise for not warning them about the change to richer food than they had for many years been used to in Britain; that M'lady had quite rightly pointed out that it was his duty to take care of all their interests, to which he had responded churlishly, and for that he now apologised to her. He then advised them not to eat too much breakfast, something solid but not greasy, and that lunch in Nice would provide similar fare to Toussous – so a light meal, such as an omelette would be wise. Dinner in Rome would be different, Italian rather than French in style but still rich, so although it would be all right to eat well they should still try to steer clear of greasy foods. He took the opportunity also to point out that, east of Suez, they should heed the age old advice to steer clear of salads not prepared by themselves (despite the heat they would surely encounter) and that water could be very dangerous unless boiled or otherwise sterilised – from this day on. They would be kept up to date daily on all those matters. As they moved out towards the small coach taking them to the airport M'Lady said quietly – 'sporting of you'.

A beautiful clear sunny day without a bump in the sky, the air seemingly washed clean by the storms of the previous evening, graced the flight down the Rhone valley at 5000 feet to Marseilles, then eastwards along the Cote D'Azur past Cannes to Nice, where the landing was on the single long runway paralleling the Mediterranean shoreline after a perfect two hours 40 minutes flight – everyone in high good humour.

The lovely new modern terminal building and restaurant were not then completed. The old bistro (warm and smelling like that at Toussous) worried no one, the Colonel seemingly fully recovered, but Jim repeated the warning about taking care what they ate. He asked M'Lady if she would be kind enough from now on to keep an eye on things whenever he and Bob could not be present – such as now for when they had to go for weather briefing, filing the flight plan, superintending refuelling, and cleaning of the aircraft cabin and toilet (there being no agent appointed in Nice) to which she readily agreed.

It was necessary to advise the passengers that they must expect rough weather, not unlike that of the previous evening at Lyons, during the last hour of the two hour 45 minute flight to Rome. They had all eaten modestly during the one and a quarter hour stop at Nice, which was just as well as, after passing the northern tip of Corsica and turning south east towards Rome, rain started in heavy drops and then in torrents from large cumulus clouds. Seat belts were fastened as Denebola started to toss around and, down to 1500 feet approaching the coast of Italy, lightning streaked the turbulent sky and thunder, clearly heard above the smooth growl of the engines, both intensified – the air becoming very rough.

Looking back Jim saw faces showing signs of strain, though so far nobody had been sick, and hoped his smile was as reassuring as intended. He told them that the flight would take about half an hour longer than planned as, due to the weather, it would be necessary to follow a valley after crossing the coast to avoid high ground, and that that did not lead directly to the Ciampino airport.

What they were not told was that there had been no radio contact with Rome, which made it necessary to circle over the coastline under the 1200 foot cloud base until some advice was received by radio (M/F was still in operation at Rome) as to time to make approach for landing as there would be many aircraft movements in and out of that very busy airport. In that sort of weather medium frequency radio is very difficult to operate, but Bob kept on patiently trying to make contact. There was no other landing ground within range so Ciampino it had to be and, if no radio contact had been made by the time of estimated arrival time as per flight plan, there would be no other choice but to follow the valley of the river Tiber and hope that visibility would not deteriorate until the airport came in sight. It could be expected that Air Traffic Control would hold any other aircraft aloft until 30 minutes after Denebola's ETA, a normal procedure in bad weather when no contact had been made with expected traffic.

There was a sudden break in the clouds over the Rome area, though lightning flashes were continuous to the north, south, and east. At the same time Bob made radio contact, getting a magnetic bearing to steer to the airport – then lost contact again as heavy rain started once more. Taking up that heading as darkness fell, and lowering to just under the increasing cloud at 900 feet, it was possible to catch sight of ground features in the recurring flashes of lightning and Jim hoped that the airport would become visible in time for him to throttle back for landing. He had not been to Rome before but knew that a steep hill or small mountain almost grew up from the eastern end of the runway, which would make a circuit difficult if he was unable to make a direct approach. The landing direction would be to the east (surface wind over the sea by the coast indicating a strong south easterly) and it had to be assumed that receipt of that radio bearing also indicated permission to land.

Then two long lines of bright sodium lights appeared dead ahead, through the rain-streaming windscreen, wipers not helping much it was so heavy. Throttling back and using only half flap, in view of the strong cross wind now obvious from the large angle of drift as the aircraft descended, bucking madly, towards the runway, he literally flew her down 10-15 mph faster than normal to ensure control until the wheels made contact, and had still to keep a little right-hand engine power on to keep her straight until the taxiway appeared, for a turn off to the south side of the airport where a green light and a marshaller with lighted batons guided them to the parking space.

Somone was sick as the cabin door was opened, unmistakable sounds of distress – the 12 year old, poor kid, probably terrified out of her wits. M'Lady already to the rescue! It was surprising nobody else was sick, for during the last thirty mintues it really had been one of the roughest rides Jim had ever experienced.

The agent, Mario, had a bus waiting drawn up close to the exit door and a huge umbrella with which he sheltered each passenger as best he could in the gusty wind and rain, and then the crew in turn into the vehicle. He himself, despite long raincoat and hood, was soaked from standing out in the rain as they taxied in but cheerfully told them that Customs had waived examination, though the police would have to stamp their passports. They would do this on the bus to save passengers getting out in the rain again before leaving the airport for the hotel. He told Jim that Air Traffic control had held seven other aircraft, regular airliners, overhead until Denebola arrived as they had been unable to read any but that one of Bob's transmissions due to the weather which, incidentally, had been forecast simply as heavy showers without thunder and lightning.

Bob's Merchant Navy experience and calm temperament had certainly paid off for them at Rome but from there on he became refuller, steward, purser, public relations officer, and generally a superb right-hand man. Twenty two years old, married, he was already a seasoned hand more usually found in much older men, and the seven-year age difference from Jim's twenty-nine was no gap at all in their relationship. Personalities were already beginning to surface amongst the passengers too, reactions becoming predictable. It was remarkable that only M'Lady of all of them had ever flown before, yet they had so far come through two experiences with flying colours that, the Rome one certainly, would not have been borne so well by many regular air travellers. Jim was beginning to get a sort of gut feeling that, no matter what problems were to come (and there were sure to be several on such a long journey) a team spirit was emerging which would cope with anything. Their stay in Rome tended to confirm it.

People dine late in the Mediterranean countries, as in the Middle East, from 8 and often 10 pm so there was plenty of time to relax in hot baths and have a few drinks before eating in the old-fashioned but comfortable hotel restaurant. Everyone was cheerful again, including the Twelve-year-old lass whose name they learned was Doreen, and for once her parents had no grumble, so it was peaceful and very pleasant. Mario gave instruction on how to eat spaghetti, with some amusing results from five of the passengers who had never eaten it before, but Doreen was very quick to master the art. She had started to come out of her shell a little, thanks to M'Lady's concern when she was sick and now to having her on one side and Bob's interested attention on the other. It seemed that her intelligence may have been submerged by what appeared to be a 'be seen and not heard' attitude from her parents, the father very moody and withdrawn and the mother tending towards hypochondria – but perhaps too early, and unfair, to make a judgement.

Scheduled departure from Ciampino was to be 9 am the following day, 1 November. Mario telephoned at 6.15 am to advise that the weather over the Appenines to Bridisi was very bad and not expected to clear for another 24 hours. After using the house 'phone to advise the passengers that they would be having a free day in Rome and that Mario would be with them after breakfast to arrange any sightseeing they might wish to do, Jim and Bob took a taxi to the airport to meet Mario. Bob went off with him to check over his radio, just in case its poor performance was due to some unforseen snag (nothing was wrong, which disappointed him) whilst Jim went to Air Traffic Control to thank them for the special effort and help they had given. They made it clear that they thought it crazy to be bumbling all the way to Australia in such an old aeroplane, offerred coffee, were disappointed to know that there were no young ladies amongst the passengers and said laughingly that, in that case, they would refrain from joining the travellers for a night out!

Despite the wind and rain a tour of the city in a small bus was arranged, started at 11 am. There were some breaks where short walks were practicable – to look inside the Colosseum, take in St. Peter's Square and the Basilica, have a leisurely lunch at a small cafe (owned by one of Mario's innumerable relatives) and throw a few coins into the Trevi Fountain – before returning to the hotel having seen a great deal of the city, some of it only through the bus windows.

That evening Mario took them to the famous Grotto restaurant, decorated inside like a huge cave, where they dined to music played by a violinist and a guitarist accompanying a superb tenor who visited every table to sing or play requests, or just sing Neapolitan songs – 'O Sole Mio' obligatory of course. Very romantic, beautiful food not a bit rich, with excellent Chianti. Doreen's parents would not come but, after much persuasion, allowed her to go in charge of M'Lady who handed her over to Bob, and the bright-eyed girl had what would surely be for her a long remembered joy. She had never eaten by candlelight before and Bob was a very good dancing partner, but so was the old Colonel for a couple of turns round the floor, and of course Mario charmed her totally. Jim was allowed one dance with her, three with M'Lady (as light on foot as a feather, like so many larger people) and one with the Colonel's lady. Doreen was never heard to tell about that evening – other than to say she had had a lovely time when her father asked the question at breakfast.

At 6.15 am 2 November Mario telephoned to advise the weather was beginning clear over the mountains but not expected to be good enough for visual flight until after midday. The passengers were advised not to hurry down to breakfast as departure would not be until after lunch, which meant a nightstop at Brindisi intead of Athens. There was a bit of flack from Doreen's father – 'At this rate we'll take a month of Sundays to reach Sydney' – which prompted M'Lady to remark that she would prefer to see where we were going and not be bumped about too much.

150

DISTANCES IN STATUTE MILES

SEA OF AZOV

THE CRIMEA

BLACK SEA

YUGOSLAVIA

ADRIATIC SEA

ITALY

Rome 2.73

Bari

Brindisi

Taranto

GREECE

Istanbul

Bosphorus

Dardanelles

Ankara

TURKEY

Izmir

Adana

ATHENS

Rhodes

Samos

Nicosia

317

Mt. Taurus (Olympus)

Beirut

Damascus Syria

CRETE

Heraklion

AEGEAN SEA

MEDITERRANEAN SEA

Palestine/Israel

236

Tel Aviv

Aqaba

Jordan

267

Benghazi

Tobruk

Port Said

Suez Canal

Suez

Gulf of Aqaba

CYRENAICA

NILE DELTA

EGYPT

CAIRO

Airborne shortly after 1 pm local time, climbing out to a cruising altitude of 7500 feet south eastwards, after an early turn to clear that mountain rising close to the end of the runway, the Palace of Godolfo (the Pope's summer residence) was seen about one third of the way up, looking very beautiful bathed in watery sunlight. They flew in and out of cloud over the Appenines, crossing over Benevento, from where so many Italian migrates to Australia seem to have originated, the air smooth enough and the scene very impressive with patchy cloud shadows in intermittent sunshine vying with the mountains and valleys. As the eastern coast of Italy appeared by Bari the sun disappeared, rain starting to fall, light and steady this time, as they decended slowly along the Adriatic coastline to Brindisi.

The manager of the hotel, once used by the Royal Navy after the fall of Italy in 1943/44, was acting as agent, Mario having called him from Rome to arrange accommodation. It seemed they were friends. Friendliness from him, his wife, and all of the staff was the keynote of a stay, not intended other than to refuel on the way to Athens, and made that an evening all were glad not to have missed.

To M'Lady's delight it seemed the Senior Service had become very popular whilst stationed there, the manager and his wife telling many good stories in very good English. He had been to Oxford and she to the Sorbonne in Paris. The Colonel, having puffed out a few Army anecdotes in an attempt to balance the atmosphere and ably supported by very amusing comments form his lady, retired early. The 'Grumpies', as they had christened Doreen's parents, perhaps unkindly, had retired right after dinner taking the girl with them. Maybe just as well, for the conversation became quite hearty as a wonderful evening went on until 11 pm when, exhausted and happy, they all went to bed for eight hours solid sleep.

The take off was 20 minutes late from the usual 9 am sheduled departure but, as it was only a three and a half hour flight to Athens on 3 November, and not intended to go further that day, no one was pressed to hurry over breakfast. The weather was overcast with no sun but without rain and the air smooth until, about an hour after take off and flying at 5500 feet over the Adriatic sea, the island of Corfu came in sight on the left, and at the same time the cloud started to break. Quite quickly the sun shone to reveal, from their peaceful gently droning observation post in the sky, a world of grandeur and magnificence as the Greek mountains rose on the left, a few topped with snow, then over the Gulf of Corinth they turned eastwards along it to the landlocked end through which the deep-cut Corinth Canal leads out into the Saroin Gulf on which, to its north east, lies Athens.

The view, as they descended slowly along the Canal in bright sunshine, then passing Piraeus the port of Athens, before seeing the Acropolis on its tall hill right in the city, was breathtaking – even for Jim who had been there twice before but never in such perfect weather. It was very warm and, due to the high hill running close and parallel to the runway with the sea on the other side, the approach was a little bumpy but did not disturb anyone. It was a perfect introduction to one of the world's most beautiful cities.

After a rather wild drive into the city to the Hotel Grane Bretagne they were met by their agent, a business man dressed in what looked like a Saville row suit, but was probably cut by a local tailor, the Greeks being past masters of the art. Mr Papadopoulos spoke excellent English and displayed perfect manners, obviously a very good business man who, among other things, was running a Travel Agency. The hotel proved to be as stuffy and stiff, yet as luxurious, as when in 1945/46 it had served as British Army Headquarters after the Germans had left, and when Jim had stayed twice.

After settling in, a stroll round the squares near the hotel ended in a snack lunch sitting outside at a pavement cafe, then return to the hotel for a short rest and bath. They assembled as arranged in the hotel's saloon bar where they were met by their guide for the evening, who introduced herself as Katia. She was very, very beautiful in a classic blonde-haired Greek manner, and spoke perfect English only slightly, but most attractively, accented. She was one of Mr Papadopoulos's staff who brought with her his apologies that he had a business engagement and hoped that they would enjoy to the full a typical Greek evening out.

She avoided possibility of complaints about the food by making sure each person fully understood what they were offered to eat and how each dish was prepared, also explaining the background and translation of the various songs to bazouki music. She maintained a sort of mesmeric charm and totally involved patter througout an exhilarating evening, answering clearly any questions, though few were put as her continuous explanations of all that was going on covered most things. The final treat was a bus ride up to the Acropolis, bathed in moonlight, from where she pointed out other ancient Greek monuments and gave their history. Happily Doreen and her parents had joined the party and seemed to have enjoyed it, Katia being careful to involve the girl personally all the time.

It was near midnight when the party returned to the hotel and Katia called for a taxi to take her home. Jim was permitted to escort her to a suburb some way out of the city, a beautiful ride in the moonlight during which she was silent except for an occasional pointing out of places of interest. Handing her out of the taxi he thanked her again for giving them such a wonderful evening, dared to kiss her firm little hand (possibly holding it just a bit long) then like a wraith she was gone up a short flight of steps to pause, a quick wave and a silvery laugh, then she was lost through the door like Cinderella from the ball. That enchanting sight remains clearly embossed on his mind to this day – a perfect finale to a perfect evening.

The weather over the island of Rhodes, the next scheduled stop for refuelling, was very bad so they had to spend another day in Athens. Katia did not reappear and Mr Papadopoulos was fully occupied in his office, so they were left on their own to enjoy another beautiful sunny day, and explore round the city based on her exposition of the places and traditions passed down through the centuries since the halcyon days of Ancient Greece. Mr Papadopoulos joined them that evening, choosing a quiet and excellent restaurant for dinner, very much silver service and quite opposite from the gay tavern of the previous evening. He came alone, quite naturally acquiring M'Lady as his partner, who was clearly delighted with his courtly manner. He was interested in doing business in Australia and the conversation centred rather on that sort of subject and world affairs.

What might well have been a very dull evening (for in Jim's experience top-class restaurants tended to be copies of each other around the world with no special gastronomic features other than superb cooking and service of what could be called top class syndrome meals) turned out to be very pleasant and led to an early bed. On the side he discovered that, as their agent, Mr Papadopoulos had managed to get a big discount on most bills and suspected that his normal commisions may have been waived, which was a pleasant surprise.

Shortly before 9 am the next day Denebola took off into smooth air, cloud cover medium high and broken, but otherwise clear enabling them to enjoy humming along at 5500 feet over the Aegean sea. More green than blue that day but still a perfect background for the myriads of small islands, whitewashed houses set in olive green, fishing boats with brightly coloured sails in tiny harbours – a peaceful sparklingly beautiful scene. Little whitecaps began to blow up on the surface as the wind began to strengthen to the 20-25 mph forecast as the mountainous island of Rhodes was approached.

The flight plan was to land at Colato, on the eastern side of the southern part of the island as, for some reason not explained, refuelling facilities at the main airport (Maritza) in the north were not available so Esso had arranged to be at the alternate airfield. It had one long asphalt runway, no terminal facilities, and was situated in a wide bay with mountains growing out of the western end, which seemed to be getting a familiar feature. There was just enough room for a light aircraft with a small turning circle, like Denebola, to approach on a descending turn to land into the strong south easterly surface wind towards the sea, the runway ending close to the shoreline. It was pretty rough for the last 20 minutes but by now the passengers had found their air legs and appeared to be enjoying the roller-coaster type motion.

Esso turned up just as the aircraft taxied to a halt on the extreme western edge of the runway. It had started to rain and lightning could be seen in the heavy cumulus clouds over the mountains, as forecast, and as there was no shelter of any kind outside the refuellers agreed to allow the passengers and crew to remain on board, a practise normally prohibited. In the 25 minutes it took to refuel, hot soup from thermos flasks and lunch boxes provided from Athens were opened and eaten in the relative warmth of the cabin. The friendly Esso crew had long departed before the one hour 45 minute stop was over, an interval thought best for relaxation and digestion. The rain had continued but become intermittent, the lightning flashes fewer, and the wind less strong during that time so it was fairly smooth after take off over the sea and climb again to 5500 feet to cruise close to the southern coast of Turkey en-route for Cyprus for nightstop. The weather had cleared completely during the two and a half hour flight to Nicosia, the magnificent sight of 6432 feet high Mt. Trudos, or Olympus, with a tiny cap of snow at the summit, sliding by on the left during descent.

The arrival time was 4 pm local time and it was very pleasant to be met by traffic staff and customs people whom Jim had known from the BOAC No. 5 Line days, Cypriots of both Greek and Turkish origin who showed no sign of the unhappy factional differences which in later years resulted in the tragic division of the island. They had booked rooms in the excellent Acropole Hotel where he had stayed a few nights during 1943/46 when operating through Nicosia (normally just for refuelling) on the Ankara-Istanbul from Cairo run. It proved to be the same pleasantly comfortable, without much fuss, place – the food plain but excellently cooked and served. There was not much to do in the evening other than to enjoy a walk under a canopy of stars in balmy air before a 10 pm bedtime, in preparation for a long three-leg day, necessitating an early start at 7.30 am for Baghdad.

On 6 November 1947, destination Lydda (now Lod) was a refuelling stop not looked forward to. Still (but only just) Palestine, Arab and Jew at deadly loggerheads, the British mandatory presence under the League of Nations being relinquished daily more rapidly, popular with neither Jew nor Arab. It had to be because Damascus, the only other place within range, was off-limits at that time. They arrived there at 9 am local time, having left Nicosia earlier than planned at 6.30 am, intending just to refuel without Jim's preferred one and a half rest at stops and hoping that 45 minutes would sufficient. Despite the

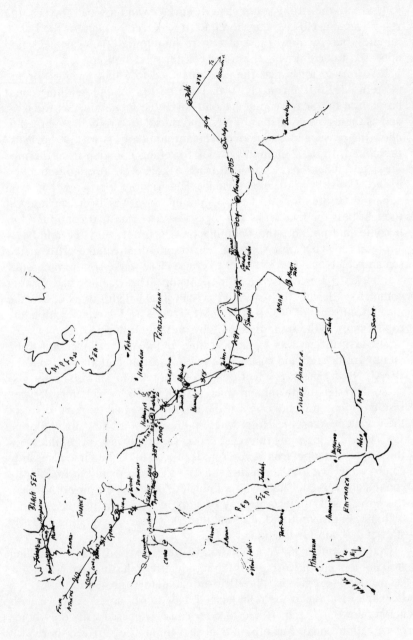

seemingly quite deliberately prolonged formalities, it was managed in 56 minutes, during which time reluctantly served coffee and cakes at grossly inflated prices were taken by the passengers, Jim and Bob both supervised refuelling and cabin/toilet cleaning, as much for security's sake as to ensure a quick turn-round. For Jim it was sad, for he had enjoyed time spent there only one or two years before, picking up sacks of oranges and grapefruit to take home to Cairo and enjoying friends (Arab, Jew, and British) when idealistic enmity had not intruded.

The climb out from Lydda took them over the parched Jordanian hills, bumpy as usual from reflected heat but not yet as it would be after midday. The river Jordan was the only sign of life as it stretched, thinly silver, down south to the Dead Sea. Then past the Jordanian capital of Amman to reach the desert – sand, sand, sand as far as the eye could see, red gold and soon to be shimmering in the heat, no vegetation, the only feature of significance the black oil pipeline from the Iraq oilfields to Haifa. At intervals along that pipeline were situated oiled strip landing grounds, to one of which (LGH3) Denebola was headed for the next refuelling. They were operated by the IPC (Iraq Petroleum Company) and provided bases from which pipeline maintenance and repair were carried out and, as before the war, flying operations were provided by Airwork.

It was not as hot after landing as it could get but, after a fairly rapid change from much cooler climates, the passengers were uncomfortable and appreciated the cold drinks from flasks filled at Nicosia. After refuelling from a tanker, which appeared from somewhere along the pipeline (to disappear back from whence it came afterwards) the tanker crew all Arabs but very friendly, joking and laughing as they did their job most efficiently, the lunch boxes and more cool drinks were taken shaded from the sun under the wings, where the temperature was really quite pleasant. It was very quiet with little wind. The smell of the desert sand (dry, dusty, musty and peculiar to the Middle East and North Africa) nostalgic to Jim but a new and weird experience for the others, was judged not unpleasant to all but Doreen's parents. She herself thought it romantic and said how identified she felt with Lawrence of Arabia, about whom she had been reading at school.

Off again, climbing to 7000 feet where the air was not too bumpy, following the black line of the pipeline over the new shimmering sand until the relief of Habbaniyeh on the left, the RAF station with its huge lake on which Service and civil flying boats landed close by the large airstrip. Letting down shortly after to cross the river Euphrates before landing at Bagdad on the river Tigris at 6.40 pm, just eighteen minutes past sunset local time, and 11 hours since leaving Cyprus. Confusion reigned on the tarmac, several aircraft having arrived close together, but an agent appeared fairly soon to introduce himself. His name checked out on Jim's briefing list, and two of his henchmen led the passengers to the terminal whilst Bob superintended refuelling and Jim started on the paperwork.

It was hot and stuffy in the aircraft so, after having completed the technical log, he took the journey log, passenger manifest and customs declaration (together with crew and passengers' passports) outside to complete, also where the apron lights gave better illumination. Normally all that would be done in the terminal building, but with so many aircraft arriving together the place would be overcrowded and Denebola's turn last in the queue. The lower wing was as good a place as any to put the various items on as they were completed in turn, including the passports. Hearing loud shouting coming from the other side of the plane Jim looked up sharply, but seeing nothing he bent down to look under the fuselage to see that something must have been dripped from the wing of the next aircraft in line, but any excitement was over and returned to his paperwork. The passports had gone!

Nothing else was disturbed, there was no wind to blow things around, and there was no sign of the passports having slipped off the wing. Obviously they had been stolen, and it was only then that Jim remembered having heard about such thefts being common, with a big trade in them being used to get illegal entry into Palestine. At that moment the agent turned up again and they hurried together to report the matter to the police, telling Bob to join them when his refuelling was finished.

Except when a few countries insist on holding all passports until the owners leave the country (Iraq at that time being one) the document never leaves its owner who is personally responsible for its safe keeping. For Jim the situation was therefore a disaster, and the police were less than helpful. Howver, they did agree to allow passengers and crew to go to their hotel on guarantee from the agent to be personally responsible for their proper behaviour whilst in the country – nobody to leave the hotel unescorted!

From the hotel, Jim telephoned the British Consul (who was out) but the theft details were recorded and an appointment made to see him at 9.30 am the following day. That was a Saturday, not normally a working day, but the matter was treated (as indeed it was) as an emergency. The passengers were, as may be expected and quite rightly so, upset, furious, and panicky in the sense of 'what will become of us without passports'. M'Lady was not very kind in her comments and Jim received a proper dressing-down on the spot, to which he could hardly raise objection though he had thought she might have been more reasonable.

Admitting that the matter was his fault he made it clear that the priority was not recrimination but to do something positive to obtain new passports, towards which he had made the appointment with the Consul. Further, a photographer would be at the hotel at 8 am in the morning to take everyone's photograph, and that he would require birth certificates and personal details for the Consul. There would be no need to accompany him in the first instance (though no doubt the Consul would wish personal interviews in due course) but, it being a weekend, it would be unlikely that things could be processed in time to continue the journey until well into the next week. Looking then directly at M'Lady Jim stated firmly that he would be much happier, as no doubt would they all, if she would be kind enough to collect and take charge of the personal papers and accompany him, with Bob as escort, to the Consulate – he was sorry to trouble her and would have asked the Colonel instead, but he was again indisposed.

For a moment Jim thought the tight lips, extra ramrod back, and furious steel grey eyes would erupt into clash number two. The ensuing silence was positively noisy with high frequency vibrations, suddenly subsiding before. . . 'Very well, I shall be happy to do that'. . . with a small smile to signify armistice effected!

The Consul was predictably very annoyed and made it abundantly clear that, being the weekend, there was no hope whatsoever of obtaining authority from London for him to issue new passports – the affair, incidentally, was ruining his own arrangements.

M'Lady promptly took over, emphasising that the theft was clearly a planned operation against which sort of thing far better security should be provided at the airport and that the local representative of the British Government should ensure this. From his home she would personally telephone a person high up in the Foreign Office (who lived a few doors away from her husband, a retired senior Naval officer) who would no doubt give the necessary authority for the issue of new passports, despite it being the weekend. She pointed out that the necessary photos had been taken and would be available later in the day, and that she held all the necessary papers relevant to the individuals concerned. As the crew were not in possession of birth certificates, (as they were not emigrating to Australia like the passengers), he (the Consul) would have to accept the personal details recorded on their flying licences in lieu.

She continued. . . 'If he would now be good enough to provide nine application forms she would return with them completed by midday, at which time please to be kind enough to allow use of the Consulate telephone for her to catch her contact between 9.00 and 9.30 am local time in London before he went off to golf. At that time he too would be able to speak and receive the necessary authorisations. The Captain had a record of every passport number and date of issue for those stolen which could be advised then for the purpose of immediate cancellation, and he and his Radio Officer would return with her in case needed to answer any questions'. . .

Jim felt a little sorry for the man but to his credit he turned the situation right round by thanking her for such valuable assistance, and for her suggestions. He then handed her the application forms and invited all three to join his luncheon party after the call to London had been made. He added that, assuming the authority was forthcoming (and he had no doubt her influence would prevail) he would have temporary passports available by Monday morning for them to continue their journey. The invitation was accepted, the vital telephone call made successfully, the garden party as it turned out thoroughly enjoyable, and the passengers told of the arrangement on their return to the hotel.

On the Sunday afternoon the Consul telephoned to advise that the passports were ready but he would feel happier if they would permit him to arrange for them to be delivered directly to the airport on Monday morning, rather than risk them being overnight in the hotel. In point of fact he brought them himself at 7.40 am in time for an 8.00 am departure, a goodwill gesture not just diplomacy (at which he had shown some skill) but believed to be a genuine desire to wish them well, for the unfortunate start to their acquaintance had reversed completely in the previous thirty-six hours. One more up to that remarkable Lady!

The flight plan for the first leg of the day, 9 November, was changed from Basrah to Abadan in southern Persia (Iran) due to forecast headwinds making a Basrah-to-Bahrein leg too long for safety. Abadan lies about half way to Bahrein, so splitting the total distance more evenly. It was hot, though at 7500 feet pleasantly warm, the air fairly smooth with cloudless skies, hazy with humidity as the Persian Gulf was approached. The track followed the Tigris southwards, over swamps just before the Euphrates joins it north of Basrah, the confluence becoming the Shatt-al-Arab which flows then down to the Gulf carrying the huge tankers with Iraq oil – the port busy with all kinds of shipping. Thirty years later (1977) Thor Heyerdahl (of Kon Tiki fame) constructed a huge sailboat, using reeds grown in those swamps, in which he proved that ancient mariners could have done the same to trade down the Gulf to India, and as far west as Djibouti in Somaliland. That voyage is recorded in his book *The Tigris Expedition*, which is fascinating to read.

Returning now to the journey in hand, they landed at Abadan after three hours 40 minutes flight. It was hot and sticky at over 90 degrees Fahrenheit, though nowhere nearly as bad as the Gulf can be with humidity often over 90° and temperatures (at the same time) well over

110° Fahrenheit. Happily there was a small air-conditioned office in which to enjoy cool drinks and eat from their lunch boxes. The employees of the Anglo American Oil Company which operated the airfield were very friendly and helpful, always glad to see fresh faces.

On the approach to Abadan Jim had noticed the upper and lower wings moved horizontally, in a sort of scissor action, when the ailerons were being operated to keep level in the very bumpy air low down, though control had not seemed to be affected. After take off for Bahrein, bouncing around in the hear of the lower air, he noticed it again though at their 8000 feet cruising altitude in cooler, smooth, air everything appeared normal again. Bob too had noticed the wing movement. Doreen asked to come up to the cockpit, too shy to have asked before. As the various instruments, switches, and controls were explained to her she said that, back in the cabin when the air was bumpy the aircraft looked like a bird flapping its wings. Descending towards Bahrein Jim watched the wings closely, moving the aileron controls more firmly than usual, and saw a small scissor-like movement gradually increase to become quite marked on final approach though, again, control response had not been affected.

After the passengers had left for the BOAC mess where accommodation had been arranged he contacted the RAF (who ran the airfield and had a big staging post operation) to ask if they had anyone on their engineering staff who was used to old fashioned rigging of biplane aircraft – that is adjustment, to explain very basically, the various wires which braced the wings and struts to give correct flying trim. A sergeant was found who had experience on types of biplanes ranging from Tiger Moths, Gladiators, even Vickers Vimys, before the war. He examined Denebola after she was taxied over to the big hangar and found that some of the streamlined steel wires had slackened off due to the heat, which had only been experienced really since leaving Baghdad.

He examined the maintenance manual carried on the aircraft, then called a mate of the same approximate age (a corporal probably late forties or more) and said. . . 'Leave it to us, Sir, she'll be right as rain in the morning'. . . And so she was, the two coming up on a 6.45 am test flight loving the old biplane atmosphere. Jim wanted to do something for them or their mess but they wouldn't hear of it, being just so happy and proud to have used their not forgotten skills.

Meanwhile, overnight in the rest house, they met with three crew members of the company's Hudson which had arrived earlier that day from Nicosia. They had arrived in Rome when Denebola was stuck in Baghdad, picking up seven from Athens – all emigrants. After leaving Bahrein they were scheduled to arrive in Sydney four days later. Doreen's father had found this out from the Hudson's captain and had made a great fuss about changing aircraft, in which the Colonel and his lady backed him wanting to reach Sydney much sooner than could Denebola, which had at least another 15 days to go without any more delays.

M'Lady announced that if that meant offloading passengers from the Hudson to make room for them she disapproved strongly. Anyway she wished to remain with the DH86, to which the single gentleman added his support (they had learned his christian name was Richard, which he asked to be used, but please not 'Dick'). It would be necessary to offload five Hudson passengers if the five defectors were to have their way. Of these passengers only one could speak any English, a Greek gentleman travelling with wife and three children a two year old and twin girls aged about six months. He was asked if he would prefer to enjoy a longer trip and see more places, but it was obviously not on with such small children. That left two more Greeks, a young lady travelling out to get married to an English ex-army officer now living in Melbourne, and an 18 year old lad. The Greek gentleman explained the situation to them and they were quite happy to change aircraft. As the Colonel was not a well man, Jim decided that the and his wife would be the two to change over. Doreen's father ranted and raved, demanded that top priority be given to finding space for the three of them, and that if only one other Hudson passenger would change then he and his family could go and the Colonel and wife remain with Denebola.

The tough Aussie skipper of the Hudson took Jim aside as the squabble continued – (M'Lady, having said her piece, had retired to read in company with Richard). he said he could offload seven passengers, Italians. They were travelling on assisted passages to join husbands who had been out in Australia since before the war started, and had had to remain there. After so many years apart perhaps another three weeks would not be that bad, and as they were not full fare paying passengers like the others he felt sure that would be in order. But how to tell them? Nobody else spoke Italian, and they spoke no English or Greek.

It was decided that there would be no point saying anything until departure time next day and then, with sign language, somehow get them to board Denebola instead of the Hudson. Joining the squabblers, the Aussie skipper announced very firmly that he had managed to make five seats available on his aircraft, but he was only prepared to accept them as passengers provided they agreed to cause no further unpleasantness before reaching Sydney. If they boarded his aircraft in the morning he would consider that acceptance of his right to offload anyone, at any stop, who created a problem similar to this evening. Doreen's father, red in the face, declared that he would not accept any such high-handed treatment, to which the answer snapped back. . . 'then don't fly with me'. . .

Jim and Bob went over to M'Lady and Richard, who had of course heard all, to advise that the other two of the seven Italians could be offloaded to make room from them on the Hudson. Both reaffirmed they wished to continue in Denebola, she saying that. . . 'After all, someone had to remain to change their nappies for them!!! '. . .

14 A multi-national 'family' – India in turmoil; Calcutta affair – Singapore, after ten eventful days.

Breakfast on 10 November was in the non-air-conditioned small hangar which served Bahrein as the terminal building at that time. Cornflakes with liquidised powdered milk, scrambled eggs with tinned tomatoes, toast with tinned butter and jam. It was hot, even at 6 am, and appetites not too good so not much was eaten. Loud complaints were voiced by Doreen's father that he was sick of eggs, eggs, eggs. Twelve days out from Britain where one egg per week per person (if lucky) was the ration, but that was only what might have been expected from him. The Hudson captain stood over him at that moment to ask if he had decided to travel on his aircraft. Answered in the affirmative, the skipper repeated his conditions of the night before. The moment was well chosen and Jim heard later that there had been no further trouble during the five days to Sydney.

The young Greek lady and the lad were joined by M'Lady and Richard and moved out towards Denebola, their baggage already loaded. The Italian lady and her three children who were to change planes were led towards the group (naturally looking bewildered) by the Hudson captain gesticulating to the effect they would now be travelling with the two Greeks on a different aircraft, and to show which was their baggage. They understood, picked out their baggage which was then loaded into Denebola, and joined the others without protest.

An enormous commotion erupted from the Hudson group, wailing and screaming as the remaining Italians realised their friends were going on a different aircraft and they came rushing over to join them. Tears all round, with M'Lady trying to comfort them with the help of the Greek lady. The extra load was no problem as there was still room for four more passengers, and their luggage very little so no trouble about Denebola being overloaded. Jim asked Bob to arrange for its transfer from the Hudson and moved into the distraught group, to be addressed in halting English by an 11 year old girl from the new arrivals. . .

164

'Why you take them?' (as she pointed to the family, clinging then back shyly to her mother) – 'Okay, you come too', said Jim, and shepherded them all into Denebola. . .

The Italians were seated in the front four rows, leaving one seat empty on the right in row four. The two Greeks one each side in row five, with M'Lady and Richard in the last row where they had been before. Now there were eleven, but everyone seemed quite happy.

Denebola's spruce-framed fuselage was covered (structurally) with birch plywood, wooden stringers being set over that the whole length of her, an insulating material then held in place outside the plywood frame by an outer skin of doped fabric stretched over the stringers. Not only was that a very effective soundproofing device which contributed largely to the extremely quiet cabin, but acted well as insulation. So, with the high top wing helping to shade the cabin in part from direct sunlight she was relatively cool inside, but Jim started the engines as soon as possible, taxiing out right behind the Hudson, whose cabin must have been stifling. It may have been fresher smelling than theirs, for the newcomers obviously lacked the sophistication of deodorants – a problem addressed at a later date.

The Persian Gulf shimmered in the heat haze as they flew eastwards towards Sharjah on the Oman peninsular at 9000 feet, where it was pleasantly cool and smooth, landing there after two and a half hours flight. The runway being fairly close to the sea, and landing to the east, the approach was fairly smooth with only a short period of sharp bumps as the coastline was crossed. The passengers were taken quickly to the old fort, built with thick blocks, layers deep and very cool inside even when 110 degree outside shade temperatures occurred. Lunch boxes, requested on the flight plan, were ready with cool fresh lime for the flasks, refreshing tea with small rock bun type cakes being provided whilst refuelling was taking place. Jim told M'Lady and Richard that the first 30 minutes or so to the three and a half hour flight to Jiwani, (by the Gwader Peninsular, which was to become part of Pakistan), would be very bumpy climbing out over the Oman Peninsular until over the Gulf of Oman then the Arabian Sea. They assured him they would help Bob with the new passengers should they become sick or frightened. After take off Bob was to take the empty seat in the cabin in row four.

Although the air was extremely rough until passing 7000 feet, and far from still even on reaching 11,000 feet (1000 feet higher than normal without oxygen) nobody was sick. A few shrieks of alarm, but then screams rather like those heard from the big dipper at fairgrounds and slightly hysterical laughter – Bob, Richard, and M'Lady encouraging them and making a firm rapport which lasted and stood everyone in good stead for the rest of the trip to Sydney. Over the sea the air became smooth again, altitude lowered to 9000 feet, and the lunch boxes were opened one and a quarter hours before descending into bumpy air again at 3000 feet over the sea, crossing the coast on approach to land at Jiwani an few miles inland.

Hot, hot, hot there – temperature over 100 degrees and very dry and dusty. The terminal building was a simple Nissen hut with no fans, but tea and small cakes again were served by one of the two Indians staffing this outpost. The RAF were in residence during the war, and still were the last time Jim had landed there in a BOAC Ensign, with 34 passengers and vegetables for the RAF, en-route back to Cairo from Calcutta. The other Indian was the Air Traffic Controller, who brought bad news.

It had been intended to go onto nightstop at Karachi, but a message had been received to say that Mauripur airport was closed from dusk to dawn, no reason given, so there was no choice but to remain overnight at Jiwani. There were no beds available and the only shelter the single Nissen hut they were then in. There was an old metal hangar which housed an electric light generator, water was scarce, food stocks low and three weeks to go before the next delivery of rations for the two people stationed there – so, there was a problem.

By using the emergency rations and water carried on the aircraft, food was available from tins quite sufficient to cover dinner and breakfast, and two quart flasks of lime juice from Sharjah had not been used so, with rationing, liquids were also sufficient. M'Lady said she would take care of the rations. The Air Traffic Controller suggested he and his colleague could camp out in the hangar, leaving the Nissen hut for the visitors to use for shelter and sleep. There were two mattresses and some blankets he thought would be clean left in the old RAF storeroom. There were six deep armchairs and a large settee also left behind and already in the hut, and the dining table might serve as a bed with some of the cushions from dining chairs and settee. The nights were not very cold, as the wind was from the north-east and dry having crossed a lot of desert before reaching Jiwani.

It was decided that Bob, Richard, and Jim would sleep in Denebola, which had been tethered close to the hut with stakes and guy ropes against the probability of the wind strengthening, and the females all in the hut, with the Greek lad in the bathroom cubicle to be on hand if necessary to converse with his lady compatriot. Toilets were no problem as the ablutions end of the hut, although without water, had four 'thunderbox' cubicles only one of which had been in use since the staff had been reduced to two. Inspection revealed that the others had clean buckets and seats and flies (by the busy buzzing coming from the one in use) not interested in those three. As darkness fell the Indians started the generator so there was light from three small wattage bulbs in the main area with another doing duty in the ablution area. The friendly and very helpful Indians retired to the hangar to prepare and eat their food and said goodnight.

Helped by the 11 year old girl and her mother (whom they had christened 'Mamma', to remain so for the rest of the trip) M'Lady opened a tin of ham, two of mixed veggies, and a packet of cracker biscuits – they had found plates, four forks, two blunt knives, six dessert and two teaspoons. Paper cups from the aircraft to drink from, and dinner was enjoyed in a happy camping atmosphere (Doreen's dad was not missed at all!!!). The child's name was Carmela, but so far the other Italians' names had not been found out, nor the Greek lady's, but the lad was called Yanni. M'Lady had a name for the Greek lady next morning, not printable, but was the reason for clash No. two with Jim – described hereafter.

There was no water to wash with and tooth brushing had to be given a miss. That did not worry the continental passengers in the least, and their odour had become pretty stifling in the confined area of the hut as cushions and blankets were arranged for the female group to settle down for the night as well as possible on the two thin mattresses, deep chairs, settee, and table.

In the aircraft the three men settled on the cabin floor, nightstop bags for pillows and, tired from the long day, fell quickly asleep. They remained fully clothed, which was just as well for just after 1 am the cabin door opened to admit M'Lady and her powerful voice to jerk them awake. It is doubtful if it would have worried her if they had been starkers for she was absolutely choleric with fury. She demanded that Jim accompany her back to the hut where, she alleged, she had been woken by heavy sounds coming from the bathroom area to find two Greeks fornicating, and that he was to express disgust and fury in such a way as to make it clear they would be offloaded if it ever happened again.

Of course the other passengers were wide awake by then, looking thoroughly scared and huddled together as the dragon lady sailed past them to confront the offenders with a sound not unlike a horse's snort, repeating loudly to Jim (with suitable gestures) what she had discovered. He asked her to leave him alone with them and, after a moment or two of silence, she departed with another snort.

The young lady, no beauty at the best of times, was in tears and moaning whilst the lad's huge brown eyes looked hurt like a whipped dog's, his arm around her protectively. Jim's private view was that their relationship was their own affair so long as it did not affect the other passengers or (particularly in the case of passing through countries, Moslem a case in point) where public morals could be offended. He got them to lie on the floor and show him what they had been doing, hoping the demonstration would not be too explicit. Shyly they lay down together cuddling close, her head on his shoulder and a leg thrown over both his. No movement (feeling distinctly embarrassed, but he had to get to the truth of the matter) at which the lad looked hurt and upset as she howled denial, he shaking his head saying what was obviously 'NO,NO,NO' in Greek. He indicated they rise and made mime that they must not lie together again. He got sulky looks in response so he pointed to Yanni, putting his hands together like handcuffing and shoved him, not too gently, into a toilet cubicle banging the door shut after him. It seemed he got the imprisonment message indicating (when let out) by much shaking of the head, putting his arms around her then pushing her away from him, that it would not happen again. She was sent back to the main room, Jim's head on pillowed hands suggesting she sleep, then he gave the lad a half smile, shaking a finger under his nose, then giving him the same sign pointing to the floor.

Back in the aircraft he found M'Lady calmed down but still indignant and upset. He told her what he had done and made it quite clear that personal relationships must be considered their own affair as long as kept strictly to themselves. She insisted that she would most certainly be seeking out the girl's fiancée when they reached Australia to ensure he knew what a slut he was about to marry, and that made Jim very angry. He said that, true or false, he had to accept that the pair denied impropriety and must take their word for it, and that he had made it quite clear that they must never be found in that position again. However, in a world of their own amongst eleven others, unable to speak their language nor they either of the other two, it must be allowed that they remain close for he believed the lass to be very frightened and needing Yanni's company. She had shown Jim a picture of the good looking man she was to marry beside which was one of a very pretty girl whom she indicated was herself, and he (Jim) wouldn't be surprised if she was terrified that the fiancée would refuse to marry her and send her back in disgrace to Greece when he saw how fat and unattractive she had become. Whatever, as long as there were no more incidents like that he, as captain, wished to hear no more of the matter and expected that M'Lady and everyone else on board would show kindness and understanding to them for the rest of the trip – remembering that the world was full of peoples with vastly different standards and customs which needed to be thoroughly understood before voicing criticism.

M'Lady rose and went to the cabin door, turning there to glare at Jim and say. . . 'I have never been spoken to like that in my life. You won't hear the last of this I can assure you – and do me the favour of not speaking to me again unless to give instructions for the proper running of this ship. . .

She made a dignified exit but he would bet she sat up the rest of the night to ensure the Greek lass did not sneak back to the bathroom. Bob said he thought Jim had been rougher than necessary and had now probably lost her goodwill for the rest of the trip, to which he said that just couldn't he helped but hoped she would come round in time. Richard felt she would and didn't see really how Jim could have acted differently. They managed a couple of hours sleep until dawn.

After untethering the aircraft, rechecking the previous day's refuelling, doing pre-flight checks, collecting a weather forecast and filing the flight plan, they had a quick snack and drink of the still cool lime juice and re-stowed remnants of the emergency pack. They said goodbye with many thanks to their Indian friends, boarded the passengers and took off at 7.18 am for a two hours 40 minutes flight to Karachi. They climbed to 7000 feet into smooth air and a clear sky straight into the eye of the newly risen sun, the mountains of Baluchistan in a sharp profile on the left, the Arabian Sea below, and the coastline parallel until it curved back towards them as the descent to Karachi started – landing was at 10.30 am local time, watches advanced half an hour from Jiwani time, five and a half hours ahead of Greenwich Mean Time (GMT).

It was learned there had been riots in Karachi, which was why the airport had been closed for security reasons overnight. Disturbances all over India (with independence from Britain and partition into Moslem Pakistan and Hindu India causing an enormous refugee problem) were escalating making it imperative to proceed across the country as fast as possible. Due to the restricted range of Denbola, refuelling stops would have to be made at Johdpur, Delhi, and Allahabad before reaching Calcutta. The traffic officer acting as agent happened to be an old friend from BOAC days, and he advised that accommodation would be almost impossible to get – especially in Delhi where the refugee problem was particularly bad. He organised a large food hamper, restocked the emergency rations, provided two half gallon thermos jugs filled with curry stews, and four more quart flasks of clean water and lime juice on top of their own, as he was sure uplift of food before Calcutta would not only be difficult but possibly not safe to eat. He managed to get a Telex message through to a colleague in Calcutta to reserve accommodation there. An answer came 15 minutes before the end of what proved to be two hours 25 minutes on the ground – rooms had been reserved at the Great Eastern Hotel from 12 November, but would be held until they arrived, even if later. The hamper and extra flasks were to be left with him when they reached Calcutta. Meanwhile, after conference with Bob, it had been decided they would fly through the night, stopping only to refuel, until reaching Calcutta. If Jim felt too tired to continue, then a short break for sleep on the aircraft would be taken after landing at whatever that place might be. Assembling the passengers in the terminal building, with his agent friend beside him, he explained in English what was planned at the same time showing on a map of the country where they would be landing, approximate flight and stopping times, and estimated time and date for arrival in Calcutta. 'Hotel' (Shake of the head) 'sleep' (indicated by head on folded hands) then pointing to the aircraft. They all seemed to understand, then M'Lady said. . . 'We are all relying on you completely and I believe you have sense enough not to go to sleep on us in the air'. . . It seemed the rift was healed!

It was 12.41 pm when they left Karachi for Johdpur, crossing the mighty river Indus whilst on climb to 9000 feet, for a flight plan of three hours and 20 minutes against moderate head winds. Midday and early afternoon in the hot dry weather crossing the 'Thar', or Great Indian Desert, can be very rough but bumps are more of a constant movement in all axes than sharp and sudden – up and down draughts like a rolling sea without crests or troughs, and the passengers soon got used to the motion, laughing and squealing whenever there was an occasional up or down 'whoosh'. Johdpur's castle on the high cliff north of the airport was clearly visible as they approached for an east-north-east landing in a gusty 15-20 mph cross wind on the surface. The hot air from rocky ground and runway added considerable updraught effect before touch down but nobody was sick, and they exclaimed in wonder at the sight of the Maharajah's Palace (the castle) glowing pinkish gold in the light of the sun sinking low in the west – it was 4.10 pm local time.

Jim told Bob he had decided to add 30 to 45 minutes to the usual one and a half hour refuelling stops. In that extra time he intended to find a quiet spot to lie down if possible for a short shut-eye in order to stretch his stamina to cover the close to 24 hours elapsed time since leaving Jiwani and estimated time of arrival (ETA) in Calcutta. In that way he hoped to retain full awareness for each of the approximately three and a half hour legs between stops – (flight time regulations in those days simply laid down a maximum number of flying hours in any one month – 120, and 1200 in any one year. Duty times had not been introduced any more than daily or weekly maximum for flying hours, nor minimum rest periods). He suggested Bob do likewise, even though his flight duties no longer included use of the radio (which was useless), as the passengers would certainly need advice and assistance during the night and it would be better if he (obviously not Jim) were not to be seen asleep in flight.

Harry Manton, the traffic officer at Karachi (incidentally an Anglo-Indian whose father had been in the Indian Army and married to a high born Hindu lady) had told Jim that the authorities everywhere would wish to examine their aircrew licences (as they had at Karachi). It was also probable that they would want (which had not happened at Karachi) to see the passengers' passports/travel documents, and most certainly would at Calcutta. In fact he had not checked on the European passengers, assuming the Hudson crew would have done so en-route to Bahrein. Whilst they were comfortably seated in the large airy airport lounge, enjoying again tea and little cakes served by white-robed attendants whose colleagues were pulling at ropes which activated beautifully coloured 'Punkah' panels high up in the ceiling to keep the air circulating (there were no fans), he checked their papers.

There were no passports, just travel document issued by Italy and Greece authorising them to enter Australia via the various countries en-route, and countersigned by Australian consular authorities in Rome and Athens. He was now able to find out their full names but, for the purpose of this narrative only fictitious christian names have been used. The lady with three children became Signora Philomena and her children Cesare aged 12½, Roberto aged 11, and the girl Gina aged 10. The lady travelling on her own became Signora Maria, and Carmela's mother retained the nickname Mamma. The Greek lady was named Zouky in fun, that being nowhere near her real (unpronounceable) name but the nickname approach seemed to bring out her confidence a little, and finally resulted in a smiling face that was quite attractive. The cheeky, fun loving Mamma he noted was only 32, the other Signora 47.

After a stop of two hours 10 minutes, during which Jim got a 20 minute break (joined by Bob) just to close the eyes and float, they left Johdpur heading north-east for Delhi, the sun just set with the twilight a short moment or two of indigo sky to the east. A smooth starlit flight at 7000 feet lasted two hours 40 minutes, during which Carmela brought sandwiches and cool drinks up to the cockpit whilst the passengers enjoyed a good meal of curry stew, which the crew intended to eat later when on the ground. They landed at 9 pm local time, but the crew meal was not to be as the shambles in the terminal was truly appalling. Refugees were lying all over the floors and furniture, half-starved ill dressed skinny children screaming, no doubt hungry, despairingly waiting to be loaded on to an aircraft (presumably destined for a Moslem part of that newly divided country) away from Hindu hatred.

The RAF were using Dakotas in the main for that airlift, an aircraft normally seating 32 or less but in that desperate emergency all rules had been waived. The lightweight refugees with miserably tiny bundles of belongings were jam-packed onto aircraft floors in numbers three or four times the regular amount. Weightwise the aircraft were not overloaded (though the wartime all-up take off weight of 32,000 lbs had been authorised – 4000 lbs above the maximum permitted British civil figure of 28,000 lbs) and, amazingly, in the many weeks of the emergency it is understood that nobody was hurt in aerial transit.

The had seen nothing of that in Johdpur, despite Harry Manton's warning, so the scene at Delhi was a dreadful shock, especially for the Italians and Greeks who wept and moaned at the sight of such misery which they couldn't understand, and the crew unable to help with any kind of explanation. Nobody wanted any papers. It would have been impossible to wade through that mob to toilets, even if those were usable, so the passengers were shepherded back to Denebola away from that evil smell and sight. She still had not been refuelled, but the toilet had been emptied so was usable for anyone needing it before flight. Bob finally rounded up a refuelling bowser, but Jim had been unable either to obtain weather report or file a flight plan.

Nevertheless, and regardless of rules and regulations (which in any case seemed to be being broken by all and sundry) he taxied out in the wake of an RAF Dakota, waited until it became airborne, turned on to the duty runway after checking no lights on the approach, and took off without bothering about a green light from the Control Tower. It had been a horrendous two hours 20 minutes on the ground. Turning right on to the south-easterly heading for Allahabad, climbing to 5500 feet in smooth air just under a thin layer of cloud at about 7000 feet so that the ground could be kept in sight and landmarks checked from groups of lights from small towns and villages, he estimated arrival at Allahabad to be about 2.20 am on 12 November.

Kaupur (Cawnpore in the days of the British Raj) came up on the left after one hour 50 minutes. The glint of the river Ganges was clearly seen reflecting the city lights, distinguishable itself as a wide silvery snake winding ever closer as they approached Allahabad, which is situated at the confluence with the Yumma river on which lies Delhi and passes through Agra (city of the Taj Mahal) about a third of the way to Allahabad. Both rivers were clearly visible as Denebola let down towards their destination, the city lights and those of the runway which lies just to the west of the rivers' junction brilliant in the clear air. A green light from the Control Tower as they circled the airport and they landed at 2.18 am local time, the crew beginning to feel somewhat jaded and hoping they would find somewhere peaceful to lie down before going on to Calcutta.

The terminal building was almost empty, there having been so far very little refugee traffic, and it seemed the airport staff were pleased to see them or at least to have something to do in their night duty. After checking the weather and filing a flight plan for departure at 5 am (which would give them a good two and a half hours to snatch some shut-eye) Jim left the passengers in charge of the traffic manager who said he would ensure they had a meal in the restaurant, and plenty of places to lie down if they wished. He showed Jim into a small room with two camp beds, normally used by the traffic staff on shift duty, where he was joined by Bob who had finished with the refuelling but reported that the right hand inner engine had used three quarters of it's oil. Whether or not this could have been a refulling slip in the chaos at Delhi they were not to know, but Bob was certain he had dipped all the tanks personally, double checking as usual. No point worrying about it at this time – rest was more important. They lay down and were wakened from deep sleep by the traffic manager, as arranged, at 5.30 am who provided them with soap and towels for a quick shower. Much refreshed, though feeling hungry as they had not eaten since sandwiches en-route to Delhi, they gathered up the exhausted passengers.

M'Lady looked fresh and bright with eyes almost naughty in expression. She had charmed the traffic manager into offering them all showers (to the horror of all but her and Richard, also looking spruce again). With a sort of one-upmanship she told Jim she had also arranged for their showers. . . 'As they hadn't thought about the passengers so she assumed they hadn't thought about themselves either'. . . – it seemed that they had also had a good meal despite the sticky atmosphere, those Punkah fans having been very effective.

The right-inner engine oil was checked again, dipped a full tank and no sign of leaks round or inside the cowling. As there had been no sign of rough running in the air Jim felt satisfied that nothing serious could be wrong, so they took off again at 5.08 am with first light brightening to sunrise. The climb was made to 9500 feet as it could be bumpy crossing the mountains in the province of Bihar, which rise to between 3000 and 4000 feet above sea level and lie about the middle third of the leg to Calcutta. Also Jim wanted to fly as high as practicable just in case No. three engine should give trouble, that is the right-hand inner which appeared to have lost a lot of oil during the last leg. So far everything seemed normal, oil pressure normal, throttle opening the same as the other three for the same revs, and running smoothly. Both crew ate some curry stew, still warm from the thermos jug loaded at Karachi, and very good it was too. The aircraft would fly comfortably on three engines, slower of course but quite safely, though would not maintain much over 6000 feet in the prevailing temperature, so a margin of 3000 feet for a slow drift down to that height would help both speed and safety margin should in fact No. three engine fail.

The Ganges drifted away gradually from the left on its way through

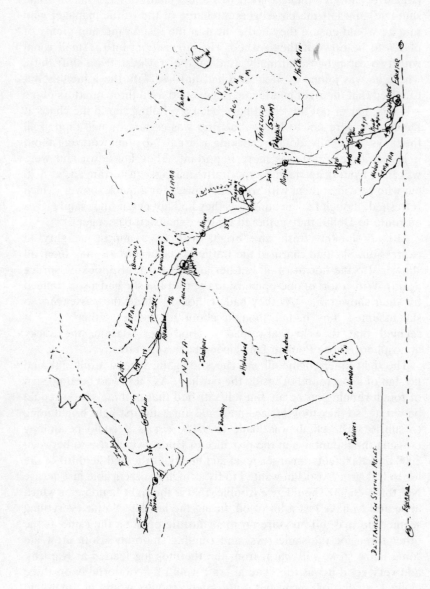

DISTANCES in STATUTE MILES

Equator

Patna to its enormous delta basin of Calcutta, to Chittagong as it flows into the Bay of Bengal after being joined by a miriad of smaller rivers on its way. Calcutta itself, always pretty steamy even at this approaching winter time lying just south of the Tropic of Cancer and surrounded by swamps, lies on the river Hoogli which also empties its sluggish brown silt-filled water into the Bay of Bengal. They had crossed over the series of lakes on the eastern side of Bihar and were over the swampy plains 120 miles north-west of Calcutta, with another 75 minutes to go, when the oil pressure on No. three engine started to waiver, settle down, then waiver again. Each time it settled at a slightly lower pressure than before and continued to fall slowly over the next 20 minutes. Jim throttled back to 1200 revs and started a slow descent, keeping the airspeed above 115 mph. The engine still ran smoothly, but clearly was not well. He didn't want to stop it altogether unless the pressure ran down to the danger mark, as the drag of a stationary (non-feathered) propeller would mean having to increase revs on the other three engines to keep a reasonable airspeed – at 1200 revs the drag was neutralised.

The uneven beat of unsynchronised propellers caused some alarm in the passenger cabin, and M'Lady moved up into the empty seat in row four whilst Richard came up to ask the question – (marvellous how those two had become so teamed up to act whenever their calming influence could help the others). The problem was explained and that, even if the engine had to be shut down completely, Denebola was safe and easily controlled on the other three (even on two) at lower altitudes. By that time they were descending steadily at 200 feet per minute, with airspeed built up to 120 mph and, with the light tail wind of 8 to 10 mph would be landing in about 45 minutes. Thumbs up and smiles, with M'Lady staying in row four and Richard sitting (uncomfortably) facing backwards on the sill of the cockpit doorway, stopped the others worrying except for the occasional hands over ears to shut out the drumming of uneven synchronisation.

They landed at 9 am, 17 minutes later than flight planned, stopping both inner engines to taxi in on the outers to the terminal at Dum Dum airport. A smiling face appeared at the cockpit window – BOAC cap, white shirt with senior traffic officer's stripes. . .

'Good morning, captain. After two years I may still beat you at chess. Welcome, Harry told me it was you'. . .

Ram Tamluk had been a real friend in the 1944/45 years of the Ensign services to Calcutta. It was a real moral booster knowing that the stay in Calcutta would be handled not only efficiently but most pleasantly for them all.

Jim introduced him to M'Lady, Richard and Bob, then to the others. Jim knew he was a linguist but this was manna from heaven – he greeted them in Italian and Greek! At long last they would be able to communicate properly and explain about the rest of the journey to Sydney. Bob had refuelled and reported that No. three engine was almost out of oil – no leaks in sight but obviously a qualified engineer had to look at it.

Ram telephoned to one of the small air companies and arranged for their engineer to check it over. Taxiing over to their hangar to meet Roger (preferring to be called Rod), a very experienced fully-licenced British aircraft engineer, Denebola was put into a large hangar where rested two of her smaller sisters – the twin engined DH 89 Rapide. These had the same type of engine as Denebola's Gipsy Six (Series I), but after the war had become known as the Gipsy Queen III, very little modified from the original. He promised a report next day but felt it might not be until the afternoon as he thought he might have to remove the engine to find the fault – probably an internal matter as there were no sign of external leaks. That meant at least a two days delay, more if new parts were needed. A crew car returned Jim and Bob to the terminal where they joined the passengers for the 25-30 minute bus drive to the city. Ram would join them for dinner at the hotel. Surprisingly it was only 10.10 am, and the passengers had been given a small breakfast whilst waiting after, for the first time, having their papers checked. The journey from Dum Dum to the city was always a nightmare. Not because the Sikh driver (nothing unusual for Calcutta taxi drivers) seemed intent on breaking the world land speed record, but because of the smell of decay, open drains, and the sickly sweet stench of rotting flesh cloying the damp air which oozed through open windows of the non-air-conditioned bus.

Most of the journey passes through hideous slums, matchstick people in filthy robes their teeth stained red with Betel Nut (the streets also where the juice was spat) eyes wild with the madness of hunger and misery. Men, women, and children alike in the final stages of dying on their feet, sitting in rubbish strewn gutters running with filth – and every few yards one or two laying, eyes fixed open in death.

The Italians and Greeks were crying, Richard and M'Lady not far from it, Bob white as a sheet, as they pulled up outside the hotel. They had never seen anything like it, and despite many previous journeys Jim had never become injured to that appalling travesty of human existence. Perhaps the driver's haste was due to desire to pass it by, not being able to look without causing a smash, though Jim had never been driven by a Sikh placid behind the wheel. Yet they are a very human race in general, saving ferocity for the fighting and daredevilry for driving, which showed as he stood by the door, clear blue eyes taking them all in, to say. . . 'I am sorry you had to see'. . . with obvious deep feeling for the distressed women and children. Jim shook his hand and said he hoped it would be he who drove them back to the airport. Blue eyes, by the way, are quite common in that proud mountain race, and not necessarily due to an injection of European blood.

After climbing up the long terraced steps of the massive old Great Eastern Hotel into an enormous lounge with high vaulted ceilings and chandeliers, deep armchairs and settees with tables in plenty, the decor basically a cool green, M'Lady had gathered the group into a quiet corner. Jim and Bob checked in at reception for them to find that rooms had been booked by Ram so that they were all together on the first floor – on a family basis. Mamma and Carmela, Philomena and her three children, Maria, Zouki, and Yanni in separate rooms as were M'Lady, Richard, Bob, and Jim with a room each. They felt that the arrangement could cause problems of community separation, particularly as they were going to have to stay at least two days, so Jim asked Bob to ask M'Lady to join him and take her place with the flock.

She agreed that there should be a change so, with endless patience, the head receptionist managed to rearrange things so that there would be two rooms with connecting door for Mamma and Carmela in one and Philomena and her children in the other. Maria and Zouki were to share on one side next door, with Bob next to them then Jim at the end. M'Lady was to be next to the families on the other side, Richard next to her, and Yanni at the end that side of the row of eight adjoining rooms. Whilst this was going on they agreed that the Europeans all must be made to bathe, shower, or whatever and get their few clothes washed, for the pong had become altogether too much. They told Richard and Bob that decision – but, how to go about it?

Up in the rooms Maria flatly refused to share with Zouki, making clear signs that she smelt bad (which brought a smile to certain faces) and marched in to join her Italian friends. The question of where the young, and not so young boys would sleep would obviously be at the discretion of the ladies and, fortunately, there was a big settee which could be made into a bed for Maria. M'Lady showed them the bathroom, shower, and toilet (which area separated the two rooms) made sure the adjoining doors were unlocked and pocketed the keys to ensure nobody got locked out/in anywhere. Then she made clear gestures, looking at Maria in particular, that they MUST shower or bathe and (making mime with cake of soap) to lather well. Squeals of protest! She just pointed to her watch, help up 10 fingers and pointed again to the watch, as she swept out with a chorus of dismay following her to the door.

They found Zouki sitting disconsolate on the end of her bed. She started to wail for Yanni brought up short by M'Lady's. . . 'Shut up girl'. . ., then followed meekly into the bathroom (all rooms being en-suite) where the pantomime about bathing was repeated. She made no protest only wanting to be shown which taps did what. It should be pointed out that both the Greeks were city people used to normal ablution facilities, but the Italians were of simple peasant stock from an area without modern facilities. Zouki clung to M'Lady begging for Yanni then Bob said. . . 'Look, let him have my room, the one next to this. Whatever they get up to is really their own affair and she is naturally very lonely and scared to be on her own'. . . Immediate agreement from M'Lady so Yanni was fetched, he and Zouki suddenly all smiles and thank-yous (if that is what sounded like 'efaristo' meant). Ten minutes plus by her watch M'Lady returned to the Italian contingent, Jim and Bob waiting outside. Commotion could be heard behind the closed door, soon to be reopened by M'Lady literally blowing steam.

She demanded that they go in with her. Protests ceased abruptly to be replaced by anxious looks. All were fully clothed . Jim walked to the bathroom, beckoning them to follow to watch him turn on the shower, adjusting hot and cold to a warm mix and getting splashed as he took soap to make lather under the running water. Leaving it running he wiped his hands on one of the huge bath towels and made mime of drying all over as though he had had a shower. Trying to look stern he pointed to the shower taking Mamma by the arm and guiding her towards it, then with Bob left the room. M'Lady soon came out again to report no action and much commotion. Thinking back, they probably took quite a risk (certainly 40 years later would possibly be charged with assault) but all three then went in and physically herded the seven of them under the shower, clothes an all. The shrieks of protest quite suddenly became giggles and happy yells. Mamma started to take her clothes off until Carmela yelled at her, pointing to Jim and Bob who were already on their way out.

M'lady followed them a few minutes later, somewhat damp but grinning happily, to announce that the two boys had refused to undress whilst she was there (probably also until the females had finished washing) but that lather was everywhere and great fun being had washing hair and splashing at each other. Now there was the matter of dry clean clothes to be tackled, which turned out to be no problem at all as the hotel had full laundry facilities. No clothes dryers in those days but a system of fanning dry warm air over the washing after wringing. M'Lady collected the soaked clothing, after leaving them to play for half an hour under the shower, handing them out to be put into two large baskets and taken to the laundry.

The laundered and dried clothing was returned by 7 pm in plenty of time for dinner which would start from 8 pm to 10 pm for sitting down to eat and finish often after midnight. Apparently the now happy families spent the interim in bed or wrapped in dry towels, of which there was always a good supply in the bathrooms of that wonderful hotel. It was not until then realised that they had no change of clothing at all, not even underwear, and none had any money with them – only a few trinkets. The Greeks did have changes of underclothes and Zouki a best dress which she wore for dinner, but Yanni had only one each of trousers, shirt, and jumper, but did have three pairs of socks.

Next day, whilst Jim went down to the airport to check on the progress with Denebola, Bob, M'Lady, and Richard walked the Italian contingent a short distance to some shops. The Greeks had met with a Greek family living in Calcutta (who had dined at a next table the previous evening, having a birthday party for the wife) and were being given a tour of the city to be followed by an evening in their home. That was good, as obtaining a change of underclothes for the Italians, possibly a dress each for the females and shirts for the lads, was subject to a limit Jim had set as funds were already running low due to delays. After all, those items were not strictly legitimate route expenses, but were cheap in India at that time and did not necessarily have to be of a quality to last.

The expedition proved a tremendous success, for a cost of £10 (including a light lunch) had covered two changes of underwear all round, a new shirt for each of the boys and a light dress for each of the girls. M'Lady had chipped in personally out of her own pocket for a dress each for three ladies, insisting on any colour but the black they had been wearing. Mamma was very gay in a flower print to match her daughter's new dress, the other two very shy and modest in plain light brown for Maria and plain dark red for Philomena.

Gina and Carmela had stopped glued to a window displaying various trinkets so Bob gave them each the equivalent in rupees of 2/6d, giving the same to the two boys who bought sticky sweets. A great treat for them it seemed, which the girls tried to share without success – temporary sulks, but Gina had a fine filigree bracelet and Carmela a ring with imitation ruby. By the next day that ring, far too tight for the finger it had adorned, was deeply imbedded in a swollen flesh and could not be eased over the knuckle, so Bob took her to a chemist down the street where it was removed using small wire cutters. There were some tears for the broken ring, but relief from agony soon won the day. Bob was able to convince that very intelligent child, who understood enough English, that it could be mended. It was in fact done while they waited, by the shopkeeper from where it was bought, then placed on a smaller finger on the other hand. From then on Bob became her hero, to a point embarrassing on occasion when her normally sulky expression would change to a very pretty face lit with adoration – no less!

Back from the airport with the bad news that the oil filter was found to be full of metal, magnetic sump plug also, Jim said that the engineer, Rod, was certain a main bearing had gone, probably one of the centre ones as there had been no noticeable vibration in flight, and no apparent loss of power either which indicated normal compressions. He had removed the crankcase cover of the inverted six cylinder motor to find that No. three main bearing had indeed destroyed itself. Fitting new bearings all round would be required and the engine flushed clean of metal bits, a job that would take at least a week provided new bearing shells were obtainable quickly. It would be necessary for the engine to be re-certified by an airworthiness inspector after the work was completed, and the only one was away up country for two or three weeks. It was now Thursday 13 November. As a possible solution had been found, which would enable Denebola to be airworthy again within two or three days, the superstitious might conclude that it was lucky that date was not a Friday.

One of the two Rapides operated by Rod's employers was in the process of major overhaul for renewal of its Certificate of Airworthiness and not expected to be ready for several weeks. Despite the engines having been designated Gipsy Queen IIIs, the serial number of one of them was 6113, earlier in production than 6441 of the faulty engine designated Series I Gipsy Six. In fact there was absolutely no difference and it was not out of hours as far as airworthiness certification went (having some 180 hours left before being due) but was nevertheless scheduled to be overhauled at the same time as the aircraft concerned.

Armed with that information Jim had approached the manager (it was a British compay based in Calcutta engaged mainly on survey work) to explain the serious problem of time delay for Denebola's engine to be made serviceable, even if his engineer would be able to concentrate entirely on the job. He asked that a direct swap of the two engines could be considered, which would take only a few hours with them to help Rod with tackle and tool handling. Jim would sign a chit on behalf of his company promising to pay for the necessary overhaul of the faulty engine, and it's new certification, for fitting into the company's aircraft.

The answer had been a blunt 'No'. Jim persisted that, apart from the long delay in their journey, the overhaul of the faulty engine would have to be charged to his company no matter whether it went back into Denebola or into the Rapide. The manager pointed out very firmly that may be, but he would not authorise release of the engine in any case after overhaul without cash payment, So Jim's employer would have plenty of time to come up with that whilst the faulty engine was being overhauled – and before reinstallation in it's own aircraft.

With so many post war business sharks and confidence-tricksters around all over the world, especially in aviation and motor vehicles, Jim had to admit he could hardly blame this caution. Indeed he really knew very little about his own employer for whom he was making promises, which he openly admitted. However, as the company was operating under the auspices of the Australian Minister for Emigration, solely to transport migrants from Europe for whom regular airline and shipping capacities were swamped, he was very sure that the company was sound and therefore felt able to make promises in good faith. The manager would not change his mind but did become more friendly as he rose to terminate the interview. Jim thanked him but asked him please to think over the whole matter, particularly the plight of his passengers, and said he would phone next day in the hope that he would reconsider. They shook hands.

Ram had not been able to join them for dinner the previous evening, a delayed aircraft requiring his attention. He joined them at 7.30 for drinks before dinner that night. He was delighted to hear about the shopping expedition, and the previous day's events leading up to it, and hoped that Zouki and Yanni would be back from their visit to the Andamopoulos home in time for him to see them for he knew the family well – in fact he kept his Greek in practice with them and other friends in that community. Wherever humans live, no matter the colour, creed, or country, there is (and probably ever will be) the 'I'll scratch your back, you scratch mine' philosophy. Jim told about the negotiations concerning the engine, Ram stopping him at the point of the manager's refusal to co-operate and excused himself for a moment. He returned after some time (during which they had shepherded their charges into the huge domed-roof dining room to get started with dinner) to where Jim awaited him with their scotch and sodas. Ram had been doing some 'scratching' (unwilling to disclose the nature of his connection) over the overseas telephone, producing total co-operation authorised by the aerial company's managing director in London for Rod to start work the next day removing the faulty engine from Denebola and replacing it with No. 6113 from the Rapide as quickly as possible. Drinks up in one and in to dinner!

That evening, through him, they were able to explain to the Italians that there would probably be two more days to stay in Calcutta before they could fly away to Sydney – chorus of 'Seednee Domani' with glowing faces, which changed quickly to disappointment as it was explained to them that they were just about half way to 'Seednee' with another 12-14 days to go, so it would not be 'Domani' (tomorrow) when they got there. Ram interpreted their excited chatter to say that they were repeating that that was the most time they had been told in Rome it would take to get to Sydney. From then on the cry 'Seednee Domani' became a daily question of hopefulness from those simple people.

Ram said that they were worried about how they would be received in Australia, having heard that Anglo-Celtic indigenous people were very intolerant of foreigners. Their husbands seemed to have done quite well for themselves and settled in (despite some difficulties during the war) without too much trouble, so he had tried to assure them they would be welcome. He said he had told them, and was about to show them a little, that to use knives and forks correctly when eating in public would help a lot towards them not being thought strange and different in their new country, and that he had promised (on the English crew and passengers' behalf) that they would help them in whatever was necessary to learn Australian customs. He then explained the reason for, and proper use of, the various spoons and other utensils, but told them not to worry about it during the rest of the journey, unless they wished to practice.

Ram organised a whole day tour for them the next day, Friday 4 November, and had managed to find a tour operator with a multi-lingual guide, a Cairo-born Armenian temporarily in Calcutta gaining experience of the Far East before returning to Egypt – his Greek and Italian were better, if anything, than his educated English. Ram, Bob, and Jim saw them off then headed out to the airport, where Bob went off to give Rod what help he could removing cowlings and things. Ram went to his office and Jim over to the aerial company's office.

He was not too well received but a pot of tea was produced over which Jim thanked the manager for his reconsideration and the help now being given. He hoped the manager would think him unaware the changed situation was due to head office instructions and would believe it due entirely to his own rethinking. It seemed to work, for the attitude softened to become quite friendly. Arrangements were made for paperwork to be drawn up setting out an agreement for Jim to sign promising reimbursement by his company for the cost of rectification of the faulty engine. They parted on a friendly note, Jim telling him that after all he was getting a good bargain as the total hours on the engine he was releasing were 9826 as against under 8000 for the faulty one out of Denebola, at which the manager laughed and wished them a trouble free journey from then on.

Rod advised that the engine change would be completed the following evening at the latest, ready then for test flight. Jim went over to the terminal to discuss the weather trends in the Met. office, wanting as much local knowledge as possible to supplement the standard conditions for the time of year down through Burma to Singapore then on through the Netherlands East Indies (NEI, or more commonly called the Dutch

East Indies in 1947) to Australia, as he had not before flown there. There he found another old friend, a forecaster two years ago when they last met, now promoted to assistant chief forecaster. He had, before the war, spent some time based in Singapore so he had personal practical knowledge of weather patterns over the whole route. In particular he was able to go through the current trend in the interaction between the Inter-tropical Front and Line of Convergence through which they had to pass between Singapore and Batavia (now Jakarta).

Simplified, the two frontal systems are like two long lines of highly unstable air running roughly east to west in which violent thunderstorms are common, particularly when the systems merge or converge closely. When dangerously active there are clear warning signs, both on the synoptic charts and by actual airborne observance of the cloud patterns, and it was the details of the latter Jim was now able to learn. The benefit later on when in that area turned out to be inestimable.

He then went down to the airport bar to find Bob already there as there was no more he could do to help Rod (who had had to break off to attend to a snag on an aircraft belonging to one of his company's regular customers) but would be returning to help again the next morning. They had a couple of drinks before taking a taxi back to the hotel. The tourists were not due to return until 4 pm, so they had a hot bath and a sleep which was broken by a 5.15 phone call. It was Ram who asked if he might join them again for dinner and could be there about 7 pm. Good news, and having rung Bob to tell him, they went in search of their passengers. They had had a wonderful day and. . . 'hear this'. . . M'Lady exclaimed, saying the others were in showers and baths preparing for dinner – no persuasion needed!

The next day was not too hot and the Armenian came to take anyone who wanted on a tour of shops and markets rather than formal sightseeing. Jim and Bob had to go to the airport so M'Lady was given funds to cover lunches, and the guide was told to bill (through Ram as yesterday) for his services. It was after sunset before Denebola was ready for test flight, completed satisfactorily by 6.50 pm, and arrangements made for departure for Akyab and Rangoon at 8 am the next morning, 17 November. They were late joining the others for dinner but Ram had once again taken the trouble to turn up, this time with his charming wife – mother of four children and greatly acclaimed by the Italians. After dinner, Ram translating, Jim (again with the help of a map) outlined the next day's programme together with the rest of the route and stopping places to Sydney. He made it clear that there would be at least another eight days of travel, which meant arrival in Sydney on 25 November, but that he expected there might be two or three days more due to possible weather conditions, so 27 November or 28 would be a more realistic estimate. The Italians once again protested, but not for long, and he suggested they all retire to be ready for a 5.30 am early rise in the morning.

Ram was not on duty the next day, and asked if they would mind him not seeing them off as he and his family were to visit his wife's parents in Patna for three days. He had left the account for Jim to settle with his senior traffic officer at the airport, and wished them a safe and trouble-free journey from then on. He could not resist saying to Jim that it was such a pity they hadn't had time for that game or two of chess at which (past experience notwithstanding) he was sure that at last Jim might have beaten him – farewells to such friends are never easy.

Passing through those awful slums on the way to the airport, after the luxury of the hotel and the very happy time during the last four days, brought everybody down to earth again. When leaving Calcutta there was always a feeling of shame and guilt that one's own condition in life was so immeasurably privileged, no matter what desperate worries or unhappiness an individual might have, for nothing, but absolutely nothing, could be so inhumanly ghastly and incomprehensibly degrading as that sight and stench. The driver was the same Sikh who had brought them into the city, Jamal Singh as Ram had introduced him during their stay and arranged for him to drive them back. Shaking hands with him after arrival at the airport and thanking him, there seemed to be a bond of understanding as eye met blue eye – remarked upon also by Bob, Richard, and M'Lady who each shook hands and thanked him for driving them again.

When Jim had settled the BOAC account which included tours and other transport, paid landing and parking fees, added the charges made for Rod's time changing the engine, and the hotel bill and meals for four days, the balance of the cash float was pretty low. He cabled the company headquarters in Sydney requesting addtional funds to be available in Singapore by 18 November at the latest.

Airborne at 8.13 am en-route to Akyab in Burma, a three hour flight in clear weather with high overcast, they landed there at 12.10pm local time, which was one hour ahead of Calcutta time. Refuelling was by hand pump from 44 gallon drums. Time on the ground stretched to two hours 25 minutes due to a really over-fussy immigration control person, who no doubt had to be sure his superiors in Rangoon would find no fault with his vetting of the foreigners. His English was poor, but who were they to grumble for that was all they had apart from Greek and Italian. (Jim has always felt that the practice of speaking more loudly than usual in English, expecting foreigners then to understand, was not only bad manners but an arrogance quite properly resented, which is why he tried always to learn at least a smattering of the lingo of places he passed through and felt in himself somewhat inadequate if he was unable to make himself understood – by mine and friendliness if nothing else).

Leaving at 2.35 pm they arrived in Rangoon at 5.20 pm after a smooth and softly sunny run down the emerald green coastline of teak forest contrasting with deep red earth, flying low at 3500 feet over the water, the spinal ranges of Burma rising rapidly to 12,000 feet on the left. Then, turning left to cross the low coastal range before letting down over the river Irrawaddy Delta, past the famous Shwe Dagon Pagoda its golden domes brilliant in the near sunset, before landing. A memorable trip of sheer beauty.

The nightstop was uneventful once the passengers had been shown that all the bedrooms in the guest house had lizards, quite harmless, running over the ceilings – bright little creatures typical of most tropical countries. Their first experience of mosquito nets, though M'Lady was able to show how to use them, explanation as to why being very obvious with plenty of the whining little bloodsuckers in evidence. It was a hot and sticky night, nobody sleeping too well, but the thrill of the day's flight scenery had put everyone into the best of moods and breakfast was a very happy one in anticipation on another similar scenic flight.

The flight plan was to refuel at Mergui, a small village on the Burmese coast – then onto Penang in Malaya before a final leg to Singapore, each taking about three and a half hour's flying time. It would be a long thirteen and a half hour day, including the two refuelling stops, so departure time of 6 am would make arrival at Singapore 8.30 pm, local time there one hour ahead of Rangoon. It didn't happen that way, though nothing really untoward occurred.

The day started sunny and smooth again at 3500 feet following the beautiful coastline over a continuous chain of green, green islands – the coastal forest denser than the previous day with the mountain spine on the left closer to the coast, though not so high at between 3000 and 6000 feet above sea level. Mergui was reached on time, and the instruction to circle the village twice to alert the refullers was carried out before landing on the tarmac strip slotted into the forest – cleared for 100 yards either side and about 1000 yards each end, though the trees were much less tall than those on the side of the strip. There was no windsock but smoke rising vertically from fires in forest clearings indicated no wind so the landing was made on what appeared to be in a slightly uphill direction.

They disembarked to shelter from the sun in an open sided structure with one long bench and bark strip roof a few yards off the edge of the runway. Forty minutes later they were joined by a petrol bowser. As usual there were plenty of refreshments on board so they were able to enjoy a picnic in the balmy smelling air tinged with wood smoke, probably teak, a mixture Jim had not smelled before – nor since. Peculiar to Burma perhaps, something like Morny's Sandalwood soap but far more romantic. The whole atmosphere was of peace and relaxation.

The two-man crew of the bowser could have been twins, with short bow legs and great beaming grins on their round teak-brown faces. All ready to start pumping, – nothing happened. Much laughing and banging around the pump area, but after 10 minutes still nothing. Serious faces, shrugging in unison of broad shoulders followed by signs (pointed to an open topped 44 gallon drum by the shelter – a rubbish bin no doubt) then, making unmistakable hand pumping signs, they jumped back into their bowser and were away in a cloud of reddish dust back where they came from.

Despite the frustration they had to laugh and return patiently to their picnic. As it seemed there would be no catching up on time Jim told them that the nightstop would have to be at Penang not Singapore, which seemed to bother nobody. Engine oil was always carried as a spare on the aircraft so Bob and Jim carried out that part of their refuelling, in which only a small amount was needed to top up including the newly installed engine which had run equally as smoothly as the others since leaving Calcutta.

A cloud of dust and this time a tray truck loaded with 10 gallon drums roared to a halt by Denebola. The same tough little men manhandled (as easily as bales of straw) six of the drums each to either side of the aircraft, produced two hand pumps and signalled that pumping help was needed. So Jim and Bob each manned a pump on one side, the locals on the other, a drum to each pump. Very hard work, especially in the heat, and not speedy as the pumps had no in-built filter so a chamois one was inserted into each tank filler neck – the rate of drain of those is quite low and care had to be taken not to overflow them. Pumping close to 60 gallons a side took the best part of an hour, with Richard and Yanni pitching in to help the crew. The Burmese finished their side a good 10 minutes before the others, even though they had taken the sunnier side – much to their delight and to that of the female passengers, led by M'Lady in clapping the win. The Burmese were given a cool drink and waved off in their truck.

Showers would have been very welcome but they had to settle for a towelling down, a snack and cool drinks, before starting up to be airborne again at 11.45am. A half circle round to the heading for Penang, making a low pass over the village for the benefit of their Burmese friends (madly waving from the jetty below) for an estimated three hours 40 minutes flight time which would mean arrival at 4.30 pm local time, an hour again to add to watches from Burmese time.

The weather forecast from Rangoon had suggested that, about half way, cloud would begin to form and the south-westerly wind increase, so a 20 mph headwind component had been allowed in the flight plan, but after a little over an hour total cloud cover could be seen ahead. The base looked between 3000 and 4000 feet though they were still in clear air, following the lovely coastline with its chain of islands. White caps were forming on the water and even at 3500 feet the air was becoming unstable. They let down to 1200 feet, where it became quite bumpy but should take them under the rapidly approaching cloud base. The white caps were whipping up and shortly after the first drops of rain fell, soon becoming heavy and continuous. The sea was by then quite white and, by the time they passed Phuket (where the Malayan coast angles south-eastwards) the ground speed check showed an average of only 95 mph since Mergui. This meant that it would average under 90 mph for the rest of the way with the surface wind indicating a speed of at least 35 knots, or over 40 mph. A quick calculation showed that the flight time to Penang would total over five hours with the present ground speed, half an hour more than the maximum fuel capacity, and the wind could easily increase further. Diversion to Alor Star was decided as, even if the wind speed increased to 50 mph, it could be reached in four hours, which still meant only 30 minutes fuel overhead. There was no other possibility, at least as far as landing grounds shown on the map were concerned.

The passengers were not bothered by the rough weather, disappointed about the scenery now dark and rain-obscured but fascinated looking down at the turbulent sea. The weather was not thundery or typhoon type, just an intense frontal disturbance probably only 150 to 200 miles deep. Visibility was quite good, despite the heavy rain, so following the coastline (now down to 800 feet) was not difficult and hopefully the headwind effect would be a bit less at that height. Jim was recalling stories about Alor Star, told to him by a colleague who had flown with Imperial Airways along that route before the war. It was then a regular nightstop and the rest house, built mainly of wood, was superbly comfortable. There were no runways as such, just a long mown strip running roughly north to south, and it was always necessary to make a low pass over it to clear the sheep which kept the whole area fairly well mown.

Three hours and 55 minutes after leaving Mergui they came over Alor Star, not far from the Siamese border. Just as his friend had related, it was covered with a huge flock of sheep. The low pass was duly made, into the strong wind to check its approximate speed (estimated at a gusty 30 mph from the apparent groundspeed – there was no windsock visible). Right on cue the sheep herded together and started to move directly to the north-east corner of the field. No dog was seen, only a single person behind them following the flock as though the procedure was rehearsed, despite the fact the the airfield had not been in use for a long time.

Apparently the system also alerted the rest house and an antiquated bus and two private cars awaited their arrival at the wood and tin shed which served as a terminal – four hours and 15 minutes after leaving Mergui. Considering there could have been no prior warning of their landing it was quite remarkable.

The overnight stay is remembered as one of the most pleasant Jim has ever experienced. There was an open fire going in the comfortable lounge, for that night was cold and damp not unlike a British winter. The dustcovers had been removed by the time they arrived from the airfield, and there was the warmest welcome from the old couple who either owned or managed the place. They and their two remaining servants seemed delighted to show the hospitality they had dispensed before the war. The dinner was superb, as was the old-fashioned cooked breakfast in silver dishes arranged on a long sideboard, from which one helped oneself. The beds were very comfortable – even aired with hotwater bottles! He could hardly belive the miniscule account he paid in the morning before saying a reluctant farewell, wishing for an excuse to spend more time there. To top it all off there were no landing or parking fees to pay, for the first time since leaving Croydon 20 days before – it was the 19 November.

It was still cloudy, but with much less wind and no rain when they took off for Singapore direct – no need to stop for fuel at Penang. The cloud was breaking after passing Port Dickson at 5500 feet, becoming less with patchy sunlight by the time they landed after three hours 45 minutes at 1.15 pm local time, giving plenty of time to settle in. KLM very kindly accommodated them at their marvellous club, the famous 'Cockpit'. Their restaurant was open to the public but accommodation was only reserved for aircrew and the occasional special passenger, but fortunately there were none for a few days. Nevertheless it was a very kind gesture and quite typical of that superb company throughout the world. Most of the hotels in the city and for some distance outside were fully booked due to celebrations for the wedding fo Princess Elizabeth and Prince Phillip the next day, 20 November 1947. It was an event that had escaped their notice completely, even M'Lady's. It was to be a festive day, with no offices open but restaurants and bars and the markets looking forward to a bonanza. Delays or not Jim declared that they would stay to enjoy the occasion. He felt it would be an ideal opportunity for his European charges to learn something about the British Commonwealth, its Royal traditions and customs, and feel part of it by experiencing such a celebration first hand. The others agreed, in fact delighted that this time the delay was to be of their own choice.

The fact that the banks were to be closed would not have mattered as they were open on the day of arrival had the funds Jim had cabled for been available. The agent (Malayan Airways in those days before Singapore and Malaya split into having separate ones) had received nothing, nor had their bank when telephoned from the airport – not even a cable acknowledging his from Calcutta. At this stage Jim was beginning to have some doubts about his company. While the passengers were having a light lunch at the airport before travelling into the city he had a chat with the manager, a retired Imperial Airways (then BOAC) captain. He would genuinely liked to have helped out with a cash advance but in view of the lack of action from Sydney he could not, in all common sense, comply. He sent a signal to his company's Sydney office to check out Jim's outfit there. Whilst he waited for the reply Bob escorted the passengers into the city.

When a reply did come it was from Jim's company's Sydney office – 'No way. Never heard of the man. Try our manager London'. Unbelievable! It was almost midday in London seven and a half hours in time behind Singapore) and even if the man who, as managing director, employed him could be found (even if he were still in London and had not taken the 15 November regular airline flight back to Sydney as scheduled when Jim left England) there would be no chance of getting anything done about sending funds from there with the Royal wedding preparations going on. There was nothing more to be done so he thanked the manager and took a taxi to the 'Cockpit' Not a very happy man, but he kept it to himself, even from Bob, not wanting their enjoyment to be spoiled.

Largely due to the very inexpensive stop at Alor Star instead of Penang (where cost would have been astronomical by comparison) he had sufficient funds left to ensure a good time for all and to cover accommodation expenses, landing and parking fees. After that there would be nothing left. That evening in the 'Cockpit' Jim met the local KLM manager – Mr Pilgrams. Over a couple of drinks at the bar (where he was introduced to the Dutch 'Bols' gin) he told him the problem and was invited to join the manager for dinner, so he excused himself from passengers. Many questions were asked about Jim's employer and the company, how he had come to take the job, and great interest was shown in the adventures of the journey so far and plans for the rest of the trip. His own history with KLM came out, covering much pre-war ground including the famous Parmentier and Moll team which took winning handicap honours in the 1934 London to Melbourne Air Race in a KLM Douglas DC2, shortly after the far-sighted Albert Plesman (founder of KLM) had acquired that revolutionary (at that time) aircraft type for the airline. Jim, as a very junior first officer in 1942, had met Captain Moll in Bristol when he was flying Douglas DC3s from there to Lisbon for KLM (then operating in exile from Holland) and had been very impressed with his modesty and friendliness.

As they enjoyed a Van der Humm liqueur (a taste both had acquired whilst in South Africa) and coffee Mr Pilgrams outlined a proposal that he would help by arranging for KLM to handle the aircraft through the Netherlands East Indies (NEI), providing accommodation and meals with credit for landing and parking fees, and transport, as though Denebola was a KLM aircraft. He would supply up-to-date briefing on airfields, facilities and fuel supplies, with a covering letter in Dutch to all authorities. (It should be noted that he was manager Far East, based in Singapore, and not just station manager for that city. He could not provide cash other than a small advance of $1000 Malayan which, with care and judicious use of exchange rates in the bazaars (particularly the Chinese) should cover any minor expenses.

Jim made it quite clear to him, in view of the day's experience with his own company, that he could give no firm guarantee that KLM would be reimbursed and that he, personally, was in no position to make up any shortfall. All Jim had to do, Mr Pilgrams said, was to sign receipts on behalf of his company for the cash and services – having checked out his authorisation as captain of the aircraft registered in the company's name, the log books, carnet de passage and fuel carnet, his signature was wholly acceptable and could be taken in good faith. KLM was big and tough enough to enforce repayment if necessary, not hesitating even to impound any or all of Jim's company's aircraft if necessary as they tried to pass through the NEI.

He stayed in Singapore again three times in 1948, having meals at the 'Cockpit', but each time Mr Pilgrams was away so he was unable to relate the story of their progress through the NEI. Sadly he was killed in an air crash not long afterwards, on his way home to Holland. Jim wondered whether or not he had stood personal guarantee for that $1000 Malayan but, as it happened that and the other costs were repaid eventually by the company. The advice about the exchange of those dollars proved excellent later on. By buying Australian pounds through Chinese traders (who were at that time amassing Malayan currency in the expectation that they might be forced to leave when the NEI became independent) a profit of a £A50 was made against the nominal £A125 to $M1000. Very little of it was spent anyway as most of the expenses were billed, as arranged, on credit to KLM. The best credit of all however was the ready help and kindness shown by the Dutch people throughout the journey through the Indies, complementing that shown by Mr Pilgrams – obviously natural and not just for the enormous respect he enjoyed wherever his name was mentioned.

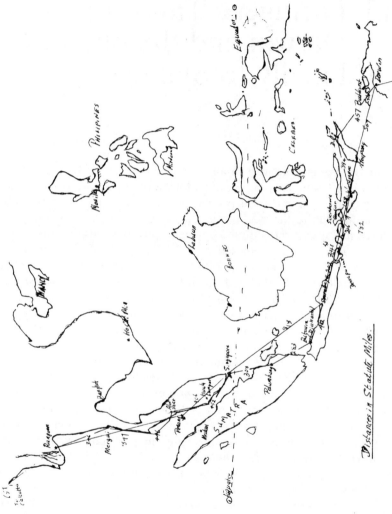

Distances in Statute Miles.

Singapore, through the Dutch East Indies – Portugese Timor to Darwin and the outback – Finally to Sydney

15

Leaving Singapore at 6.15 am on 21 November the first leg of two and a half hours, crossing the Equator on the way, was to Palambang in Sumatra – an active oil producing area with refinery. It was also notorious during the war for its Japanese-run internment camp for Dutch nationals, who suffered appalling privations – in particular the women and children, separated from their menfolk. They were later to meet a family who had suffered there. It was raining when they arrived with thick layers of cloud, but the airfield lay close to the coast so was easy to find. During the one hour 45 minutes spent there the sun started to break through, the earth became steamy, and the air very sticky.

The weather deteriorated during the two hour 20 minute flight to Batavia (now Jakarta), the rain becoming very heavy and continuous though visibility remained quite good – good enough to see some very spectacular explosions of lightning out to sea to the north which, as the afternoon wore on, would become impossible to fly through safely or close by. The Intertropical Front and Line of Convergence were close to each other at that time of the year with their interaction becoming violent in the afternoons and evenings in particular, so flying was confined to the mornings whenever possible whilst in their vicinity. Landing at Batavia was at 12.50pm, late enough in the circumstances, so they stayed there the night.

The Dutch Army, fully armed, was in evidence everywhere. Officials were suspicious of everything and everyone so they had a long progress through customs and immigration checks, were warned not to leave the hotel to sightsee unless properly escorted, and certainly not at all after dark. The insurgent war was getting very close to flare-up and evacuation of the Dutch. KLM officials could not have been kinder or more helpful and had arranged for an excellent hotel where a good night's rest was possible, despite the oppressively sticky heat. The process of boarding the aircraft next day was almost as lengthy as for the arrival, despite KLM's traffic staff giving every assistance, but departure at 6.30am was achieved en-route for Soerabeia at the eastern end of Java. Arrival there was just after 10.00am, looking forward to a late breakfast as coffee and rolls were all that had been obtainable at 4.30am before leaving the hotel.

The military presence was very much in evidence again and officials as suspicious as at Batavia, but the KLM staff got them through into the airport restaurant by 11.15 where a rather greasy bacon and egg meal was served by very surly Indonesian waiters. No smiles, no response to attempts to communicate and, if it hadn't been for the KLM traffic officer who had remained with them, it is doubtful if they would have had any service at all. It was uncomfortably obvious that the local inhabitants were resentful and rebellious against their Dutch Colonial masters, their escort being extremely abrupt in his manner to them. it was a long and not very happy two hours 15 minutes before taking off for Bali.

A lovely flight of just over two hours, low around the rugged coast fo north-east Java into sudden sunshine, through the straights of Bali to the south side of that fantastically beautiful island, its deeply green extinct double header volcano cones rising from a narrow coastline, fringed with palms and brilliant white beaches, to 10,305 feet (Agur) and 7465 Feet (Batukau). The airfield at Denapasar lies on the south coast, a long east/west runway made of crushed coral gleaming pinkly as they approached to land westwards at 2.30pm. The air smelled warmly earthy and vaguely spicy, the wind gentle from the west, as they disembarked by the small palm-thatched open-walled Terminal, to be met by the Shell representative who doubled as KLM agent. A huge blonde Dutchman with kindly blue eyes, a very deep voice, and gentle friendly manner. (It should be remembered that fuel carnets issued by one company were honoured by all, so their Esso was acceptable where that company had no facilities).

His name was van Dyke, christian name Haas. Holland and Dykes go together – the marvellous story of the little boy holding back the sea with his thumb came to mind, with the thought that Haas's thumb might be large enough to hold back the Roaring Forties pouring through a manhole! An exaggeration of course, but as a barman (using the old fashioned hand-held measure) he could have made a fortune if so inclined. He drove the old bus without windows himself as they travelled slowly through the forest on a brownish-red dirt road the twenty minutes into the small town, really a village surrounding the Temple. The large hotel on the outskirts, whitewalled with reddish-brown wooden doors and window frames, eaves and verandah supports, roof shingles and even furniture, contrasting breathtakingly with the deep green of the rain forest surroundings.

There had been squeals and giggles from the European passengers on that marvellous drive as they passed local natives, mostly women bare to the waist, carrying large loads in baskets on their heads. The beautiful golden brown of their skins, peculiar to the natives of Bali compared to those from other parts of the NEI (from Sumatra to Timor in the west), shone in the patchy sunlight filtering through the trees. Older ladies with breasts as firm as the young, all with happy smiles and greetings as they passed by. The Balinese people were without doubt, to Jim anyway, the most beautiful in their delicate facial bone structure that he had ever seen – or has seen since. Men and woman alike, with their skins gleaming with perfection of complexion rather than perspiration, are exemplified by the local art of carving (in teak, so similar in colour to their skins) head and shoulder to the waist of both sexes.

These were the days before the dreadful invasion of multi-national tourism and high-rise luxury hotels. The atmosphere was very relaxed, with none of the suspicion and surliness they had experienced in Java. They had had to suffer no officialdom of any kind, the whole scene being one of beauty, peace, and warm welcome. It was discovered that special permission had to be obained to visit the island, as there were no customs or immigration formalities, a Dutch Resident Officer the only official. KLM had fixed clearance for their visit. There was a wide choice of courses on the dinner menu from wonderful fresh fish to curry, the very hot Indonesian style Jim enjoyed even more than his previously favourite West African ones, and various pork dishes.

The Balinese raise pigs as their staple meat, those and cock fighting being the main interests (apart from fishing for food rather than pleasure) in their happy community-oriented existence. Plenty of dogs, but clean (unlike the starving Pidogs of India) who lived well alongside their human friends. After the meal Haas took them the short walk down to the main street. Lots of stalls offering all kinds of local produce, in particular the Batik work for which Bali is famous. A Chinese money changer happily converted the £M1000 to £A175, a £50 bonus over the normal exchange rate as mentioned previously.

Then it was on to the Temple where they were stunned by the exquisite dancers as they moved hands, arms and legs in incredibly graceful eurythmic type sinuous motion to the strange, yet thrilling, clash of cymbals. A stringed instrument sounding much like the Indian Lyre provided the tune which seemed monotonous to ears not used to such music but, once concentrating, almost mesmerised by the atmosphere, innumerable small variations on the main theme could be picked up. The dancing was not unlike that common in India with the Hindus, but the local religion is believed to based more on Buddhism – in any case far removed from the largely Moslem type in the rest of Indonesia. The performers, they were told, were all very young girls, the most senior 13 to 14 years old, at which stage they leave the Temple where they have lived and trained since early childhood. Their costumes were fantastic – high conical headdresses bright with colour, encrusted with jewels and beads, arms and legs covered in bangles clashing in time with the cymbals. Full length costumes matching the headdresses, which swayed in contrasting rhythm above delicate necks, their heavily made-up faces almost gaudy – but not hiding that beautiful bone structure. All this, under a starry sky in balmy, spicy air is memory which remains vividly alive whenever recalled. Haas told them he went regularly, before the war too, and never tired of the performances.

Returning to the hotel, where the bedrooms were in a number of self-contained bungalow type buildings, M'Lady, Richard, Bob, and Jim stayed up on the verandah for nightcaps with Haas, whilst the others retired. He then gave them an interesting outline of the Dutch influence in the region. Since the 18th century they had discovered, traded and colonised from Sumatra to West Timor, the Portuguese founding East Timor. They had brought development and prosperity to the Indies (with Holland benefiting greatly from its exports) and law and order – albeit with a pretty heavy hand. The Japanese occupation had forced the Dutch out, or imprisoned many including whole families in POW camps. On 17 August 1945 the Japanese surrender was taken by the British, whose troops and administration became virtually an occupying force for the time being. The Indonesian people under Suharto had however unilaterally declared the country independent and actually fought with what forces they had against the (legitimate) temporary occupiers. Many casualties were sustained on both sides, most due to a major clash near Soerabeia, (this explained the open hostility shown there).

With the British came Dutch forces, together with their nationals who had pre-war interests, properties, and businesses of all kinds, and their administrators, to re-establish their pre-war Dutch East Indies. The Indonesians rebelled violently, the current state amounting to full scale civil war, with arms and supplies being smuggled into the region for the Idonesians by all sorts of opportunists of many nationalities. The experience in Java had been different from that in Sumatra where, at Palambang, the Dutch had restored the oil wells and refineries and their influence was very strong. Also the local Indonesians had witnessed the inhumane treatment by the Japanese of Dutch women and children and their separated menfolk, and had far less antagonism than the Javenese. It appeared that the inhabitants of the many islands to the east of the two main ones had far less nationalism in their way of life and seemed quite content, indeed close and happy, with their Dutch overseers to whom they looked as protectors and providers. That rounded off a most interesting and pleasant evening as they finished their drinks before drifting happily off to bed.

As a footnote, in the light of later events, it was not until 27 December 1949, four years after the 17 August Japanese surrender and Indonesian unilateral declaration of independence, that agreement was reached in the United Nations for the State of Indonesia to be recognised formally as a fully independent nation. Nevertheless, the Indonesians celebrate annually their Independence Day on 17 August.

The van Dykes, mother and two teenage children, had organised breakfast for them next day in that quaint opensided thatched-roof building at the airport for 6.15am. A simple meal of rolls and coffee. They had also made up lunch boxes, and a large box of varied items to enable a proper meal to be cooked should they have to nightstop before reaching Dilli in Portugese Timor. Saying goodbye to the gentle giant and his family, and to those happy and smiling islanders (all covered up as the day had not warmed enough to warrant removal of tops) was a nostalgic affair.

They were airborne at 7.10am heading out past the rocky bulk of the island of Lombok (peaking at 12,250 feet above the sea) towards the island of Soembawa. Here they landed on a grass strip (quite long as it had to have enough room for the DC3 supply plane) at Soembawa Besar at 8.50 am local time. The Dutch Resident, his wife, two boys aged 12 and 10, and a nine month old baby girl, met them with cool drinks and a welcome as warm as the van Dykes' with whom they had been long time friends. Ten gallon drums of petrol were offloaded from a truck and preparations made for refuelling. Denebola was the first aircraft to require fuel since the Japanese left, as the supply plane had range enough to cover the entire flight between Batavia and Koepang in West Timor, landing at various islands en-route. Jim discovered that the drums contained Japanese motor fuel left behind them. The Resident said it worked perfectly well in their transports, was all they had, and had tested out at 86 octane before they had used any of it. Denebola's simple engines ran normally on 90 octane but would no doubt function perfectly well on the slightly lower rating. However, the hand pump contained no filter and there were none on the island. A felt hat from the local store would have done just as well as a chamois, but a search found no such thing.

With any petrol a filter is vital when refuelling aircraft, ensuring that any water and small impurities are separated before clean fuel enters the tanks. With the age of that petrol a filter was even more important than usual. The island's radio link was used to contact Haas in Bali, who did have a filter and would lend it to them. Nothing else for it – Jim and Bob had to fly back the one and a half hour trip to collect it then return to Soembawa Besar, where a night would now be inevitable. The Resident organised the opening of a rest house, cleaned after the Japanese left but not since used. Providing clean bedding and ensuring the water supply was flushed through (though no hot water was piped on) was quite a task but with their help did a marvellous job, and by the time Denebola returned the passengers were installed and a meal in preparation. Richard opted to eat at the rest house though he had been invited with M'Lady, Bob, and Jim to dine with the Resident and family, but he was feeling very tired after the late night at Bali on top of (for him) a sleepless one at Batavia.

Before that there was the job of topping up the fuel tanks, one at a time with only one pump and a single filter – a large one, but flow through such filters is necessarily slow though surprisingly little debris or water was in evidence. During this procedure it was realised that the drums contained about eight gallons, not ten, so the contents must have been based on the American gallon (five sixths of the Imperial measure) or a Japanese measure coincidentally similar to the American. That surprised the Resident, and explained why his petrol vehicles had an apparently high consumption – it had never occurred to him that the drums were other than ten gallon ones and he had never actually measured the contents.

Refulling completed eventually the engines were started, warmed up during a deliberately bumpy taxi up and down the runway to effect a complete mix of the two petrol types in the tanks, then run up to full power with every indication that all was normal – including acceleration. They then went to the rest house to clean up for dinner.

A jug of hot water had been supplied from the reopened kitchen, some of which was poured into a spotlessly clean wash basin and cold added before Jim bent to sluice his face. As he did so something moved, causing him to jump back. As well he did, for a large scorpion crawled out of the overflow slot and was smartly despatched with the heel of a shoe. Shaken, and hardly believing his good luck not to have scooped the thing into his face, he helped himself to a good measure of Scotch before poking around that slot with a ruler to flush out a possible mate.

It was a good starter to the dinner conversation. The superb meal was cooked personally by the Resident's wife. They described the horrors of life in that Palambang prison camp – she and the two elder children in one part, he in another. That and their pre-war lives in the

Indies, their post-war return to Holland (where they could not settle down) then the return to the island which had been their old, much loved, home kept their guests spellbound. Such people, such courage privation and faith, must humble anyone meeting them.

Quite casually, and more or less in passing as they said goodnight, Jim asked if the fuel situation at Waingapo (their next refuelling stop) was the same as here. The Resident stopped in his tracks to ask his wife if she had heard the Resident of the island of Sumba (where Waingapo lies) say something about fuel supplies when he had passed through Soembawa Besar on the supply aircraft two days before. It appeared he had ordered more fuel to be sent on the next supply ship, as his stocks were very low – just in time to catch the next ship before it left Soerabeia to call at the islands. That news caused a major problem, but it was lucky that they had it for they could have been stuck in Waingapo for many days until that ship arrived there, and there was no known accommodation other than the Resident's small house.

Maps and charts were examined to see if an alternate route could be found. Denebola's range was insufficient to overfly Waingapo to Koepang on the south-western tip of Western Timor. There were two islands in the long chain where fuel stocks were known to exist, and were within range – but from either of them to either Koepang or to Dilli the distance was also out of range, and they had to land at either of those two places before they could cross the Timor Sea to Darwin. Clearly they must assume that Waingapo had insufficient fuel stocks, even the relatively small amount of about 80 gallons needed to top-up Denebola before continuing for a three and a half hour flight to Dilli.

There were three possible things to do. Firstly to fly the passengers back to Batavia and transfer them to a regular airline for Sydney, the crew remaining there until fuel became again available at Waingapo – in possibly two weeks or more. Financially that was impossible for the company, and Jim was not prepared in any case to sign on its behalf in the unlikely event KLM would be prepared to extend futher credit.

Secondly, to stay where they were, or back at Bali where supplies in general were plentiful (unlike at Seombawa Besar) but still an expense he felt the company might be unable to cover – even if KLM were prepared to accommodate and feed them on credit for that two or more weeks, a matter Haas would most certainly have to refer back to Mr Pilgrams in Singapore. Being still in the NEI however (and under the original credit terms no time limit had been imposed) it might just be a possibility. Here M'Lady had a word to say – quite simply she felt that, as far as the passengers were concerned, a lengthy further delay would prove totally unacceptable and could possibly result in legal action by their families and/or sponsors in Australia, though she and Richard would find an extended holiday in Bali quite acceptable.

The third alternative would be to carry sufficient fuel in the aircraft to Waingapo to refuel either for a short hop to Koepang before going to Dilli, or enough to proceed direct to Dilli. The former would require two drums of petrol, the latter eight drums, form Soembawa Besar. To carry any fuel at all as freight (and it would have to be in the passenger cabin as the cargo hold was too small to load even one drum due to size and shape) was totally illegal and against all safety regulations. Even if the aircraft was flying solely as a freighter, a special permit would be required and not given easily except (perhaps) in cases of dire emergency. So if, and it was a mighty big 'if', drums were to be carried it might as well be eight as two and fly Waingapo to Dilli direct – the aircraft would still be 89 lbs under maximum all-up weight with the eight drums. In either case an accident would involve a high risk of fire directly in the cabin.

M'Lady was asked to think the whole matter through and discuss her thoughts with the very sensible Resident and his wife (their names have quite deliberately not been used). After all they did represent KLM and might face blame for aiding and abetting an illegal act. Jim and Bob went outside under the stars to discuss the situation. Ther former well aware he could lose his flying licence over it and Bob, not in that way affected, would be taking an extra risk with his own life. That was also a consideration for Jim, but he was much more concerned about his responsibility for the safety of his passengers.

It was after 10.30pm when they joined the others. M'Lady considered the accident angle unimportant – she felt that Denebola was obviously a very safe aircraft unlikely to be involved in an accident over just one leg of the journey unless it was a very major one, in which case the carriage of petrol would probably make no difference to the fate of all on board. She was, however, very concerned about Jim's and Bob's careers, as were the Resident and his wife. They (the crew) had agreed outside to load eight drums, for the number carried was immaterial if any at all were to be loaded, provide M'Lady and Richard (when consulted in the morning) concurred. It was agreed that they sleep on any decision, consulting Richard in the morning after his good sleep before taking the matter any further. Jim made it quite clear that, in everybody's interests, the matter must not be divulged to anyone but themselves – or even talked about should any of them meet in the future. Obviously they could not communicate with the other passengers in any properly explanatory way, and were sure they would not know fuel should not be carried. Fortunately, only Jim smoked and that was not on in the cockpits of those days, so a thoughtless light-up would not be a problem.

In the morning Jim said that, having slept on it (and not too well either) he had come to a different conclusion and couldn't think why it had not occurred to him the night before – perhaps it was the urgency expressed about no further delays for the passengers. There would, however, be one more day's delay while the petrol was flown to Waingapo as freight, without passengers, the aircraft returning that day for nightstop before leaving normally with them the following day. The eight drums needed for the Waingapo leg would be supplemented with four more to top up Denebola at Waingapo for the return trip to Soembawa Besar. The Resident agreed to lend a hand pump for that purpose in case one was not available at Waingapo. The passengers would eat lunch from the boxes brought from Bali and kept overnight in the Resident's cool room. The extra box of provisions from Bali in case of an unscheduled stop could be used for dinner, so that local stocks were not further depleted.

Jim would have managed on his own, assuming some labour help would be available at Waingapo, but Bob insisted on going with him. It was a pleasant good weather flight and they were met by a light coloured gentleman in white duck suiting, the red dot on his forehead indicating Hindu origin. In lilting Indian English he greeted them formally on behalf of the Resident who (as they knew) had gone to Batavia, introduced himself as 'Icky' and was so sorry there was no petrol until supplies arrived in 'just a few days time'. He was quite surprised to see they had brought their own fuel but helped to offload the 12 drums, eight of them being stacked in the open-sided thatched roof shelter so typical of that part of the world at small airstrips, and he promised they would be safe until their return next day.

As Bob and Jim were pumping fuel into the tanks from the other four drums Icky said that the local pump was locked in a store in town and the key locked in the Resident's house (where he lived alone) so that meant no pump for tomorrow unless they brought their own. The borrowed one would have to be returned to Soembawa Besar so tomorrow's refuelling would have to be by humping up the 70 lbs or so weight of the drums to tip fuel into the filter direct – a job for two, with two others to lift the drums up to them. At least they had been forewarned and were able to prepare Richard and Yanni for the task if no other help was available.

Back at Soembawa Besar nobody seemed put out about the extra day's delay, and it was a relief to all that the passengers had not been put at risk. The petrol freighting may have been illegal but, in the circumstances, Jim was confident there would be not repercussions. However, he did suggest that the less said about it the better. (Later, in 1948, there was a precedent set in the Berlin airlift, but that was quite different).

Next day they landed at Waingapo at 7.45 am, met again by 'Icky' who had donned overalls over his white ducks to help with the refuelling. It was hard work but done in one hour 25 minutes. A small crowd of ill-clad natives, much darker skinned than the Indonesians previously seen and with features more resembling New Guineans, gathered just as refuelling was completed. Fortunately it was not very hot, but the crew were pretty exhausted none less as they started to top up the oil. Not much was needed, but Jim lost his grip on his quart bottle as he was securing the tank cap, and away down the wing it slid spilling about one and a half pints. Those natives immediately came alive, running, chattering shrilly to crouch under the wing and drink the oil as it dripped off – a sight which made them all wonder if their eyes were deceiving them. Jim wiped the wing clear of oil, pushing it down with a rag to drip off the trailing edge to add to the feast below, feeling that it was not being wasted as obviously it was a gastronomic treat for those scruffy fellows.

He was glad nobody laughed, though the Italians and Zouki looked horrified and made 'yucky' noises as they boarded and seated themselves. Icky (maybe such a scene had caused him to be just that, thus to have the nickname) was having trouble chasing the natives away but they ran off in a bunch as the engines were started, the tail swung towards them with the slipstream helping them on their way.

Climbing away to 7000 feet, heading north-west towards Dilli, the upper cloud had thickened and lowered and to the north heavy cumulus was building up – through it soon to be seen a long line of thunderstorms. Denebola's track was well to the south of that so the three hour 15 minute flight was without incident. The grass airfield was half-saucer shaped (yet another with a steep-sided hill climbing high almost from it's circumference) and probably only just big enough for a Dakota to use – certainly nothing bigger or less manouvreable. The landing time was 12.55 pm local time, 25 November.

The Australian Consul met them, an exceptionally pleasant young man, to say that the company had called him from Sydney to ask him to act as agent whenever they arrived – (perhaps it had been recognised, at last, that Jim and troupe actually existed!). However, the Consul had (from Air traffic telex messages) not only been aware of their existence but had followed their travels since they had left England. He was bursting to hear tell of their adventures. That evening he and his wife dined with Jim, Bob, and Richard at a rest house in the hills where he had arranged their accommodation, bringing with them M'Lady who they had put up in their own home, and were suitably entertained by their stories.

Accommodation was very short in Dilli but the other passengers had been found two large rooms to share in the only hotel, with Yanni in an attic, but it was clean and the food good. In the rest house the three had to share a large airy room where they left a totally exhausted Richard for a siesta while they (Jim and Bob), in a crazily driven taxi, went to check that the passengers were happily settled at the hotel. They were over the moon (the Italians) that spaghetti was on the dinner menu not having had pasta since leaving Rome in the Hudson 18 days before on 7 November. Zouki and Yanni were looking forward to the fish course.

The next leg was to Darwin, over the Timor Sea and longest of them all – three and a half hours in still air. Forecast headwinds had to be light enough to enable a maximum estimated flight time of three hours 45 minutes, which allowed 45 minutes remaining fuel for emergencies, detours round heavy weather (common in that area for the time of the year, cyclone time) and possible diversion to an alternate field. Take off the following day was delayed until 8.45 am for an up-to-date wind forecast to come in from Darwin, though in fact stronger headwinds were experienced – so much so that they passed Bathhurst Island (chorus of 'Owstrilla, Owstrilla' from the cabin!) at the same time as they should have been over Darwin, where they finally landed in heavy rain at 12.55 pm Dilli time (1.55 pm Darwin time) after a four hour 8 minutes flight.

The crew were as pleased as the excited passengers, finally to have made it after 28 days. Jim recalled that that was a day longer than it took Ross and Keith Smith in their Vickers Vimy in Nov/Dec 1919 to reach Darwin from England, but then they were pioneers so it could hardly be considered a big deal not to have done better with more modern facilities and a route so well defined and serviced. All the same, Jim and Bob both felt it had been a satisfying achievement.

Dinner (which was lunch) was served to them at a long trestle table in one of the huge hangars by two strong looking buxom ladies, and appeared to be a 'Welcome to Australia' event. They were so kind and bursting with welcome, especially for the Europeans in the party (which Jim thought tremendous public relations) that it was unfortunate the two large mutton chops on each plate defied the knife and, when finally hacked-off bits found the mouth, teeth could chew but not masticate except for the generous coating of rubbery fat. The pumpkin was good, though strange to the Europeans, long beans and boiled potatoes excellent, the gravy delicious, and the mutton-flavour strong but (to Jim anyway) enjoyable. The Italians had to abandon knives, the Greeks following suit, and fingers picked up the chops to chew.

The two kind ladies were by then looking less than happy, so Jim went over to them and explained that none of them were used to so much meat after the meagre ration at home since early in the war and were finding it hard to assimilate but (as they could see) the vegetables were being thoroughly enjoyed. That cheered them up again, and plates laden with blobs of well-chewed meat were removed to be replaced with others containing large wedges of apple pie with thick custard, which disappeared in no time at all. There was strong tea to finish off with – powdered milk, fresh being impossible in that hot humid time of the year only 18 degrees south of the equator (and refrigerators few and far between all over Australia until some 10 years later). That good old Australian 'tucker' was a bit of a shock to the travellers, but to him no more than expected. However, they were all so happy to be almost there it was a laughing and excited crowd that went in taxis to the Darwin Hotel for the night.

The appointed agent in Darwin the local taxi firm operator. A six foot four inches giant of a man, with hollow legs when it was time to enjoy Darwin 'stubbies' – the fat large capacity beer bottle produced specially for the local thirst. He had a tremendous sense of humour and twinkling eyes, ever ready to mock anything and anybody in good natured banter. Clive Keetley was what the locals would call a 'bonzer bloke', as gentle as he was kind. It showed in the first instance when he told Jim he had arranged for them to eat in small dining room normally used for the hotel staff. It was some way from the main one as he did not want the Europeans ('or you Pommi bastards for that matter') to be subjected to drink fomented abuse from the 'front bar' off which it opened – possibly overhearing such terms as wogs, dagos, poms, and balts issuing forth from that off-white tiled area, (in that era closely resembling, to look at, the public toilets in Piccadilly Circus!).

There were no other overnight guests in the first-floor bedroom area, but the better rooms in the front were over that huge bar so theirs had been allocated to the rear of the hotel. Not so comfortable maybe (minimum of two sharing) with a very small separate one for M'Lady which Clive had persuaded a young female kitchen hand to vacate for the night when he realised that she (M'Lady) was a bit different. There was absolutely nothing but good humour throughout that conversation – just a lot of practical common sense and kind thought.

After the 6pm meal, rather heavy schnitzels after soup and again the delicious 'sweets' of homemade apple pie, Clive invited Jim, Bob, and M'Lady to his home to meet his wife (Richard had again declined the invitation, preferring to sleep) and enjoy a yarn over few drinks – this time Scotch. After he had given them the news that the Department of Civil Aviation (DCA) had organised full M/F radio facilities throughout the route to Sydney day and night (normally then used for emergency communications only) which was the best welcome to the country Bob

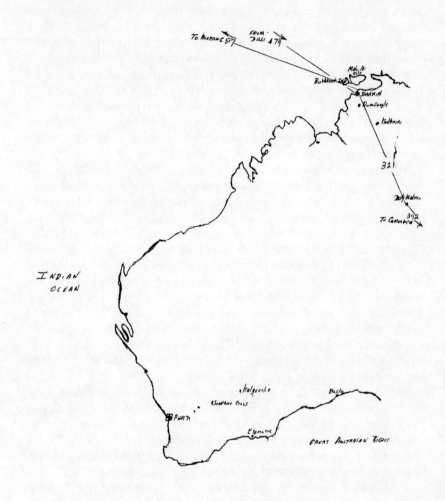

To MELBOURNE 577   FROM DILLI 479

Melville Isle

Bathhurst Isle   DARWIN

Pine Creek

Katherine

321

Daly Waters
To Cambridge   392

INDIAN
OCEAN

Kalgoorlie   Eucla

Southern Cross

PERTH

Esperance

GREAT AUSTRALIAN BIGHT

SOUTHERN OCEAN

Distances in Statute Miles.

could have had, they listened to a string of yarns. Most were hilarious, some even sad, but all most enjoyable. Then he took them back to the hotel in his big Buick from that attractive little wooden home, built on stilts – a common form of architecture in the Northern Territory, and also in Queensland.

Breakfast of ham and eggs, strong tea, bread, tinned butter and jam, was at 5am – again in that hangar at the airport, the same two ladies officiating. It couldn't have been better. Scheduled departure was 6am, 27 November, from when it was planned to fly all day, through the night now that they had radio facilities, to arrive in Sydney about 5pm local time the following day – 28 November.

Whilst filing the flight plan with the Darwin Air Traffic Control Jim received his first lesson in Aussie English. The officer in the (then) wooden briefing hut wore a wide-brimmed hat, an open-neck shirt with sleeves neatly rolled up. He had a generous drooping moustache and was very tall, with enormous knotted brown hands in which the pencil taking down the plan details was almost lost. Asked for the aircraft registration Jim pronounced G-ADYH – (aitch). He was fixed with steady blue eyes as the pencil poised (raised) after the 'Y' and, in a very firm voice 'Hightch' issued forth, which Jim tactfully repeated before the pencil descended to write that letter. All finished, the blue eyes fixed his again. . . 'You'll do cobber – good trip'. . . with a small but friendly smile. Jim liked that – made him feel welcome.

Airborne on the dot of 6am, Bob clattering away happily on his morse key for the first time since leaving Rome raising contacts and receiving messages, they flew south for two hours 40 minutes to Daly Waters, still in the Northern Territory, to refuel. The airstrip was in a large field some cattle browsing in another near by, a solitary large shed in one corner with a windmill in the background. As they taxied towards the shed a battered utility (pick-up) arrived. The shed door was opened by a very tall man in short-sleeved vest, complete with battered wide-brimmed hat and a large drooping moustache, who rolled a 44 gallon drum out towards them. By this time they had disembarked to be fixed with another pair of bright blue eyes, towering from above, as he stopped by the wing opening the drum to slide in a wobble pump (hand operated), undid the cap from the right-hand tank and, with a deep voiced 'G'dye', started to pump. He was obviously well verse in the aircraft type, which used to be operated in Australia alongside its twin-engined smaller sister the DH89 Rapide and that one's forebear the DH84 Dragon - the latter still being operated by the Flying Doctor Service.

Strong thick braces held up his trousers (sorry, 'strides') up to belly button height. The crew were obviously superfluous so joined the passengers sheltering from the sun in the shadow of the big shed. A second 44 gallon drum was run out for him to complete the refuelling. . .

'Name's Jake – sign here'. . . as he presented the refuelling form to Jim. Then using the top of the drum as a table, he started to take down the flight plan details for the next leg, to Camooweal in Queensland. Pronouncing the 'Hightch' as instructed in Darwin (surely this must be that chap's twin brother) Jim got a piercingly steady blue-eyed look then a wide grin which made him (Jake) look half his apparent age and a. . . 'you'll learn'. Jim was tempted to ask if the Darwin fellow was a relative but did not, feeling that the information would be offered if he was supposed to know.

. . . 'Mate of mine'll meet youse at Camooweal – good trip'. . . a huge paw extended to crush both Bob and Jim's hands as they boarded Denebola, topped with a huge grin and fond pat of the wing. . . 'Pity they chopped 'em'. . . Obviously he had some nostalgic memories of the DH86 Express Airliner, which type had been withdrawn from the Australian register by mandatory regulation of the DCA after the war finished. They had been used extensively during the war, particularly in supply to and evacuation of people from New Guinea, operated by Qantas.

10.25am, after a surprisingly short one hour 45 minutes on the ground considering Jake did all the refuelling on his own (they being clearly not wanted to assist), course was set eastwards for the three and a half hour leg to Camooweal, climbing to 9000 feet. The weather had become hot and dusty, a complete change from the damply overcast skies at Darwin, and the air becoming quite bumpy. A feature of the terrain below was the amazing number of windmills (pumping brackish water from bores into the artesian basin which lies under a large part of the Australian Continent) into huge dams or troughs, standing out clearly against the pinkish-brown land. Yet they saw only four homesteads in the huge area over which they flew.

They had to keep a sharp eye on the drift and compass course as the terrain stetched parallel to their track in waves, looking exactly alike, so it would be no use selecting one to follow as that could easily be the wrong one. Camooweal is just over the border into Queensland and they landed there at 1.40pm Central Australian time, putting their watches forward then to 2.10pm Eastern Standard time which would apply for the rest of the trip to Sydney.

Jakes's mate (now they were certain triplets had been born!) met them. The same nonchalant attitude as he refulled Denebola – three 44 gallon drums, but this time on a utility. A lady, presumably his wife, led the passengers to a wooden hut, flies abounding, the screens full of

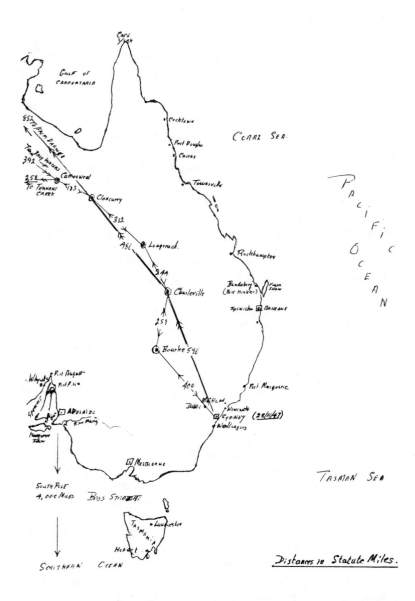

CAPE YORK

GULF OF CARPENTARIA

CORAL SEA

PACIFIC OCEAN

857 To NORTHERN DARWIN

To N.T.N. WATERS
392

258
To TENNANT CREEK

Camooweal

133

Cloncurry

312

Cooktown

Port Douglas

Cairns

Townsville

456

Longreach

344

Charleville

Rockhampton

Bundaberg
(Port Hinkler)

Fraser Island

Ipswich

Brisbane

259

Bourke 546

400

Port Macquarie

Whyalla
Port Augusta
Port Pirie

ADELAIDE

River Murray

Kangaroo Island

Maitland

Dubbo

Newcastle

SYDNEY   (28/11/47)

Wollongong

MELBOURNE

SOUTH POLE
4,000 MILES

BASS STRAIT

TASMAN SEA

SOUTHERN OCEAN

TASMANIA

Launceston

Hobart

Distances in Statute Miles.

holes, where a meal had been prepared. Jim and Bob joined them after signing for the fuel and completing the flight plan to Cloncurry. The 'Hightch' elicited another electric blue stare, but this time no smile – maybe he thought Jim was trying to take the mickey out of him. Those braces over the woollen vest hitching strides up to navel were fascinating, but no doubt there would be some very practical reason for the outfit. He followed into the hut, wide-brimmed hat still firmly in place, to help the lady serve the dinner.

Oh dear! – mutton chops, wet cabbage, sloppy boiled potatoes covered with thick gravy, and thick mugs of strong tea with powdered milk – (flies everywhere). It really was awful by any standards, and it was hot, dusty, and stuffy. M'Lady, Richard, Bob, and Jim deliberately tucked in, glaring at the others who seemed too stunned to start which achieved a semblance of them having a go at it. To their credit, (Mamma in particular who was always the instigator of complaint and comment), no derogatory signs or remarks were made but Jim felt certain they all wished they had never left Europe. He thanked the couple for taking so much trouble to cook for them in that heat explaining that, of course, none of them was used to that which was why they could not do justice to the hot meal.

The still-loaded plates were removed, with apologies from the lady who then produced cold apple pie with warm custard in a jug. That was very nice indeed, Richard after tasting the custard saying loudly to them all that it tasted jolly good, and giving the couple a big smile of thank you. He meant it too, not just a tactful remark, and Jim and Bob followed suit making the same appreciative noises for it was a real homemade custard, not packet stuff – it turned out the couple kept chooks.

The chickens and a goat were displayed for them, kept close to a small wooden house (on stilts) a hundred yards or so from the airfield shed where they had eaten. 'Shirl', as the kind lady introduced herself, and 'Ben' had lived over twenty years there, she on her own for the three and a half years he had been away in the Army during the war, returning home wounded early in 1945. It was only then they realised he walked differently due, she said, to an artificial right leg below the knee. They left them then, feeling very humble, and glad that their visit had been an exciting major event, for they saw very few people year round except the Flying Doctor and a few droppers-in driving through the Barkly Tablelands between Tennant Creek and Mount Isa (where the couple managed at most two trips a year for a day or two).

They stood, waving, as Denebola took off, surprisingly only one hour 20 minutes after arriving, at 3.30pm. The terrain below was similar to that of the previous leg, only even drier and dustier, but the same

208

reddish-brown earth with windmills in plenty. There was only one homestead, seen far south of their slightly south of east heading, during the short one and a half hour flight to Clomcurry.

Bob, happy as a child with a new toy, clickety-clacking on his morse key received confirmation from Air Traffic Control that the rooms they had booked for a short rest after the evening meal were ready, also that the M/F radio system would definitely remain open for them all night. Landing at 5pm they were soon on a dusty ride in a bus into the town to enjoy a meal of huge T-bone steaks, eggs and salads, more apple pie (this time with ice cream!) and the inevitable strong tea, though with real milk.

The town was quite large the centre for a vast area of cattle country – somewhat reminiscent of their film-educated imagination of the American wild west. They were told they were lucky they had arrived on a Thursday because the town was always crowded and very noisy Fridays and Saturdays. They slept after the meal until woken as arranged at 1am by 'Jolly Joe', the hotel proprietor, to enjoy sandwiches and tea prepared by Shelley (short for Michelle) his pretty blonde wife. She looked very fit, tall and solidly built, making him look small yet very nuggety. The travellers were finding Australian hospitality, though different, warm and genuine and full of good nature. The Italians and Greeks were seen by now really to appreciate and feel comfortable about it.

Take off was 2.25am, climbing to 5500 feet heading south-east in the still cool of the night. The sky, laden with stars, seemed so close overhead in the startling clearness of the Australian atmosphere and everyone was relaxed and peaceful in the knowledge that 'Seednee' was 'today' – no longer a fickle mirage 'domani'. They were heading for Longreach, the 1920 birthplace of Qantas (Queensland and Northern Territory Air Services) and also the inland headquarters of the Royal Flying Doctor Service. There is a famous aviation museum located right on the airport which unfortunately was closed when they landed – at 5am.

During the 50-minute, bowser-operated, refuelling stop they ate more sandwiches prepared by Shelley and had soup she had put into two of their vacuum flasks, saying that they would find it very cold at night. And that was very true, for it was almost freezing outside and there was no heating in the airport building – with the aircraft heating available the cold in flight had not been noticed. Jim and Bob were enjoying not having to superintend refuelling, that being attended to by the highly efficient airport staff – just having to sign the chit. They didn't have to file any more flight plans as, from Cloncurry, they had been able to file for the whole of the rest of the journey to Sydney via Longreach,

Charleville in south-western Queensland, and Bourke in northern New South Wales – having simply to advise by radio their airborne times and ETAs at destinations.

The pink glow of dawn appeared in the east as they took off heading south-eastwards for Charleville, and soon the red-gold orb of the sun rose stately and dazzling from the eastern horizon. A perfect cloudless day, so far very smooth and remaining so as they let down onto the long brown, white-marked, grass strip at Charleville at 8.15am. A very neat well-kept looking airport as they drew up on an oblong of tarmac by a large double hangar. Surprisingly a hand pump from a small bowser was used for refuelling, but that was because of a breakdown of the motor pump.

Two large cars for the ladies, and for Jim. Bob and Richard a ride in the back of a utility bouncing dustily, which took them into an attractive little town to draw up in front of the hotel – a white trimmed with green, very clean-looking structure of stucco-covered stone or brick. A warm and friendly dining room provided bacon and eggs, snags or sausages (as you like), real tomatoes, toast and, for the first time since arriving in Australia, a choice of tea or coffee, also fresh butter and a variety of jams – all homemade. What with that, and toilet facilities with hot water, soap and towels (spotlessly clean), they would not have minded a stay there. But, 'Seednee here we come' – at last! So back to the airport for a 10.00am start south-south-east towards Bourke and New South Wales.

The weather was clear and not very hot, the ground below showing signs of green as they neared the Queensland/New South Wales border, approaching to land at Bourke at 12.10pm. There it was disappointing, and hopefully not to prove typical of the State of New South Wales – even the refuellers just doing their job, but with none of the friendliness experienced all the way at, and since, Darwin. There were no refreshment facilities or shelter (at least the single shed and a small wooden building were locked up) and no toilets. The aircraft toilet had to be used by anyone needing it and, incidentally, they were advised that it could not be cleaned or the contents emptied or refilled. A few months later Jim had to have a nightstop in the town and found the same unfriendly attitude – even in the shops and hotel. Apparently strangers were less than welcome in a town which, all over the continent, had become known as 'the last before the Black Stump' or 'Back-O-Bourke'.

They got away after an hour, at 1.10pm, Bob opening the emergency ration pack for anyone feeling hungry. Fortunately four of their eight flasks still held water or cordial, though the excitement of 'Seednee-next-stop' (in about three and a quarter hours) surmounted thirst and any hunger pains. Heading south-east again on that very last leg of the 30 day journey they climbed to 7500 feet in clear air with a forecast, received on Bob's radio, to remain so all the way. Weather reported from Sydney at 1.30pm indicated no change, the ETA of 16.25 hours acknowledged with instruction to report when over Dubbo (expected to be 1500 hours or 3pm). Mascot, the international airport for Sydney, was as busy as most European major city airports, so it will be accepted that the 24-hour clock system (universally used in flying), though expressed in GMT no matter where in the world it may be, rather than in local time as used here) will be used from now on in this narrative during the flight sequences.

If you have read so far there should be no difficulty in identifying with events during the last hours of the journey. There was merriment and singing from the cabin, Mama doing something like an Italian jig in the aisle (Carmela looking disapproving as usual) and M'Lady clapping and joining the light-hearted fun. Bob grinned across at Jim, both relaxed and happy in anticipation of a hard job soon to be finished. It just had to be that there would be another bit of drama before that finish.

Approaching Dubbo (on the western side of the Blue Mountains) cloud was seen ahead of them to be total cover, thickish-looking strato cumulus as far as the eye could see. The forecast winds had been from the north-east, backing gradually to south-east by midnight or late evening. A gut-feeling, plus that first and second generation training allied with his own experience, told Jim that the wind swing had arrived very early, the sudden di-da-dah-ditty morse heard from Bob's earphones confirming that the surface wind was now south-easterly 12-15 knots. Further, that the cloud over Sydney had become total cover, at 2000 feet with rain in the distance. There was no point trying to get under that cloud ahead especially with one mountain over to the left identifed as a 4500 foot peak in the range. M/F ground facilities did not have cathode ray direction finding equipment and Denebola had no radio beacon receiving equipment (radar was not in use anywhere in the world then for civil operations).

Jim assumed that the upper winds had also changed to south-easterly, on the nose and probably strengthened, so he calculated overhead Sydney time to be 15 minutes late at 16.40 hrs. To that he added a further 10 minutes for unforseen circumstances and Bob radioed the change to advise they would start let-down through the clouds at 16.50 hrs – heading out to sea to break cloud before returning under it for ETA Mascot 17.10 hrs. The message was acknowledged and permission given to approach as planned, to contact when estimating overhead and beginning descent. Still flying in clear conditions and bright sunlight it must have seemed odd to the passengers when they were told of the delay and why, though the Italians and Greeks probably understood nothing and went on enjoying themselves as before. M'Lady and Richard went on joining in with them, and in any case were not worried about the weather (any more than the crew were for that matter – after all it was only just a nuisance that their first sight of Sydney would be of yet another airport instead of a view of the fabulous harbour!).

A slow descent from 7500 feet was started as they passed over Dubbo at 15.12 hrs, still clear of cloud, the 12 minutes late confirming the wind change and checking with Jim's revised ground-speed calculation. Keeping the cruising power on during the descent would help to reduce the revised head-wind effect (by providing greater airspeed) giving a further safety margin to make sure the mountains were well and truly cleared before entering cloud on final descent.

At 16.50 hrs Mascot was advised that they were about to descend from just on top of cloud at 3500 feet, heading south-east out to sea, and would call when breaking below before returning under visual flight rules to land. To their original overhead time of 16.25 had been added 25 minutes to allow for increased headwinds, and now a further 10 minutes was to be added to that at least before expecting to break cloud over the sea, then reversing course to Mascot. These precautions are being emphasised, for, as they broke cloud in steady rain, Sydney Harbour Bridge was directly below them! Shrieks of delight and much clapping from the passenger cabin, as though that was a special surprise put on for their benefit. Jim and Bob looked at each other in simulataneous disbelief (and relief!), and were not surprised when Mascot Control advised the surface wind to have increased to 20-gusting-30 knots (23-35 mph) for the upper wind speed (headwind) since passing over Dubbo must have reached at least 50 mph at 3500 feet to have slowed them 33 minutes between there and reaching the Harbour Bridge.

Their luck had held out again, aided by only just enough caution as it turned out, or they would have otherwise descended straight into cloud covered mountains. A green light from the control tower as they circled gave them permission to land, pretty rough it was too in that strong gusty wind, but safely down at 17.27 (5.27pm) Australian Eastern Standard time, Friday 28 November 1947, 30 days and 12,434 statute miles since leaving Croydon, in a total flight time of 126 hours 41 minutes.

To greet them was one Allan Wardle. the company's office manager, a lugubrious character with an easy sense of humour who led them through immigration and customs. He asked Jim to move Denebola right away (after clearing the officials) to the parking area by the Aero

Club as Control wanted the apron for incoming aircraft, some of which had been held overhead until Denebola had reported below cloud and visual. Jim had wanted first to say goodbye to the passengers, but the movement was urgent. A car brought him back 20 minutes later, but M'Lady and and Richard had already left. Bob had seen them off, explaining why Jim could not, and M'Lady had left a note with him for them both. The Greeks had been met by their Consul and they left with him after waiting for Jim, Zouki tearful as the Consul translated their thanks for taking care of them and bringing them there safely – much handshaking.

The Italians had been met by their relatives – there must have been twenty or more with an equal number of friends. They had been put into a separate lounge, Jim suspected a VIP one, as Bob led him there. Cheers, clapping, and quite a hullaballoo greeted them. Mamma rushed to kiss both of them on each cheek as she introduced excitedly a very short man wearing a sort of curly-brimmed bowler hat and a black-and-white-striped shirt with red bow tie. He had a Ramon Navarro style moustache, and his flashing smile revealed white teeth flecked with a deal of gold – Carmela's Papa, Mamma's husband, who repeated the cheek kissing. Then there was enthusiastic hand shaking all round.

Carmela still looked disapproving but, probably encouraged by Mum and Dad's perfomance, then shot forward to reach up to Bob, who presented his cheeks and gave her a big hug. Then she came to Jim, looking him in the eyes with those golden-flecked dark olive ones of hers, smiled shyly and offered her hand, which he kissed to the cheers of the crowd, and she scuttled blushingly back to hold her parents' hands. Sudden silence as Papa held up both hands, removed his bowler, and addressed the crowd in Italian (at some length) before turning to Jim and Bob to say in English. . . 'We all thank you for bringing our loved ones safely to us. We wish you God's blessings for ever. We wish you joy and happiness and many safe journeys. We wish you many children and long lives to enjoy all God's blessings'. . . Then they all crossed themselves before again breaking into clapping and cheering.

It was really very moving, and not embarrassing for they were such simple people and clearly genuine. Jim was obviously expected to say something. . . 'We wish you well and happiness and great success in your new country. We shall remember you with much affection in our hearts. Thank you for being no trouble to us during our long voyage. Arriverderci and good luck'. . .

No doubt the message was translated later, but at that moment the airport staff wanted them out quickly to make room for another party.

M'Lady's letter was brief and to the point. . . .'Bob; Richard has asked me to add his thanks to this note. I'm sorry there was no time to say goodbye to your captain but please include him in our thanks for a voyage which we both enjoyed very much, despite the various tribulations – indeed probably as much because of them. I have admired very much the constant support you gave your skipper, without which I think he might have found his job much more taxing. Also, the manner in which you have shown great patience and understanding, which helped to bridge several gaps, has shown a maturity much greater than your age. You deserve to do well in life, which I hope will be a long and very happy one for you. Thank you both again. I hope we shall meet again one day'. . .

The taxi ride through Sydney's less salubrious districts (always depressing) to the hotel the company had booked for the crew in Kings Cross (close to the company's office) was somewhat of anti-climax, both Jim and Bob feeling empty and suddenly very tired. Being on the boil for 30 days reduces the oxygen and adrenalin factor quite remarkably as the heat is removed. They fell into bed, slept through the night until late the next morning, showered and dressed (out of uniform and relaxed), to venture out into sunshine for a short walk down the hill to the beautiful Elizabeth Bay then back into the Cross to enjoy a large and excellent ham, cheese, and pineapple salad in the Arabian coffee shop before reporting in at the office.

It was a pleasant start to the adventure of discovering Sydney and its cosmopolitan lifestyle.

16 Idle days – Aerial contrast – Sydney to Cyprus return – Deception – Return home to Britain

On 1 December 1947, the 'Boss' finally arrived from England in a Lockheed Lodestar bought from BOAC, with 14 passengers from Britain. The registration was G-AGBU and one of the aircraft in which had flown many hours in 1943/46 when based in Cairo with No. 5 Line. His arrival straightened out much of the misunderstanding about Jim's position, and his pay became regularised than on an advance on request basis. Allan Wardle had been very good about that – seeing Jim and Bob did not go short, but now regular payments could be sent home to families in Britain.

There was work to do in the office organising the production of route manuals to assist the aircrew with their operations, and the obtaining of a new full passport to replace the temporary one issued in Baghdad. Then it was Christmas, so different in heat from the ones enjoyed at home. Nevertheless the old traditions were duly observed – Christmas trees, turkey (hot) and ham, Christmas pudding, crackers (bon-bons in the local jargon), paper hats and all-round bonhomie which didn't need (but of course did have) the stimulus of alcohol.

Allan and his marvellous wife invited Jim and Bob to join his party for Christmas Day where they met some wonderful people whose ensuing hospitality into the New Year, then very real friendship thereafter, made Sydney a very happy place to be and, coincidentally, provided entry by introduction to several nightclubs.

On 24 February Jim obtained his Australian Commercial licence (No. 2336) which then entitled him to operate Australian registered aircraft, but as things turned out that was not to be. There was no flying for him to do, which was part of the unfortunate position the company was getting into, though he continued to make himself useful in the office. It was of course a time with loads of spare hours, even during weekdays, to enjoy Sydney's wonderful beaches (Bondi, Manly, and other smaller more secluded ones) and take endless trips by ferry round the fabulous harbour – something he never tired of and, in recent years when the opportunity has arisen in rare visits to the city, he still finds tremendous pleasure doing.

It was a very happy time and late in February he was advised that his family would soon be travelling to Rome to join a chartered company flight to Sydney and should arrive by the end of March. Great news, especially as he was told he would be in command of the migrant charter aircraft concerned which was a Douglas DC3, owned and registered in the Philipines and currently in Darwin with an American crew. In the company's interests the Boss had arranged that Jim should take over command, retaining the American crew but with the addition of one of the company's radio officers who was a very soft-spoken Australian with some experience as a navigator. It should be noted that the Boss forgot, or failed to have confirmed as part of the charter deal, that Jim's licences were validated by the Philipine authorities, which caused some bother at a later date.

On 2 March dear old Denebola was removed from the Bankstown aerodrome hangar which had been her home for the last three months to head off for Darwin, with Jim in command, a co-pilot who was to fly her from Darwin to Penang (for what reason he hadn't been told) the new radio officer, and two of the American crew who had been on leave in Sydney. Also on board was the Boss's rather autocratic mother (though very nice) and her nurse who were to travel all the way to Britain – she was well into her seventies, but sprightly enough for all that she suffered considerably from rheumatics and a heart problem.

It was an afternoon departure so only one leg (to Bourke) was flown that day. The nightstop has been mentioned in Chapter IX so no need to repeat how bad it was. Cloncurry was the next nightstop, via Charleville and Longreach, which was very pleasant and great to see Shelley and Joe again. The next day it was on to Tennant Creek at the western end of the Barkly Highway where it joins the Stuart Highway (built during the war from Alice Springs to Darwin by the Americans, a point which the two Yanks on board made much of) then on to Darwin arriving in the early afternoon of March.

The C47 (Dakota to Jim) was being serviced and having a carburettor fault rectified. The American captain was none too happy about Jim taking over command, but that was the deal and they managed to get on reasonably well. The aircraft was ready for test flight on 11 March and Jim took that opportunity to get his hand back in on the type he had not flown since February 1946, two years ago. As as matter of interest that also was the last time he had flown G-AGBU, the Lodestar, before flying her to Cyprus for this company. The American captain kindly came with him for a landing, then left him to it with a particularly nice Philipine flight engineer on board to put in a few more practice circuits. It was good to experience the Big Moth handling again and the easy floating-off taking to the air so typical of that marvellous machine – a few still in regular service with airlines over 50 years since Douglas Aircraft produced the first one in the USA in the early 'thirties.

She floated gracefully away the next day en-route for Koepang in West Timor (after a night take-off at 4.30am) to land there at 6.45am local time. When lowering the undercarriage before landing it took longer than usual and, by changing over the hydraulic pumps, it was found that one of the two had failed. That could not be put right until reaching Singapore, no spares or servicing facilities en-route. There were no fare paying passengers on board so to continue with one pump only was permissable. This was subject to the captain agreeing, which Jim of course did, but that was delayed until the next day to give the flight engineer a chance to see if he could fix the faulty pump. Unable to do so, they continued to Bali arriving just before sunset.

It was decided not to fly on in the dark, just in case that single pump also failed, when a forced belly landing at night at Soerobeia would be very dicey. In any case there would be no point as they had to land there for fuel, the distance from Bali to Singapore being too great in the weather conditions prevailing. The undercarriage was left down on the short leg to Soerabeia, leaving only one leg for a single up and down operation for the lone pump to cope with before Singapore, which was reached just before 4pm local time.

The hydraulic pump was fixed three days later, but the day before the Philipine owner of the aircraft arrived and, in a pretty tense interview, advised that he needed to use the machine himself for a week or two before it could continue with the charter flight to Rome. He also told Jim that no approval had been given for him to continue any piloting functions (his licence not having been endorsed by the Philipine licencing authorities) so when the charter continued it would be with his American pilots doing the flying.

Jim went immediately to the Australian Consulate and then to the Singapore Department of Civil Aviation to try to have the aircraft impounded (by reason of a legal charter agreement having been broken) at least until his company had had the opportunity to take what action it thought fit. It was to no avail. As to his own licence endorsement position he could not argue as, obviously, his Boss had not made the arrangements he said had been done. He telephoned Sydney, was told to remain with the aircraft as tour manager (whether flying the aircraft himself or not) and to advise when the aircraft returned from whatever it was going to do. In the meantime they would start proceedings for damages in respect of the broken charter.

It was fortunate that two of the American crew were left in Singapore for the 25 days until the aircraft returned from wherever it had been, it's owner having gone back to Manila, and that they had funds to pay the bills. All but the Boss's mother and nurse had had to move to a Chinese hotel (much cheaper and cosier) not far from the 'New World' entertainment centre. It was actually much more fun and far more interesting than in the more luxurious hotel, and the food was excellent. The two Americans (the ones who had flown in Denebola with them to Darwin) were both very pleasant fellows so, apart from four weeks of idleness, that enforced stay was interesting and a lot was learned about Singapore and it's multi-racial inhabitants. How much that delay contributed to the company's final demise was never found out, but must have had a considerable effect.

Leaving Singapore on 8 April the charter continued, arriving in Athens three days later after having flown 11 legs without stopping for rest, two crews having shared the flying and resting alternately in bunks provided in the aircraft. They decided to stop in Athens two days, before going on to Rome then back to Athens and on back to Australia with as few stops as possible. That would at least help to catch up a little on the very delayed schedule, but Jim was far from happy how the company's passengers would fare – they would include, he expected, his wife and two young boys amongst them as promised.

He telephoned home to be told that the company's agents in London had refused them passage to Rome, quite simply because they hadn't been paid for weeks for their services and were not prepared to expend any more funds until they were. Further they had told his wife that, in their opinion, even if she paid the fares herself they felt that the company was not going to be long in business and to think it over very carefully before she started on such a journey.

She told Jim she had received no payments from his Sydney bank account for the last five weeks. Obviously, no money had been paid into his account by the company since he had left Sydney so the allotment to his wife could not be covered. He told her he would ring back in a few hours. Straight to the BEA office to book a single seat for the next day, the local manager trusting him to pay the fare in London on arrival. He then went back to the hotel to advise he was leaving the company as of now and would contact their head office after reaching London. Interestingly, the captain of the Vickers Viking (BEA) the next day was an extremely pleasant young man who had been seconded from the RAF to BOAC's No.5 Line in Cairo, and as co-pilot had flown with Jim quite a lot.

He was met at Northolt by his mother, who had kindly paid his fare and had been staying with his wife helping out with finance pending receipt of funds from Australia which, of course, never happened. They had been trying for all those weeks to contact him in Singapore but nobody knew which hotel he had been staying in – something it had never occurred to him to advise, though he had written. All the news they had had was the two letters from there telling them he was delayed, but without a proper address.

Well, it was certainly nice to be home. A phone call to the boss in Australia demanding payment of £A 196/8/4d back pay due to date of leaving Athens was refused, point blank, on the grounds that Jim had left without giving notice. Technically correct, but as it turned out there were no funds to pay any staff for several weeks previously, so the money could not have been paid anyway. Bob, having found work from time to time in Sydney, finally got back to Britain. Whether he worked his passage on a ship or by what other method he managed Jim never found out. He, very sensibly, left radio operating on his return and went into business in radio and electrical goods, for it was not long before radio officers on aircraft became redundant due to rapid, and considerable, improvements in pilot-operated systems. They were a special breed of men, sadly missed by those who had crewed with them for many years. The chartered Philipine DC3 did return to Australia without further delay – in fact in three days from Rome without any nightstops!

Out of work again it was August 1948 before new employment was found, Jim and family moving once again to the refuge of his parents' home in Lancashire. No matter what the pros and cons (the latter not a bad word for it!) Jim still treasures the memories and events of the 'trip that should never have happened', and believes it to have been perhaps the greatest adventure of his flying career.

PART III – (1948 to 1965)
On Course (I & II) – Diversion – Back on Course – Alternate – Return to Schedule for Final Approach – Landing and Engines Off

17 On Course I – Private Pilot

Unlike so many others trying to find flying jobs in the depressed situation at that time, Jim was very fortunate in having parents able and delighted to have their grandchildren around for some months.

He wrote endless letters, answering advertisements (of which there were extremely few), and making contact with every known flying firm to try to get on their books even if no work was available immediately.

On Thursday 5 August 1948 an advertisement appeared in the Daily Telegraph for pilot, radio officer, and engineer qualified on Lockheed Lodestar aircraft. It was for a large trading company, Mitchell Cotts and Company Limited. A 'phone call was followed by train to London for interview, and amazingly he had the job – to start Monday 16 August when he would meet the rest of the crew who had already been engaged.

Jim would have liked, of course, to have had a hand in the selection of the other crew members, but it turned out that they were very competent at their jobs and excellent team members. They were of widely differing ages, the engineer ten years older than Jim and the radio officer six years younger (ex-Merchant Navy), and they had totally different temperaments. The engineer was a real Cockney Londoner, the radio officer lad a true Liverpudlian, their banter with each other constant and lively and amusing (agreeing about practically nothing) yet they became close friends within a short space of time.

The job itself was to fly the company's chairman and senior executives, whenever required, mainly through the Middle East where several trading posts were established – many long before the war. That meant permanent stand-by, for very little notice was given as to when the aircraft would be needed. She was registered in South Africa, and this time Jim made quite certain the authorities there officially approved him operating on his British licence – a letter of approval being delivered to the company's head office on 16 August, his date of joining.

In the ten days between his acceptance for the position and starting work he was measured for his uniform (which was ready for final fitting on the day) and returned to his family, who were to remain with his parents until the pattern of his work had been established, and until his first pay (to be credited monthly to his bank account was received).

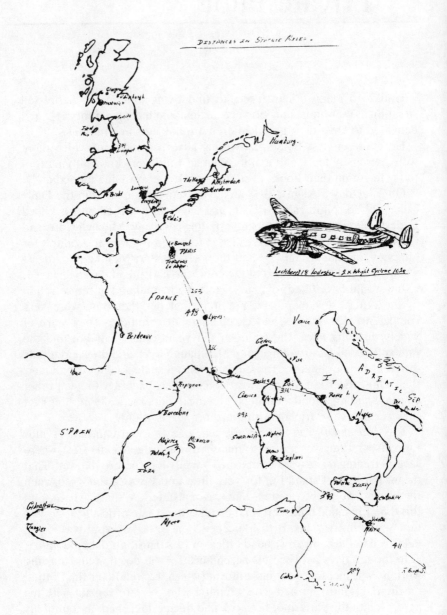

DISTANCES IN STATUTE MILES.

Lockheed 18 Lodestar - 2 x Wright Cyclone 1029

The aircraft itself was, externally, just like any other Lodestar but was fitted with the smaller Wright Cyclone G-102a engines of 1100 bhp (still having 9 radial cylinders as for the more powerful G-205as of 1200 bhp fitted to the BOAC machines) – the same engine type as fitted to the BOAC No. 5 Line Ensigns. Fuselage and wings were highly polished, gleaming silver, with the company's logo on the nose – no flashy flashes down the sides. Inside was a different world altogether.

The upholstery was dark green, patterned curtains at the windows, a huge couch down the left side which could be made up as a bed; two sets of single seats on the right side (one facing forward the other aft) with a table between each pair – those four armchairs able to swivel round to face the couch for conference purposes. Up front on the left there was a large, softly polished, wooden desk with real silver inkwells. Opposite that on the right, was a single seat with typing desk for use when a secretary was part of the passenger group. Toilet and galley were at the rear of the cabin, with a comfortable seat there for the steward whose main duties were valet and chauffeur to the chairman. He was one of the warmest people Jim had ever met and they soon became close friends, they and their familes remaining so for many years.

The chairman himself was a mild mannered, considerate, and thoroughly pleasant man – quite unlike the popular image of powerful executives of very large companies. There was no doubt at all, however, that he was very much in charge of affairs; treated with tremendous respect by all and sundry wherever he went, and not just because of his gentlemanly manner. He had, unfortunately a heart condition which necessitated flying at the lowest practicable altitude – as little above 5000 feet as possible.

The aircraft had been at Prestwick, where Scottish Aviation had been fitting a modified brake system. The crew collected her from there on 23 August, after making their first flights together whilst testing and checking her equipment on the 21 August. She was based at Croydon where, during the next four days they polished up the wings and fuselage, and the interior woodwork and became familiar with every nook and cranny as well as settling down with each other. Having worked with them all the time with the polishing, Jim made it clear that he would not be asking either of the others to do anything that he was not prepared to do himself (other than their specific jobs) and their manner started to ease a little.

Both were very strong left-wing socialists and it had not been lost upon Jim that they had been stiff and suspicious of him (clearly conservative in attitude) and he made a mental note to steer well clear of any political conversation. They were clean, well mannered, and conscientious and had strong senses of humour, each in his own way, and Jim found himself warming to them. By the time they took off on 28 August bound for Cairo to pick up the chairman and his party, the three of them had become a happy and cohesive team. There were no passengers so they would have plenty of time to settle in together operationally in the two-day trip.

Croydon to Marignane (Marseilles) then on to Malta for nightstop. The next day it was via El Adem to Cairo arriving 3pm local time. They were met by the chairman's valet, George, whom Jim introduced to Arthur, the radio officer, and John the engineer. The chairman had asked that he meet the crew (who were invited to join him for drinks before dinner that evening) – a very pleasant three quarters of an hour before he suggested George join the crew and take them out to dinner and get to know each other. He suggested a well known and expensive restaurant telling George to sign for the meal to be billed to the company's Cairo office – that is unless they had other plans, but in any case for George to settle the account. They followed his suggestion, enjoyed a superb meal, and by the end of the evening were firm friends.

The next morning, 30 August take off was 8am, with the chairman, a finance director from the South African office, and an accountant from the Benghazi office as passengers. A four hour flight direct to Benina for a two hour stop for inspection and short conference (dropping off the accountant at his home base) – a good lunch for the crew whilst that was going on – then on the Castel Benito for a nightstop in Tripoli. At both places the crew were introduced to all the local employees of the company. On 31 August the day's journey was to Rome via Malta, not so much for refuelling but for an hour's meeting with the company's man in Valetta.

The Rome stop was for three nights (two whole free days for the crew whilst a major conference took place) which John and Arthur enjoyed immensely, being their first visit to the city – Jim showing off a bit with his slightly superior knowledge. He was able to contact Mario who acted once again as guide, though this time as a friend. He learned that at least he had been fully paid up for his efforts for the Australian migrant charter company – probably because his accounts were handled through the British travel agent, which finally refused to do any more themselves.

On 3 September there was a short flight to Marignane for a nightstop in Marseilles, then on the next day to Paris where the company office was a major one and where the chairman had a permanent flat (his charming wife was French). Jim was able to renew his acquaintance with Toussous le Noble aerodrome, but it simply was not the same without Jacques being there. Then it was back to Croydon on 5 September.

On 14 September they were off again to Paris, this time to Le Bourget airport where future flights would route as a new agent had been appointed there. It was closer to the city too, taking half the time by road than from Toussous. This time the chairman had his wife with him and another executive, also with wife, and the stay was for two and a half days. The crew enjoyed that lovely city, lazing about in the sidewalk cafés of the Champs Elysée in beautiful weather and visiting most of the places of interest – historic and entertainment.

Aircraft used solely for executive purposes often spend a lot of time not flying. However, when they are needed it will usually be with very little notice so they must always be kept maintained right up to the minute and test or check flown regularly. They are very much a prestige luxury and are an enormous expense, though in the case of Mitchell Cotts in those early days of post-war airlines there were not the vast number of world wide services available as there are today (1980s). Also very few airlines operated pressurised aircraft, which the chairman would have had to have had if flying with them, for they could not have been restricted to 5000 feet type flying for him.

Finally, most of the places he needed to visit his company's considerable number of overseas offices were not served at all by other than charter aircraft. These remarks are being made to help in understanding why the company had an aircraft, and a costly crew on permanent paid stand-by. Otherwise none of the following would be comprehensible in respect of plain common sense.

Arriving back at Croydon on 16 September it was to be almost seven months (to mid-April 1949) before the Lodestar was again to be used on company business. The crew were retained throughout on full pay and allowances, but feeling guilty about it (which they did) did not alter the fact of the matter. The only alternative was to resign and try to find another job with more action in a market for all kinds of aircrew (and ground engineers) where jobs available were as rare as hen's teeth.

For no doubt a myriad of good reasons, it was fortunate for the company to say the least that the chairman did not in any case need to use his superb aerial carriage until the middle of April the following year. So the sequence of events after arriving at Croydon from Paris that September of 1948 did not inconvenience him, although the expense of them must have given the company accountants migraine.

A mandatory strengthening of certain wing panels had been recommended by Lockheed Aircraft, in view of some stress fractures found in a few machines. That work, after a delay in receipt of the modification kit, was completed by Scottish Aviation by 19 October, after which just one more short trip was made to Paris, before it was decided to have all the latest radio aids fitted which were required by a new regulation barring any aircraft not so equipped from landing at major airports in bad weather. Airwork did that job which was completed on 23 December 1948. The crew dispersed for Christmas and New Year, Jim back with his family in their Croydon home.

Almost unbelievably, on 8 January, new regulations were introduced making it necessary for the aircraft's anti-fire systems to be modified (extensively!) so once again it was up to Prestwick, and that was a mandatory matter inescapable if the aircraft was to retain it's Certificate of Airworthiness. The work would have taken less than a week had the parts for the modification been available, but it took three months, to 13 April 1949, before she was again ready for the chairman's use!

What John and Arthur did in their paid holiday time goodness knows, though Arthur did get married to a Liverpool lass to whom he had been engaged for some time. Jim occupied a good deal of his time, firstly making up a comprehensive route manual from which the chairman (and the secretary who was responsible in London for planning the use of the aircraft) would be able to calculate easily approximate route times and payloads, subject to prevailing conditions at the time of flight. Also he designed an accounting system (for his own use) in respect of the operation.

One of the duties the captain of that aircraft was required to do was the keeping of double entry accounts for all running expenses, crew allowances and advances, hotel and food bills, landing and other charges. A monthly report which had to be submitted to Johannesburg accounts department, with a copy of course to the London Office. There were six accounts, a day book, and a currency exchange book (in which seven different currencies recorded sums received from various transactions en-route, cross-referenced to the sterling float and against each other). Perhaps it was fortunate that, at the time of leaving Airwork, he had started a correspondence course with a view to membership of the British Institute of Export, the initial exercises being in bookeeping and accountancy. He never completed that course, but what he had done certainly made the current task very much easier.

It was during this time that the Ministry of Civil Aviation (as it was then known) and the Air Registration Board in Britain started to tighten up on every aspect of the regulations governing safety of flight and operation, in particular of commercial aircraft. They had been working on it for a long time and the result was a far-ranging change in construction, maintenance, engineers and aircrew licence and operational standards, and company operating procedures. Jim's company, being a private aircraft operator, was not tied so strictly as commercial operators but their executives, the chairman in particular, were very valuable people so every conceivable modification and addition of full equipment had been carried out – regardless of cost.

Part of the new regulations was that pilots operating in bad weather into major airports (not just commercial pilots, for whom it was mandatory) must hold an instrument rating which covered their expertise in using the latest navigation and landing systems and had to be renewed by in-flight examination every year. Similar qualification had been in force in the USA before the war (where radio navigation aids – radio ranges in particular – were installed extensively all over the States and Canada) and had been recently introduced in Australia. This gave Jim the opportunity to undertake a full course (with Scottish Aviation who had all the necessary simulator – link trainer in those days – facilities) to achieve the necessary standard to obtain that rating when the time came in January 1950. Meanwhile, practice on the company aircraft kept his hand in.

Finally back in operation the Lodestar was required (between 14 and 19 April 1949 to fly two shuttles to and from Amsterdam (Schipol). In May, Rome and Marseilles were visited again, followed by two trips to Paris before (yet again) going to Prestwick – this time to have new carpets and curtains fitted, also a new galley/buffet unit. On 23 June the chairman was picked up in Paris before starting a long trip to Khartoum via Lyons, Rome nightstop, Malta to Tripoli the next day (where four days were spent on business), then on to Cairo, arriving 7 July for a three week stop-over when the flight to Khartoum was made via Wadi Halfa.

On 1 August they returned to Cairo, that time via Luxor to visit yet another Mitchell Cotts outpost. Ten days were spent in Cairo before the return to Britain started, via El Adem and Benghazi where three days were spent. Then on to Tripoli (two days) a short hop over to Malta (four days) to Rome for a single nightstop, then back to Croydon, via Lyons on 21 August 1949. Throughout the entire trip all flying had to be done under 5,000 feet, the chairman's health having deteriorated and his doctor insisting he must not fly otherwise. Fortunately at no time on the routes followed was there high enough ground to prevent keeping to that restriction. Apart from that he remained all the time his usual courteous self, and obviously showed no sign of deterioration in his business acumen. That trip was to be his last. There had been investigations into having a Dakota (DC3) modified to incorporate a pressurised compartment for him, but the costs and especially the time taken to design and obtain an Airworthiness Certificate were quite impractical.

It had been exactly one year to the day since the first flight, during which a mere 150 hours had been flown. That should be measured in terms of value the chairman had to his widespread organisation, not as an extremely inefficient and costly use of an aeroplane. His death not long after must have been a major blow to the company.

Despite the frustration involved in having to hang about waiting to fly, it was a privilege to have been employed by that company. All the staff, wherever Jim went, and not just the chairman himself, were a real pleasure to have known. The decision to discontinue the aircraft was not finalised until the middle of November. The crew were retained all the time then given two months pay in lieu of notice in addition, which was generous in the extreme. However, with jobs still very scarce, it was more than welcome and typical of that company's consideration for its employees.

Jim's flying time had crept up to just over 6000 hours (4420 in command) by this time so he had plenty of experience to sell should a position become vacant. He was lucky to find work with Silver City Airways, not as a pilot but as manager of their cross channel car-ferry service, operating from the pretty grass airfield of Lympne (Kent), not far from Folkestone. The operation was relatively new, carrying up to three cars in Bristol 170 freighters over to Le Touquet in France – just a 30 minute flight, the car passengers in a comfortable cabin in the rear.

He was able to get in a few hours flying the company's twin-engined Airspeed Consul (civil version of the famous Oxford) and single-engined Percival Proctor, a few trips as co-pilot in the Bristols, and an occasional charter in an Auster operated by a small company at the same airfield – Air Kruise Ltd.

Otherwise he ran a small office together with a young, and very efficient, traffic officer. It was interesting, a particularly pleasant place to live and work, and the staff had the courtesy of use of the beautiful Lympne Country Club.

That was situated just outside the airfield boundary and had been owned and run by a friendly, charming couple since way before the war. Those were the days of a flying club and also a refuelling stop for Imperial Airways HP42 Hannibal type aircraft, en-route from Croydon to Paris (or return) whenever there were strong headwinds.

It was a happy four months, then the offer of a permanent flying job came up, based at Croydon, with Transair Ltd. They operated night mail and newspaper services with Avro Anson I type aircraft fitted with two Armstrong Whitworth Cheetah IX engines of 365 bhp each.

18 On Course II – Night mail and newspaper services

TRANSAIR (I)

Work with Transair started 9 June 1950, and was the beginning of an association which lasted fifteen years to June 1965. There were two breaks in actual employment with the company, (both Jim's choice), but there was never loss of touch. The owner and managing director, Gerry Freeman, was the best boss Jim ever worked for (with respect to most others, but Mr Freeman stood out head and shoulders above any other) in his flying career. A shrewd, brilliant businessman, he was also a kind and very understanding person, concerned for all his staff. They were strongly loyal to him, as he was to them, the majority remaining for many years with the company.

In 1947 Mr Freeman had acquired seven Avro Ansons from RAF war surplus stocks, a type which had been used mainly by Coastal Command during the war. It is believed two of them were still in crates – new at the time of purchase. Whatever, war surplus prices were relatively low and, by selling them to his company through a hire purchase firm at a price close to proper market value, he created a viable working capital with which to start operations. Out of the seven, five were assembled to obtain Certificates of Airworthiness and their civil registrations.

Contracts with the Post Office (Royal Mail) and with newspaper companies had been obtained and the night flights to and from Paris, Brussels, and the Channel Islands (Jersey and Guernsey) were started to which, later on, was added Belfast via Manchester.

A proud record of reliability had been built up by the time Jim was privileged to join, with only two flight cancellations having to be made over the previous three years, (a cancellation was considered to be when a load could not be delivered within 24 hours of schedule). Weather did of course affect some flights, causing delays of lesser time factor, but these had been very, very few.

The Anson was a stolid, reliable, and simple machine to fly, cruising at 135 knots (150 mph – having been used by Coastal Command the airspeed registered in nautical miles per hour). It had docile handling qualities, wonderful manoeuvrability, and a low landing speed. The crews were very experienced and long practised in bad weather flying conditions. The engineers were top class, also very experienced, so the background for reliable operations was well and truly built in.

The Anson I was a simple machine in more ways than one, in fact two of its features were downright primitive. The crew of captain and radio officer (there were eleven of each and all happily 'mixable') would share most of any chores outside their particular basic function.

Engine starting was achieved by insertion of a crank handle in the engine nacelle, behind the propeller, and winding away (after operating a Ki-Gass primer pump) whilst the pilot activated a booster coil (from the cockpit) until the engine fired. Too much primer, and it could be critical, meant turning the propeller backwards eight turns or more to blow out the over-rich mixture, then going through the crank-winding procedure again. The r/os were pretty expert at that job, so it was not often a second go had to be made.

Somewhat dishevelled by the time both engines were going and he had settled down in the right hand seat in the cockpit, going through the check list with the pilot to ensure all pre-take off actions were done and correct (this whilst taxiing out towards the runway) he would just about have got his breath back after becoming airborne, when a second bit of primitive mechanics had to be activated. The undercarriage retraction method involved the winding of another crank handle 136 turns. If the pilot was not too busy on instruments he could sometimes assist for a few turns (the handle being on the right side of his seat) but that meant bending down quite a bit unless he was tall with long arms. After that the r/o would start his main duties by letting out the trailing aerial before operating his morse key – (there was a small VHF voice/audio set fitted for short-range communication, but the main radio link was by morse).

Before landing (either before or after winding down the under carriage – the weight of that did help the winding process even to a point where, should the hand slip off the crank, that could whip around and fetch a wrist or arm a good thwack) the trailing aerial had to be wound in. That was not hard work but, if forgotten (and it was on the odd occasion) the row of lead weights trailing 100 feet or so below and behind the aircraft could do damage to personnel or ground equipment before landing. The aerial and weights were, as a secondary consideration, quite expensive and rarely retrievable. When that happened it was the pilot as much as the r/o to blame, for he (the pilot) must surely have failed to check the trailing aerial in with his mate before making final approach to land.

The brakes were operated pneumatically from two air bottles. There was no compressor fitted to the engines so they had to be topped up whilst on the ground. Due to the low landing speed the brakes were rarely needed to slow down (except on a very short field, when they were very effective) but were needed for differential steering during taxiing. That could use quite a bit of air, so bottle-topping was important.

There was no de- or anti-icing equipment so, in winter, the leading edges of wings and tailplane were liberally daubed with an anti-icing paste. Certainly when fresh it did help deter ice formation but the airspeed suffered somewhat. Fortunately the old ladies were able to cope with quite a lot of ice formation without falling out of the sky.

Carburettor icing was a serious problem in the earlier days and there were several incidents, including a serious accident which occurred at night flying over Belgium in a heavy snowstorm. Both engines quit, together, leaving the pilot nothing else to do but glide straight ahead from 2000 feet, snow build-up on the windscreen part blinding him, the landing lights reflecting back off the snow, to belly land. Fortunately the field was flat where they slid on at a shallow, no flap, glide angle. A ditch (or fence) brought the machine up sharply and it was a write-off. The pilot had his right foot badly injured otherwise, incredibly, there were no other injuries. After a long period in a Belgium hospital it was feared he might lose the foot, but a famous Scottish bone-surgeon (engaged by Mr Freeman) saved the foot. With a slight limp and some occasional pain for the rest of his life the pilot was able to carry on with a flying career which became really exceptional.

It is he to whom this book is dedicated, and of whom more is written later on.

Modifications were made to those carburettors pretty smartly after that, and there were no more icing problems with them. Perhaps it would be fair to speculate that, at the low level over-the-sea type of Coastal Command operations, carburettor icing may not have been a serious problem – otherwise no doubt modifications would have been made earlier. The Transair operation exposed the aircraft to very different conditions, particularly in winter.

The newspaper flight to Brussels involved a short sleep there. The accommodation provided on the airport was interesting to say the least (or best might be a better description). The company had regular contract work but as yet was unable to pay high wages or provide luxury accommodation for its crews. It was a measure of the entire staff's high regard for their boss that they not only made the most of some pretty primitive conditions, but actually enjoyed feeling and knowing that they were playing an integral part in the building of a great company.

Anyway (to revert to the Brussels nightstop arrangements) there were two iron bedsteads, with firm mattresses and an adequate supply of ex-army blankets, in a Nissen hut, an end area of which was partitioned off from a storeroom. Duckboards laid a path to the entrance and formed partial flooring inside to, and by, the beds. In winter, or any time it rained, the inside boards would be awash but, with knee high flying boots, the feet remained dry. Once perched on the bed the boots were taken off then hung from either top or bottom bedrails. Clothing was not removed, and heads went down on pillows (with cases provided from Croydon, changed weekly by the Wednesday crew – nobody worried about sharing the increasingly grubby pillow cases; it was, after all, in the family so to speak) for a three-to-four hour kip from the 2am arrival time to when the airport noises grew too much for sleep.

Some crew members actually brought sheets from home, but for Jim that seemed impractical as they would be cold and absorb damp (of which there was plenty) and plain blankets are warmth engendering and retaining. He did, however, always take a hot water bottle with large flask of water, boiling when filled at home, to hurry the warming process. The crew would breakfast in bed (what luxury!) from flasks of hot beverage and whatever was found in the package made up at home the night before. There was no hurry, the return flight starting around 9am via Lille (a 40 minute flight) to load textiles, which arrived at the airport there at any time in the first part of the morning – usually in time for a departure for Croydon somewhere about 11am. When that freight was on board there was room on top for the crew to crawl over it into the cockpit – the r/o getting a bit more exercise than usual after winding up the engines!

The flights to Paris, two per night, were quite different. The mail aircraft went out and back the same night, with the same crew who would then often continue in the early morning with newspapers to the Channel Isles. The newspaper craft changed crew at Le Bourget, arriving about 2am, for the previous crew to take the flight back to Croydon and, if necessary, be available to do the early morning Channel Isles run in the event the normal crew were delayed, sick, or unable to operate it for whatever reason. Because of having had 24 hours rest in Paris that returning newspaper crew were fresh enough to undertake any special daylight flight which might have come up – the trip up to Benbecula in the Hebrides for lobsters (described in detail later on) for instance.

The hotel, just across the road from Le Bourget, was a very small one – oddly enough not very noisy. It was very typically French in a non-luxurious way, simple but clean and cosy. Madame brought breakfast – a bowl (not cup) of strong black coffee, butter and jam, and a fresh warm croissant – when the bell was rung, so there was all the time in the world to sleep as long as the individual wished.

A few yards along the road was a marvellous restaurant, again small and quite unpretentious in decor, but with some of the best cooking Jim encountered anywhere. The chef was the owner and his wife waitress and barmaid. They were good friends to all the crews, and remained so years after that particular schedule ceased, in particular Charlie Coates, himself a gourmet cook amongst his many other gregarious attributes, who kept in touch with his chef friend whenever he visited Paris over the years ahead.

There was time to go into the city during the day, get back for an early meal, then top up with sleep during the evening. The incoming crew's rooms were different from the outgoing so, unless the hotel needed the two rooms for other guests after 11pm, the didn't have to change the bed linen of the outgoers until the next day. The reason for that schedule (possible crew availability options described above) was tied in with mandatory rest periods and maximum duty hours in a day, week, and month, and to enable the company to use their crews as economically as those rules allowed.

The newspaper flights to the Channel Isles started about two hours before sunrise, the trip times averaging one and three quarter hours and so landing about 15 minutes before dawn. Neither Jersey nor Guernsey had instrument landing systems at that time and, as weather seemed always to be bad in the early mornings (at least unreliable compared to the general forecast, as is often the case with islands) it was more sensible to arrive when able to have light to make approach and landing. That, very often, could mean very low circuits in strong winds under scud clouds only 100 feet or so above aerodrome level which (at Jersey) was close to 200 feet above sea level, the western edge of the single runway dropping away near vertically to the coastline. Prevailing winds would be from the west or south-west, so approach would normally be from the east where the land, fortunately, was pretty level with the aerodrome. With the superb low speed manoeuvrability of the Anson the exercise was nowhere near as dicey as it may sound. In fact, when landing from the other direction in easterly winds on to the runway whose threshold was right on the edge of that vertical cliff, the up/down draughts could be quite violent and the task much more difficult than for a landing the other way.

Sometimes there was freight (such as flowers from either island or tomatoes from Guernsey) for the return trip to Croydon. Whatever, there was always time for a good breakfast, provided in their own home by the newspaper agent and his wife. It was a popular run with no rush or hassle.

There were some charters, and two Airspeed Consuls (the post-war civil version of the famous RAF Oxford), with normal passenger seating, were available. One of the Ansons was modified to have self-starters and fitted with seats, also used for passenger charters. Those three aircraft were still used for freight work, with the seats removed, which was most of the time. To have said that seats were put in place when passenger charters happened would have been more appropriate!

Uniforms, provided by the company, were based on two pairs of trousers, with a battledress jacket for freight work and a single breasted brass-buttoned tunic for passenger work. They were navy blue with gold rank braiding (epaulettes for the battledress) and after every flight were placed in a cupboard for the company to have cleaned at their own expense. That practice continued over the years until, in 1960, Mr Freeman retired. He was making sure that none of his crew members would ever appear shabby on duty – especially with passengers, and he kept a keen personal watch on the condition of uniform caps too. It was not that he didn't trust the attitude and personal pride in appearance of his staff, but simply that he considered (when off duty) they should not have to spend time on what was, in effect, a company business – taking and picking up (and paying for) company property to/from the cleaners.

The most interesting of all the charters was the freighting of lobsters from Benbecula (the small island separating North from South Uist in the outer Hebrides) and crayfish from Shannon in Ireland. The flight to Benbecula was empty, via Prestwick to refuel and (vitally important) to check the latest actual weather at Benbecula before the actual one and three quarter hour leg time. It could change very rapidly from foul to impossibly so, and in Jim's experience it was rarely even marginally pleasant. Once down and in the warmth of the airport (yes, it was so categorised!) a good hot lunch was provided in the terminal building whilst 39 cardboard boxes of crustaceans were loaded and the aircraft refuelled. About an hour of warming through before venturing into the raw air for take off. His first trip there was only six days after joining the company, and it was 16 June 1950. The story of it follows, and may be taken as a blueprint of five more.

The flight up to Benbecula was without incident. However, on the return trip, it was decided to refuel at Squires Gate (Blackpool) instead of Prestwick – due to a bad weather forecast for Croydon. The flying time to there was the same as from Prestwick to Croydon (two and a quarter hours), leaving only one and three quarter hours of the four hour total trip time from Benbecula to Croydon to fly, thus having greater fuel reserves in the event of being unable to land safely at Croydon. In fact those reserves would be sufficiently safe to fly direct to Le Bourget, the final destination of the load anyway. It should be appreciated that live lobsters are very delicate (in fact they must be flown at as low an altitude as possible to avoid excessive loss of fluid) and have a very limited lifespan once packed into boxes – and they had to arrive live and well or no more charters!

Normally another crew took over at Croydon for the leg to Paris, for

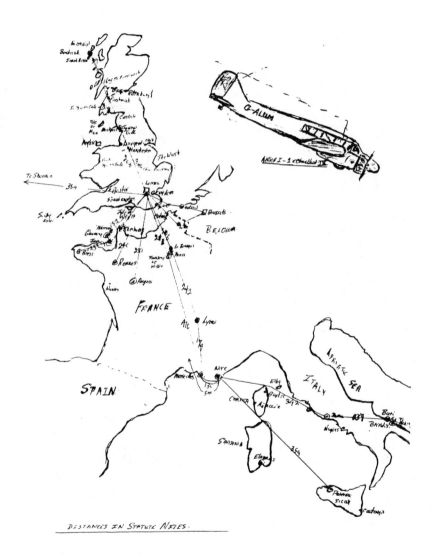

G-ALUM

ANSON I - 2 × Cheetah II

DISTANCES IN STATUTE MILES.

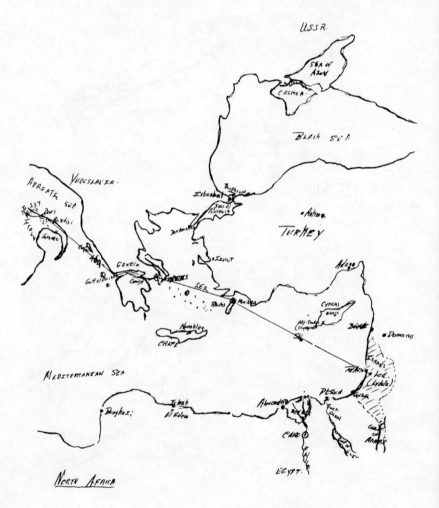

DISTANCES IN STATUTE MILES.

USSR

SEA OF AZOV

CRIMEA

BLACK SEA

YUGOSLAVIA.

ADREATIC SEA

Istanbul   Bosphorus

Sea of Marmora

Dardanelles

TURKEY

Ankara

Port Brindisi

ITALY   Taranto

GREECE

Izmit

Gulf of Corinth   Corinth

ATHENS   SEA

Rhodes   Marmaris

Aleppo

Cyprus   NICOSIA

Mt. Troodos   X   Olympus

Beirut

Damascus

Monemvasia

CRETE

SA

ISRAEL

Palestine Jod. (Lydda)

MEDITERRANEAN SEA

Benghazi

Tobruk   El Aden

Alexandria

Pt. Said

Suez Canal

GAZA

Gulf of Aqaba

CAIRO

Gulf of Suez

EGYPT.

NORTH AFRICA

the day's duty time Croydon/Benbecula/Croydon was long enough to make a mandatory rest period apply in Paris if that extra leg had to be flown by the same crew. An unnecessarily costly procedure, and loss of potential air-time for the aircraft – a very vital factor (to this day) in that an aircraft not flying is a tremendous waste of capital cost and efficiency. As it happened, in this case, it was in fact possible to land at Croydon and change crews.

As a very nice gesture to crew members on each load from Benbecula (or Shannon for that matter) two good specimens, with claws fastened by rubber bands, were placed on top of the boxes at the rear of the cabin for the crew to take home. It was not unusual (as in this case) for one or both of the monsters to be found halfway up to the cockpit (claws miraculously free) by the time Croydon was reached. After landing there this time (with the help of the SBA aural blind approach system, and a fortunate break in the low cloud) Jim and his r/o made their way down the narrow alleyway between the boxes (now soaked with the incredible amount of moisture those creatures lost during the flight) and grabbed their personal live gifts, on top and behind the claws, eventually (and on a bus at that) getting them home and into the pot without getting nipped. Oh, didn't that very fresh lobster taste delicious, and how superior Jim felt to those Parisians and the tourists who might be enjoying their feast as much, but paying a small fortune for it. The value of the pay one receives for the work one does bears great relationship to the joy of the perks!

The effectiveness of the Anson's brakes has been mentioned. They, as with most other aircraft, are essential but less so than with the others. Taxiing with none (in the Anson) was simple, using differential engine power and given a wide enough taxi track clearly defined. However, one dark night Jim landed at Le Bourget with newspapers, rolled almost to a stop by a taxiway intersection to find no brakes available for steering so, using the engines, he was able to proceed towards the parking area. No problem, but to enter safely that area (clustered with parked machines) without brakes was impossible. So, he shut off the engines on the final taxi strip, uphill a little bit, to roll to a halt. That halt was in long grass to the right, as he had intended, but in the day or two since his last visit a ditch had been dug (without any markers) into which the aircraft dropped, almost at nil miles per hour.

It was not badly damaged and the crew were unhurt, except for the r/o who had a small cut (bleeding profusely as such do) on his forehead. With its undercarriage locked down it was flown the next day back to Croydon, by another crew, for a repair lasting few enough hours for it to be flying again the same night on a similar newspaper service. This minor incident is quoted mainly to illustrate the type of person the boss was. He had a strict rule that he must be the first person contacted in the event of anything serious going wrong – not matter what time of the day or night. So Jim rang him at 3am that morning at home. The first thing he said was. . 'Are you and Chris all right?'. . . no query about how, why and what had happened, his only worry about their wellbeing. After being told he said . . 'Okay Jim, don't worry, go to bed and get a good sleep'. . . He never changed that attitude, and Jim never saw him lose his temper – get angry, yes, the voice and eyes hardening like steel, not a decibel above the usual even tone but the message abundantly clear, never to be repeated!

Shortly after that first lobster run, still in the June he joined the company, there was a delivery flight made, with an Anson, to Israel – now a fledgling country in its own right. A co-pilot, a Dutch-born Jew and an excellent fellow (who would be introducing the type into local short distance operations) came with them. It was truly a fun flight, the first stop at Nice being protracted due to a radio fault which took two clear days to fix. That lovely, to Jim, small intimate baby city, loaded with atmosphere, panache, and beautiful food, freely abounding yet unpressurised nightlife, and incredible views will always remain a treasured memory. Subsequent visits over the next fifteen years confirmed, and added to, that first impression during that protracted stay.

Additionally, a first and only ever nightstop in Rhodes was experienced. The weather was perfect and the night air scented with a pithy mixture of geranium and jasmine.

The route followed was Toussous le Noble, Nice, Bari, Athens, Rhodes, then direct to Lydda – not by then renamed 'Lod'. One only nightstop in Tel Aviv, where the incredibly tough food shortage seemed worse than anything experienced in Britain during, and especially immediately after, the war. Some fish and lots of potatoes were the main offerings in restaurants. The shortages underlined the hardships of a new nation struggling to accommodate an ever-increasing population of refugees with, at that 1950 time, not a great deal of help from outside. El Al, the new Israeli airline provided with a Lockheed Constellation aircraft from the USA, had a strictly austerity flight as far as Paris for Jim and his r/o, who went to Croydon appropriately stretched out on the mailbags of the normal Transair night service to Croydon. It was a good trip.

19 Diversion – A big frog in a little puddle

At the end of June 1951 Jim left Transair for a job with Air Kruise at Lympne, a firm with whom he had had a close relationship during the time he was employed by Silver City. It was an opportunity to try his ability in the management field of aviation as operations manager and chief pilot. Admittedly a big frog in a little puddle as the saying goes but nevertheless a start into what he envisaged as his real and final niche in the business. He was 33 years old, had almost 7000 hours flying experience in diverse fields, and felt the need to settle down in work which might provide more stability for family life which, in recent years, had become a bit fraught with the difficulties of settling down to the routines and stresses of the situation – after nigh on twelve years (for he and his wife) of footloose and fancyfree existence.

They bought a house (on mortgage of course) high on the chalk hillside near Folkestone, eight and a half acres of it above Cheriton with a view over the Channel to the south and of Lympne to the west. It was dilapidated, four storeys in the French style, and one of the first examples of metal-tied double brick construction in Britain – early 1900s. What better place for a young family to settle, with an antique-minded wife whose hobby was scraping or sanding down old furniture to renovate to its original pristine glow. All those acres of steep hillside for the two boys to run in – and to cultivate into a champagne grape vineyard!! Well, that was the plan, and why not? It didn't work out, but never let young readers despair for it could, and should, have.

The job, which lasted for three seasons (or summers) two and a half years longer than any other since the war, was very basic. The owners and managers were a delightful couple, married after a romantic meeting on a troopship returning from Burma and India at the end of the Far Eastern war.

The job was flying De Havilland 89 Rapides (twin-engined sister of Denebola) to and from Lympne and Le Touquet 35 minutes away across the Channel in France, plus a deal of joyriding in them; a couple of single-engined Austers, and a Miles Messenger with three instead of the Auster's two passenger capability. There were two Rapides, two Austers (one of which was owned by Skyfotos which took low level photos of ships transversing the Straits of Dover) and the single Messenger. Piloting the Skyfotos Auster, with the cameraman hanging out of the removed rear window on the left side, was one of his duties – an exercise much enjoyed, and requiring a certain amount of skill to get the machine positioned just right for the required angle of shot.

He replaced a single pilot who had left to become a first officer with BEA (and later a captain), but two more were soon employed to cope with increased traffic demands. Several tourist coach companies had started operations to the Continent (in co-operation with French companies) and the short airborne channel crossing was the cheapest and quickest connection. One of the companies, Wallace Arnold, based in Halifax, Yorkshire (amongst not too many others) must be mentioned for they were the bread and butter of the summer operation – cross channel as well as local joyriding. Their customers, mostly from the north of England (Yorkshire and Lancashire in particular) were similar to those happy holiday people Jim had enjoyed so much when joyriding at Southport – outgoing, determined to enjoy themselves (not too difficult because they were game to try anything and hardly ever seemed to grumble no matter what failed to go to plan); sometimes boisterous but still good-natured, and great fun to be with.

During the six-month season the job was seven days a week, starting at 7.30am helping engineers roll out the aircraft, refuelling, then checking the day's operational plan ready for the first trip to Le Touquet at 8.45am – followed by another before a snack lunch. A typical day's schedule would then include two and a half to three hours joyriding in the Rapide, covering nine 10 minute trips carrying eight or nine passengers at a time – around 72 passengers all told. Then there would be the final return trip to Le Touquet, landing back at Lympne 9.30pm to hangar the aircraft by 10.00pm, often helped by the boss, owner and managing director. An ex-wing commander in the RAF, he had fought in the Battle of Britain and in various other theatres throughout the war, ending up in Burma. His attractive and charming wife was secretary, and a very effective public relations front for the company. They had an exceptionally loyal young man, called Walter, who performed almost any duty from batman through driver and baggage handler to refueller and marshaller. A permanently happy, smiling, calm fellow – even in the times of greatest flap when something went wrong which, in the contant pressure of those hectic seasons, was not infrequent. He and Jim soon became good friends.

During the winter months Transair employed him, on a freelance basis in agreement with Air Kruise, for periodic weekly spells relieving for pilots on leave. Not only did that keep Jim's hand in on the Ansons, and constant instrument flying, but it enabled him to have the annual

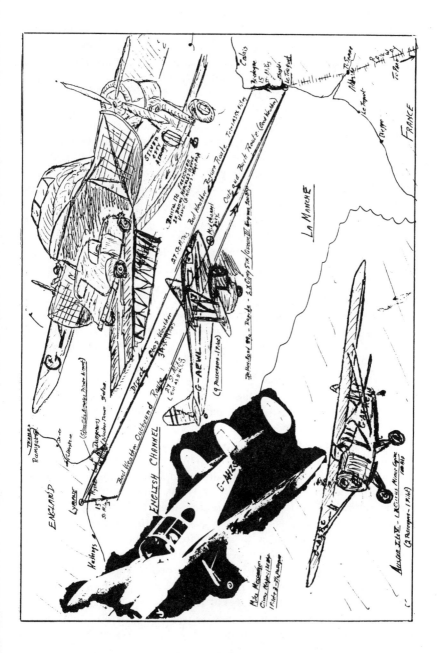

test for renewal of his instrument rating (the chief pilot being a qualified examiner, as had by then become the case with most firms). As companies progressed and grew bigger, there would often be more than one examiner approved by the Air Ministry for that purpose. A new addition to Transair operations was a contract with the RAFVR for some of their pilots to fly as co-pilots (after being given flying training on the Ansons) to gain practical experience of civil type flying. Most of them were in normal jobs but, in one case in point there was a BOAC engineer working up hours and experience towards eventual qualification for a commercial pilots licence, at the same time satisfying his commitment to the RAFVR. There were a few others doing the same thing. It was an exercise benefitting the company, the reserve pilots and the RAF and was enjoyed by all – especially the r/os who were relieved from undercarriage winding and quite a lot of engine cranking too.

Back with Air Kruise – on days when joyriders turned up individually as opposed to loads, the Austers and Messenger were used carrying respectively two or three passengers at a time. In the height of the summer holiday period those machines flew over to Ramsgate to provide joyrides from there – occasionally a Rapide would be needed also to cope with weekend demand.

The Le Touquet passengers at the weekends were mainly those going regularly to the Casino – from business men with or without wives, to film stars and directors, not necessarily together it should be understood.

Then there were a few charters, also varied in character. John Houston and Sam Spiegel at the time of the making of the film *Moulin Rouge,* Elizabeth Taylor, ill and unhappy seeking peace after divorce from Conrad Hilton, and a few regulars from the film and stage world, every one of them delightful, pleasant, and unassuming. It seemed they travelled that way because it avoided publicity, allowing them to relax, and because of an almost universal dislike of airline flying. The intimate little trip, low across the Channel in a very quiet, safe little airliner, never bumpy and lasting just 35 minutes, was ideal for them.

Some charters to Paris, in the off season for the company but which were very much in season for that city, provided a few enjoyable nightstops. At the end of one season there was an unusual charter to Marseilles with an exhausted Egyptian Channel swimmer after having had several failed attempts – he needed a bit of peace on his own at least part way home to Cairo. A particularly pleasant one was early in January 1952 with a British ballroom dancing team (the Morley Dancers) to the Hague, Holland where they won an international competition. Four most enjoyable days in a city Jim had always wanted to see, and a bonus in a complimentary ticket to watch the competition.

The log book covering February 1952 to May 1954 has been lost (out of nine all told), so details of flights cannot be told for that period. However, the general routine never varied much so no matter, but there is one thing Jim remembers clearly without the book. During that period, after many years of research, an internationally approved mandatory use of a new phonetic alphabet was introduced for use with the radio telephone (r/t) communication system. It did eliminate, very largely, the possibility of misunderstanding the pronunciation of English spoken by aircrew of other nationalities-English having been the accepted international language for use on the r/t. It was a very good introduction and not difficult to master but, to Jim at that time, it was an insult to his favourite aircraft whose registration (G-AEWL) had been known on the r/t as 'Willy Love'. It now became 'Whisky Lima', all affection and romance gone, so (for a short and very silly time as he freely admits, and only locally at Lympne and Le Touquet) he used 'Scotch and Lime' as the call sign, which caused a certain amount of amusement on that local VHF frequency for a while – other pilots had similar flutters with their call signs, the light relief soon fading away as the distinct advantages of the new system became rapidly self-evident. Locally a case in point where one of the cross-channel pilots was French (with a very thick, deep and gruff voice) whose spoken call sign in English had been totally unintelligible – not so now!

Unhappily those three seasons in two and a half years had somehow (the long hours and seven days a week no doubt contributing) had a bad effect on marital relations which, in retrospect, also affected Jim's attitude to others – to a point where relations with his employers became strained and the job untenable, for all concerned. It was very largely his own fault that a very happy period with that company ended in bitterness and the loss of a friendship with two splendid people. He hoped that he learned a lesson from it for the future, but not enough to save his marriage which broke up eighteen months later. There would be no point going into details about any of it – it was a mess with no one to blame but himself. However, it is good to be able to record that he and his wife both re-married and have maintained cordial, friendly relations ever since.

In February 1954 Transair were kind enough to accept Jim back into their happy fold. By that time the Ansons had been replaced by Douglas DC3s (C47s, Gooney Birds to the Americans, Dakotas to the British) which, in the Transair modified version was called Dakmaster. The night mail and newspaper services continued, with much greater load capacity, the Brussels service continuing on to Frankfurt returning next day (after a super and luxurious nightstop – those primitive ones of old in Brussels had paid dividends in the long run) via Paris with the US

Services newspaper the *Stars and Stripes*. Group tours, freight and passenger charters had been added to the operation, and air hostesses employed for the first time. Apart from his personal affairs he was very happy to be back amongst that congenial band of efficient, friendly brotherhood of aircrew, engineers, traffic and other staff, and their guide and mentor Mr Freeman.

Back on course – more night mail and newspapers – passenger tours – Berlin and West German internal air services – long distance freight charters.

20

TRANSAIR (II)

There were six Dakmasters, to which two more were added in May and August of 1954. For passenger carriage there were 32 seats (eight rows of four, two seats either side of a central gangway in each row) though one machine was converted and licenced to carry 36 passengers; the extra row for four being obtained by doing away with the radio officer's compartment and moving the cabin bulkhead forward to directly behind the pilots. All the seats were easily and quickly removable (or re-installed) for freight carriage, so conversion either way took very little time (a night freighter ready for early morning passenger departure for instance) so the aircraft all had extremely small ground time – very efficient. The fleet expanded further to a total of twelve until, in the 1960s they were phased out with the acquisition of Vickers Viscounts.

With the Daks requiring two pilots for commercial operation the aircrew had more than doubled, so Jim was employed this time as a co-pilot until such time as a command vacancy should occur – that was not until January 1955. It was in fact a good thing for, in his 7461 hours total to date only 1080 had been as co-pilot, and he had to adjust his thinking and actions to a support role. That did much in those ten months towards his appreciation of and attitude to his future first officers. It was all made easy for him in any case as his skippers were mainly colleagues from the Anson days (when they were all in command without co-pilots) so he just took pride in trying to be the best first officer in the fleet, though there were such a good crowd of them he supposed he was no better in fact than any others. Anyway, he enjoyed the exercise, was quite sure he benefited greatly from it and certain that, when he was restored to command, he would be the better captain for it. He had benefited from observing other captain's methods and experiences, also in crew relationships where the relatively new scene involving air hostesses was concerned.

The moment has come for Jim's eulogy to the air hostess – stewardess if you like; same difference. His log books record the names of 662 of them, including the two with Airwork in 1946/47. He remembered the faces, and characteristics, of every single one of them when read out to him – now that's a recall percentage clearly illustrating the value of the lasting impressions they made on him (and they were not all Marilyn Monroes by any means!). Christian names for some he has forgotten, particularly the German girls who are mainly recorded as Fraulein this, that, or the other in his logs, though many are recorded.

The hotesses were essential and still are for their immaculately trained importance in the event of emergency (even unusual) situations requiring firm, tactful, and competent handling of passengers, for which they are regularly checked out. Their value in public relations, both airborne and on the ground, ensuring passenger comfort and flight enjoyment (and countering the occasional difficult one) is immense. They certainly were not, any more than today, simply airborne waitresses. In the era covered by this narrative (before the advent of wide-bodied jets) when passenger loads were relatively small and individual attention could be given, the peace of mind for the captain (knowing that the passenger cabin was in firm control no matter what the flight conditions) cannot be over-estimated. Jim considers it a privilege to have flown with them, known them, and here records his big thank you – knowing full well that honest comments such as bullshit and silly old bastard may result from some, if they happen to read this – (of course, from others, it is possible that comment could be unprintable, but one can't win all the time!). Wonderful, supportive, and very, very valuable crew members.

Tours flights to Innsbruck, Salzburg, Vienna, and Klagenfurt in Austria – Lourdes, Toulouse, Perpignan and Basle in France – Majorca, Barcelona, and Bilbao in Spain, were a regular part of the summer holiday routine. Also Pisa/Italy and Alghero and Cagliari (Elmas) in Sardinia. The night mail and newspaper bread and butter schedules ran all the year round, and they were supplemented by quite a few long charter flights – to Karachi with a load of phosphorus, for which a 200 gallon long range tank was fitted in the fuselage. To Singapore with two Bristol Hercules engines for the RAF at Changi, returning with two needing overhaul, and it was on this one that once again the boss (on holiday in Nice) showed his concern for his people.

The trip landed there one day ahead of schedule, and would have continued on to RAF Lyneham that day, a Sunday. Gerry Freeman, as ever, had followed the progress of all but the regular flights even when, as on this occasion, on holiday. He met the crew at Nice airport to thank them for carrying out a long job well, let alone ahead of schedule. He suggested that they stay overnight in Nice, as arrival on a Sunday in England would mean that there certainly would be no offloading facilities available, and a not so comfortable night for them on the RAF station. Needless to say the captain agreed, his original intention to go on to Lyneham being in line with the company crews' thinking at all times – it would have saved the company money. The boss had anticipated that this suggestion would be accepted, had already booked accommodation, and gave the skipper a fistful of francs to ensure the crew enjoyed to the full that unexpected nightstop.

Then there was a trip to Columbo in Ceylon with ship's spares. Another to Nairobi with rolled cans made in France, returning with pineapple in completed cans. To Aden with ship's bolts, to Malta with passengers and general freight, to Lisbon to pick up 31 passengers from an incapacitated flying boat – a sad event to Jim, whose love of flying boats remains dominant in his mind, for it was the last flight of the last boat company to operate from Britain, Aquila. There was a charter to Israel for their national airline, El Al, involving two shuttle flights between Athens and Nicosia. To Amsterdam with the Plymouth ladies choir, and to Le Mans for the 24 hour race. Those were but a few – the ones Jim flew as co-pilot in those first ten months of return to the company he enjoyed most of all. There were many more made in the same period, a measure of the tremendous expansion and consolidation experienced under the shrewd direction of its managing director.

On 19 January 1955 Jim was back in command, having done a little over 700 hours as co-pilot since rejoining the company and having enjoyed every one of them. His pay was once again in the thousand a year (£1100 to be exact), soon to be increased along with everyone elses' to £1200 per annum. In addition (and this was ever since the firm's beginning) Mr Freeman had at Christmas given a bonus to all his staff – subject to the company having made a profit. A percentage of net profit (after tax and the usual business provisions towards reserves) was divided equally amongst the staff – no loading for seniority or importance of position, just an equal flat sum each (and that could exceed a week's wages for the most highly paid staff) for it was a reward for the whole team effort, that put in by the most junior member being adjudged just the same as that put in by the boss himself; salary differentials took care of any day to day differences in skills or whatever.

That man knew how to appreciate his staff without thought of bribe or incentive. Of course that bonus was an incentive, but it was his

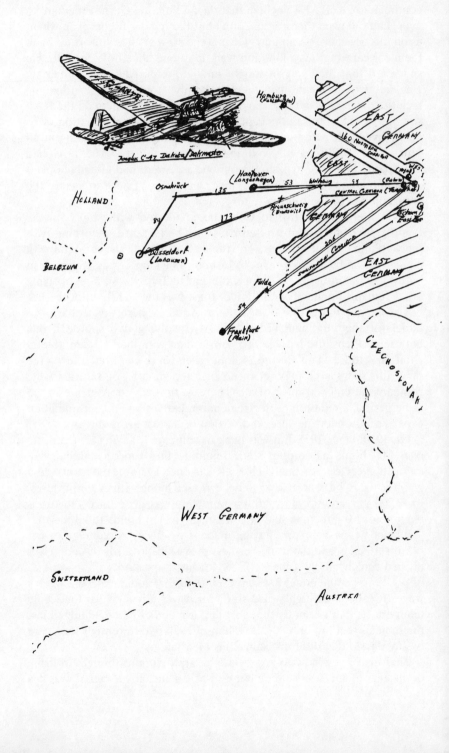

Douglas C-47 Dakota Dartmaster

Hamburg (Fuhlsbüttel)

EAST GERMANY

160 NORTHERN CORRIDOR

EAST GERMANY

Wisp

Hannover (Langenhagen)   53   Wolfsburg   55   Gatow

Osnabrück   135   CENTRAL CORRIDOR (Tempelhof)

HOLLAND   Braunschweig (Brunswick)   Berlin (East & West)

89   173   GERMANY

BELGIUM   Düsseldorf (Lohausen)   204   SOUTHERN CORRIDOR   EAST GERMANY

Fulda

54

Frankfurt (Main)   CZECHOSLOVAKIA

WEST GERMANY

SWITZERLAND   AUSTRIA

constant care and feeling for them, particularly if they had personal problems, that was the biggest incentive of all. Little wonder his team would do literally anything for him, their families backing them up wholeheartedly, and the company they were all so proud to work for.

On 11 June 1955 began an entirely new era for Jim, operationally and personally. The company had been awarded a contract by Air Charter to assist them to operate passenger flights from Berlin (Tempelhof) on internal routes through to West Germany via the ten-mile-wide air corridors over Russian occupied territory to Hamburg, Hanover, Dusseldorf, Frankfurt, and Koln Bonn (Wahn). The main contract was with British European Airways (BEA) who operated throughout the year as the British National Airline (alongside Pan American and Air France for their countries) on those routes – in accordance with the four power agreement governing the occupation of Berlin. Air Charter was owned and managed by the redoubtable Freddy Laker (now Sir Freddy) and had played a major role in the Berlin airlift in 1948, so their aircrew were very experienced in the far from simple air corridor operation. That saved many headaches for the Transair crews (being able to learn from them) for to stray outside those narrow corridors (with an upper limit of 10,000 feet) was to invite interception by Russian Mig fighters and a probability of being forced to land in Russian controlled East Germany.

Passengers were mainly German, West Germans on business, occasional film stars making films in Berlin and their directors and, outbound, vast numbers of refugees from East Germany for whom extra flights were put on. The Daks carried 32 passengers and Air Charter's Douglas DC4s nearly twice that with their four engines. BEA operated 32 passengers Dakotas and Pan American (also out of Tempelhof, which was under the control of the USAF) Douglas DC6s with greater capacity still. Air France, operating out of Tegel airport in the French sector of Berlin, used Lockheed Constellations. Gatow, in the British sector, remained mainly for the RAF but was available as an alternative in the event of bad weather conditions at the other airports.

Tempelhof airport must be unique in the world, situated in the American sector of and right in the centre of the city itself. In the shape of a wide oval, surrounded on three sides by four or five storey flats and the tall semicircle of the airport buildings to the north, the south side bounded by the 'S'-Bahn (a circle-line type railway which runs through both East and West sectors of the divided city). There were two runways, neither very long but enough for aircraft as big as the DC6s and DC4s (and military aircraft such as the Lockheed C34s operated by the USAF MATS network). The main one, running due east/west, was approached from the east through a narrow gap in the blocks of flats on that side called the 'slot', and was fairly open on the west side.

The secondary runway had blocks of flats at both ends, not more than 200 yards from the thresholds, and could be used only in clear weather and with a very steep final approach. Running round the northern side were the airport buildings, in the central third of which was the apron on which aircraft parked to on/offload. That bit was covered with an enormous cantilever roofing (completed in 1932) which is surely one of the engineering marvels of the world. It was wide enough to shelter three aircraft abreast – that is two and a half wingspans of a DC6 or about 350 feet, thus allowing passengers from three aircraft to board or alight without getting wet.

Instrument approaches (and they were very much in the majority all year round, the winter being close to 100%) were made using ILS, the pilot operated visual instrument landing system (in either direction on the main runway) or GCA, the ground controlled approach system using radar operated by controllers working in a caravan or hut close to the runway and guiding pilots by voice direction down the glide slope on to the centreline of the runway

It takes quite a lot of trust for a pilot to put himself in the hands of an outside influence for control in really bad weather approaches – by that is meant cloud base of 200 feet or less, allied with runway visibilities (RVR or Runway Visual Range) down to 600 yards, often with gusty crosswinds. Many pilots still preferred in those days to use the visual ILS display in the cockpit and their own judgement. Jim's experience generally (in the very tricky Tempelhof situation in particular) preferred a system which allowed him to relax and follow the directions of highly trained competent operators. These were in fact doing most of the sweating of intense concentration and interpretive effort to guide several tons of aircraft travelling at speeds around 130 mph to a position right in line with, and the correct height above, the runway threshold to a safe landing - the pilot becoming visual only seconds before touchdown.

Being in the American sector, control of the airport was the responsibility of the USAF, whose personnel operated the GCA unit, the senior controller being a non-commissioned officer with a Mexican sounding name – and looks too. In Jim's opinion, shared by many of his colleagues, that man was quite the best of any – and he has a great respect for all (both civil and service) controllers wherever in the world he had used their services. His voice, distinctive as it was clear, unhurried and radiating calm confidence, never varied or sounded excited no matter how far from heading or glide path a pilot might stray. That approach (through the gap/slot) still in cloud with very gusty wind conditions not unusual, posed some difficulty for pilots with consequent tension, as might be expected. This condition was much alleviated by the steadfast calm of that voice as it guided them down with unfailing precision. He was not the only one, there were one or two others equally skilled and precise in their guidance, but the power of that hypnotic voice remains a vivid echo in Jim's memory to this day.

However, use of the ILS on those night and all weather freight operations with both Ansons and Dakotas had provided the opportunity for the pilots to practice (in good weather, with either r/o or co-pilot monitoring and able to have a clear view of the operation) landing the aircraft without looking outside and away from the instruments. Both types had handling characteristics ideally suited to achieving what, today and only at a limited number of major airports in the world, is done automatically with the pilots monitoring triplicated computerised equipment.

With landing flaps settings selected (and therefore control trimmers needing no further adjustment) and a steady rate of descent controlled by slight throttle changes, concentrating entirely on the glide path and direction needles (integrated flight control system in more modern times) and avoiding interference with concentration by turning down the headset radio volume, either type would fly gently down on to the runway – at which point the pilot could look up from his instruments to control the landing run visually. There was nothing clever about it. It was practiced by most of his colleagues on a regular basis rather than (in good weather) making a visual approach and landing.

Obviously, in bad weather and at any time with passengers on board, instruments approaches would be broken off to 'visual' at or before reaching the legal cloud base and visibility limits which up until his 1965 retiring date, for the types of aircraft he operated, remained (for airports fully equipped with ILS and/or GCA facilities) at 200 feet and 600 yards runway visual range – that is the visibility as seen along the runway and not that pertaining to any other part of the airport or its environs.

Before going on with the general description of the Berlin operation, and to remain in context with the somewhat technical aspect of the foregoing whilst it is still fresh in mind (or easily referred back to), the value of that practice was soon to be illustrated in stark reality – on a scheduled night flight from Berlin to Hanover on 15 October 1955 with a full passenger load.

The weather forecast at the 7pm scheduled take off time was for marginal landing conditions at Hanover, possibly deteriorating within two hours. The normal flight time was one hour 10 minutes, but in the event of earlier deterioration diversion to Hamburg, Dusseldorf, or even Frankfurt could be made with the fuel reserves carried – or for that matter return to Berlin, but with most of the passengers refugees it would be preferable to land in West Germany. Hamburg forecast was similar to Hanover, but Dusseldorf was expected to remain well above minima, as was Frankfurt, and Berlin itself to remain open until at least the early hours of the next day.

After changing over from Berlin to the Hanover control at the border (just past half-way and before passing over Wolfsburg, the famous Volkswagen factory) they reported visibility less than 400 yards with a vertical visibility (no clearly defined cloud base) 200 feet and deteriorating. Hamburg was reporting closed, weather below all limits. Dusseldorf was then contacted and reported their visibility reducing rapidly, already less than the 600 yards minimum. Jim decided that, if Hanover had not improved by the time they got there (to within the legal limits) they would have to divert to Frankfurt which, weatherwise, was forecast to be clear of the synoptic situation further north. Hanover control acknowledged that decision and gave permission to descend and approach to land if, when on final approach, conditions proved to be within limits. After a couple of minutes they came back to advise that Frankfurt airport had been closed due to totally unexpected deterioration in their weather, and that Berlin had stopped the departure of a Hanover to Berlin flight because their weather had become similar to Hanover's and was deteriorating even further.

Short of remaining airborne until running out of fuel in the vain hope that the weather would get better somewhere within range, there was only one decision to be made – a totally blind landing at Hanover whilst there was plenty of fuel to make several atttempts. Jim's co-pilot had done several of these landings with him in the good weather practice previously described. Hanover had a line of flashing strobe lights on the approach path, in addition to particularly strong sodium runway lighting, and was thus easily the best of all possible alternatives in the area. It did not, however, have GCA operating so the well-practised ILS must be used.

Hanover could not, in the circumstances refuse permission for the attempt to land even though by then the runway visibility was reported less than 50 yards and vertical visibility less than 100 feet. Jim reported when established on final approach and requested total radio silence to help him maintain concentration. Perhaps he should have removed his headset for, as 300 feet was passed (on the glide path), there was a blast in the earphones – from another aircraft reporting its position over Ghent (miles to the west in Belgium) on the same frequency which, as can happen, would have been due to the phenomenon of a freak radio wave 'skip'. There was nothing for it but to put on full power for an overshoot, his concentration badly distracted and, although the glow from the runway lights had been signalled ahead by his co-pilot, he dared not continue for a blind touchdown.

The second attempt went smoothly, the Dakmaster greasing on at just over the 100 mph she liked best for a smooth power-on landing. Keeping straight on the directional gyro until the tail was down and the tailwheel lock operative, helped by the comfortable feeling of being in the middle of the bright glow of the sodium markers (but now wishing to look up in case of becoming disorientated by the swirling fog – as car drivers will appreciate only too well in such conditions) they came to a rest somewhere along the runway to wait until a control car found them to lead the way to the parking apron. The taxi-in behind the car took over five minutes – to do what took normally about one minute. Jim never had to do another landing like that again, but kept on with those fair weather practices until retiring.

Back in Berlin, which like most cities (even some small individual places) had a distinctive smell of its own, changing little during the seasons. The atmosphere heavy with interior warmth, contrasting in winter with brisk cold outside, was the main difference. Rich gravies, strong cigars, and the scent of leaves rotting down to compost, all overlaid with a freshness from the vast areas of trees, parks, and lakes – that was the year-round background on to which would be superimposed variations engendered by individual life styles. It was bright, gay, and bustling. The bus conductors, on the very efficient, cheap, and wholly adequate services to all parts of the city, had a humour as outgoing and dry as their London cockney counterparts. A friendly and safe-feeling place for all its isolation amid the dour ruins and poverty of East Berlin and Russian occupied East Germany. It was virtually a new city – built-up from almost total devastation by the merciless nightly thousand-bomber raids (then the Russian shelling as they occupied the city in 1945) by sheer hard labour, to become a thriving, wealthy metropolis.

An exciting place with which Jim fell instantly in love and spent all his spare time wandering about away from the main streets, finding marvellous little cafés and pubs and everywhere openly friendly people despite the fact he spoke practically no German, and many of the simple people he met no English.

One night, during the first two week stint and having the next morning free of duty, he wandered into a very local pub near Sonnen Allee. It was a Friday (pay day) and the place was seething with boisterous workers, smoke, and unbelievable noise – happy, raucous laughter being the preponderant feature. The three-deep bar crowd politely made room for Jim to order a schnapps and a small beer, making it clear from their friendly attitude he (though obviously British) was very welcome. As he eased out towards the less crowded part of the place he saw a man sitting alone in one of the wooden booths with a chess set in front of him, but no partner – probably getting a drink. Their eyes met and, with a big smile, the fellow beckoned Jim over pointing to the chess set. The invitation was clear, and he did play a moderate game, so he sat down and shook hands after putting down his drinks. The man's name was Willy (pronounced Villy), and he spoke no English, yet, and it is extraordinary but communication between sympathetic natures does so rarely depend on the spoken word. By the end of the evening the two were feeling the very best of friends and made (date written for the following Friday) arrangements to repeat the meeting – Jim had won two to one; Willy indicated he would reverse the situation next time.

Because this was a time probably the most important in his personal life, indeed had a marked effect also on his future career, the narrative is deviating for a while from aeroplanes as such, though they do have a part to play – the very next afternoon for instance, on the Berlin/Dusseldorf/Berlin schedule.

The weather along the central corridor (it was June, and long before the October incident related before about Hanover, deliberately out of sequence) though not really bad was cluttered with very heavy cumulus cloud, some of which was growing in the heat of the afternoon into thunderstorms. As was the normal drill before starting the engines the air hostess (an employee of BEA who provided all the hostesses on those internal services, all of them German) reported to the captain that various actions had taken place, one item of which was that the outside control locks on the Dakotas had been removed and placed on board with the undercarriage ground-status steel locking pins – but she failed to mention the latter, said . . 'yes of course sir' . . when Jim asked and was promptly sent back to make sure and then bring them up for him to see. She was clearly furious at what was admittedly a pernickety order (though it was after all a matter of safety as much as discipline) but of course complied. Before she returned to her passengers Jim, having politely said 'thank-you Fraulein' . . . . ., told her that the corridor part of the journey would probably be pretty rough and, please, to make sure she was properly strapped in after ensuring the passengers did so when the warning light went on. High coloured and tight lipped she said . . 'yes sir, of course'. . . and went aft.

Sure enough, within twenty minutes and some thirty-five more before clear of the corridor and able then to manoeuvre round the heavier storms, the crashing and banging and bucking started in earnest. There was no way it could be avoided, and it was perfectly safe, but certainly very uncomfortable. All over after clearing the corridor, Jim went back to talk with the passengers and reassure them if necessary (a normal procedure in those days) to see there, in the rear double seat on the right side, an apparition of two long slim legs topped by a flash of brilliant white undies up over the back of the empty seat in front, hands gripping the seat arms, blonde hair all over the place, struggling to sit up – obviously she had not been strapped in. Perhaps she had been trying to help a sick passenger, thought Jim, anyway he quickly turned his back to speak with a passenger to give her a chance to recoup, which took her very little time at all. His face may have been expressionless, but his eyes certainly were not as they met two huge grey-green brown-speckled ones; there was laughter in both pairs.

Jim's invitation to a cup of coffee when they had returned to Berlin was accepted, turned into a glass or two of red wine and, after changing, a visit to a nightclub, and an intimate candlelit meal. He had a day off before returning to Croydon, the next day, and they met for lunch then she invited him home to meet her parents. A small world is so often proved right – her father was Willy! He was 17 years older than Jim, but they were like brothers. It was the start of a change of view and of life for Jim – a wonderful change which lasted for 25 years and a marriage which produced three children, the first of which was born in Berlin in 1958, and a lifetime of happiness – it was short, for she died in 1980.

After that initial two weeks Jim returned to Croydon to operate the normal route until on 17 July he was posted back to Berlin as managing pilot for the three months to 17 October 1955. The two latest additions to the Dakmaster fleet were registered G-ANTB and G-ANTC – phonetically Tango Bee and Tango See to the crews (Tango Bravo and Tango Charlie in the international code). Air Charter's DC4, registration ending in YB, was Yankee Bee. The three formed a happy and totally co-operative team, their crews all based in Berlin. BEA (to whom they were under contract) changed their crews regularly so, apart from a few, there was unfortunately little contact though, operationally, that did not matter. The German traffic staff, employed by BEA, were highly efficient and very keen. They soon became great friends, even to a point of rooting out of bed any crew member who may have overslept and not turned up in time for the 6.15am first departure, then after the final flight of the evening joining together for drinks and often a meal at one or other of the two major-chicken-rotisserie restaurants – the Huhne Hugo or the Weinewald.

All the air hostesses (stewardesses in BEA, but what's in a name) were German girls employed by BEA, as noted before, and trained in their very tough school in London (Heathrow). They were totally dedicated to their work, in true Teutonic fashion, spoke excellent English, lived in Berlin, and were absolutely superb at their job. It is not surprising that several of them married pilots and ground engineers based in Berlin – including the one who became Jim's second wife. It was in consideration for her that he again left Transair, in November 1955.

Although she was willing to return with him to live in England, he felt it unfair (until he was divorced, even though he had split with his first wife some time before their meeting) to jeopardise her work opportunities in her own country for, apart from BEA's much sought-after-work, Lufthansa were just about to be allowed to restart operations (ten years after the war in accordance with the conditions of the German surrender) and many new hostesses would be required there. So, whilst she continued to fly with BEA, they enjoyed a wonderful Christmas and New Year together, living in Berlin in an attractive flat right on the edge of Grunewald – the vast parkland/forest adjoining the Havel Lake.

Then it was down to the serious business (necessity) of finding a job in Germany and, after much to-ing and fro-ing, he started on 29 February 1956 (leap year) with the first of the two new west German air charter companies based in Dusseldorf – the other was based in Frankfurt. Previously owning a bus service on tours, Karl Herfurtner (in conjunction with the tours agency – Tigges Fahrten/Tigges Travel – with whom he had worked most with his buses) had acquired four Vickers Viking type aircraft, powered by two 1690 bhp Bristol Hercules engines – like those fitted to the Bristol Freighter. Jim was engaged as a senior line captain, working under another Englishman who was operations manager/chief pilot. His job was to help train German pilots who had not flown since the war into the up to date techniques of airline operation (at the same time fly the aircraft on tours) with a view to having sufficient trained and competent crews for the company to be staffed entirely with German nationals. It was thus a temporary position expected to last about a year, but presented quite a challenge – as was to be found out when getting down to the nitty-gritty of it!

21 Alternate – training west German airline pilots – The first post-war German air charter operations

Karl Herfurtner/Tigges Fahrten's operations manager, chief pilot, training and check captain was a very experienced English airline pilot – a man of high principle and top class ability. He was also a very nice person, with a charming wife and two bright daughters. His job was to engage and have trained into modern flight techniques (1956 stage) West German pilots who would form eventually all the company's crews. They were mostly ex-Luftwaffe (German Air Force) pilots, having flown Junkers 88 and Heinkel bombers during the war and with very little, if any, flying practice in the ten years since. There was one very experienced Prussian who had kept in practice in Egypt since the war and had been with Lufthansa before the war, and he was flying in command already with the company (long cigarette holder and all, like a cartoon figure; a 'Von' – and as it happened a very nice man indeed). There was another pre-war Lufthansa pilot, out of practice so flying as a co-pilot, who was also a very nice chap but extraordinarily humble-though proud enough of a pretty ancient heritage.

Jim's job, as senior line captain, was to take over en-route where the chief pilot left off with base flying training. In this he was assisted by a brilliant young pilot from Britain, engaged as senior first officer. Between the three of them, with two freelance British captains, a very full programme of tours flights was operated which gave the German lads concentrated and valuable on-the-job training, to which they responded well.

The chief radio officer was German, very experienced (German Merchant Navy trained) and an excellent operator and crew member – he had a tremendous sense of humour, was very modest, and had an insatiable appetite to a point where working when hungry was nigh impossible, so a special supply of sanwiches was provided for him on board on top of the normal food arrangements. He was very slim into the bargain. He was supported by four freelance British radio officers.

To complete the staff list as it was on 29 February 1956 there were two excellent (and perfectionist) ground engineers, both German, with a British one on temporary assignment until they were fully trained and licenced on the airframe and engines. On the longer trips, where engineering work might need to be done en-route, they came along and acted also as stewards in flight – to that date the company had no other cabin staff.

That was soon rectified. Jim's lass was persuaded to leave BEA for the position of chief air hostess and was, initially, to select and train four other hostesses. It was a responsible job, would give her invaluable experience if she did eventually wish to apply for a job with Lufthansa (or any other airline for that matter), the pay being almost double that with BEA. There was a contractual stipulation that she fly only with Jim or (in 'emergencies') with the chief pilot.

There was no shortage of applicants and in a very short time she had picked four girls, all speaking excellent English (though that was not necessarily a priority as all passengers were German tourists) who very quickly became proficient to fly without supervision. She had not found it easy to break away from Berlin and BEA, but at least she was employed in her own country (should anything go wrong between her and Jim), and there would be plenty of jobs open for air hostesses for a number of years with the resurgence of German aviation. The work with Herfurtner was extremely hard, particularly as there were no flight time limitations yet in West Germany, so working and living together in a pretty pressurised situation was certainly to be a strong test of their compatability.

The German pilots soon settled back into their old flying skills and the main job in training them, whilst flying en-route as co-pilots, was in modern airways techniques and the use of both navigational and instrument and landing systems – none of which they had seen before. It began to look as though the estimate of one year to bring them up to captain proficiency would be achieved with little trouble.

They were joined in March by the ex-chief test pilot for Willy Messerchmidt. Apart from the well known ME 109 which formed the backbone of the Luftwaffe's fighter force, he was one of the few who flew the twin-jet engined ME262 as well as the rocket-powered ME 163 fighter – he had seven emergency parachute escapes behind him!! He was a very quiet, modest little man who was, initially, quite nervous and lacking in confidence in himself and his ability to cope with the new techniques. It did take some time before he got back into line but, after being with the company until it went out of business in 1957, became private pilot to the managing director of a large chain of West German department stores – flying a twin-engined executive jet. He became a very close friend with Jim and his lass, and with the British first officer who too found work as a private pilot with a German executive aircraft after Herfurtner went out of business.

The entire staff were treated by Karl Herfurtner as family. He had two sons and a daughter, and a very nice wife who ran the hotel in Dusseldorf city centre which served also as the company headquarters. He was immensely strong physically, and hard headed – a rough, tough bus operator who stood no nonsense from anyone, but was also a big-hearted, kind, even sentimental character. He worked harder than anyone else (it was wondered if he ever slept) and would see off and meet every aircraft no matter how early or late in the day or night. He did have some difficulty understanding why an aircraft could not be flown if it had some minor fault – in fact his idea of minor was a bit like a bus overheating; able to stop to cool off before starting again, and keep going thus until there was time and facility to fix it. Technical delays (of which there were really very few) had him pacing around the machine literally chewing his nails with frustration until it was airworthy again.

Everyone got on well with everyone else and the atmosphere was cheerful, optimistic, and totally inter-compatible between the two nationalities – a very happy outfit.

It was a measure of the newness of the Germans being once again permitted to operate their own airlines that the chief pilot had no.2 Air Transport pilot's licnce issued for North Rhine and Westphalia – Jim had no.3. No.1 was held by a pilot with the newly formed Lufthansa, their new aircraft being crewed by BEA pilots who were training the Germans the same way as Herfurtner and the second charter company, Luft Transport Union (LTU), based in Frankfurt and operated by crews from Airwork Ltd. – also with Vickers Viking aircraft.

The Viking was an aircraft which might be called different. It has been given some very unkind names by pilots (the Flying Pig the worst) and someone once likened it to a petrol bowser to which some idiot had attached wings, fortunately powering it with two reliable engines. It was not a machine which seemed to fly naturally, but it was solid and, with faithful grumble-rumble Hercules engines, reliable. Once the landing technique had been mastered, a comfortable if clumsy old lady to fly. In the 36 passenger cabin the aisle was wide (half as much again as the Dakmaster) which was good from the cabin staff point of view, the cockpit roomy and comfortable.

Performance-wise it was distinctly uncomfortable in icing conditions, of which there were plenty. The wing leading-edges had strips built in which oozed out anti-icing fluid when required but it was not very effective and, aerodynamically, it did not take much ice to create instability and marked loss of airspeed (which increased power did little to help) plus a sloppy reluctance to maintain height. It was simply a matter of avoiding icing conditions whenever possible, and making sure the anti-icers were switched on well ahead of time if anticipated. It is the only aircraft (in 26 years of all-weather flying) in which Jim had been struck by lightning when airborne, and that happened no less than three times in each of three different aircraft of the same type in the ten months flying with Herfurtner – perhaps he was lucky with all the other types. Incidentally, it is not a dangerous situation (for the machine in flight is not earthed to the ground) but can cause serious compass deviations, and almost always affects radio equipment.

The first route to be operated was from Dusseldorf to Palma (Majorca) via Lyons each way to refuel, with further stops on occasion at Frankfurt and/or Stuttgart. It was at the latter one day that an incident occurred, in a sense amusing yet arising from deadly serious intentions of super-efficiency. The aircraft had flown, from Lyons then over Switzerland, in heavy snow and unavoidable icing conditions. After landing the engine nacelles were still full of snow and ice, the ground temperature at Stuttgart well below freezing, but the still running engines as they taxied in to the apron very hot and giving off great clouds of steam. Before reaching the parking area the airport fire truck came tearing across, red lights flashing madly, fire officers waving furiously for Jim to stop the engines (which of course he did instantly not knowing where the fire might be – somewhere out of sight?), then came great jets of foam over both engines, the cockpit in the middle copping it too with quite a dollop of foam entering through each partly opened side window.

Shame to say (in retrospect Jim has to admit, though already for that day in the sixteenth hour on duty and having just had an extremely unpleasant flight from Lyons, and nerve ends a bit ragged) the invective heaped (in German – he had by then mastered the lingo fairly well) on the fire chief's head was long, loud, and violent. They stood eye-to-eye, almost toe-to-toe in rigid silence for what seemed like minutes after the hysterical performance had petered out, the fire chief backed off and ordered his men and truck away then turned back to say . . 'Entschuldige, Herr Kapitan'. . with immense dignity. Jim realised of course that he should have been the one to apologise for behaving so atrociously – the chief had simply done what he honestly believed to be correct, and had furthermore reacted with his men very fast and efficiently had there indeed been the engine fire he thought taking place.

Jim did the only thing possible – held out his hand and thanked the chief for his prompt and, as he now understood, perfectly correct action, offered his apologies for behaving with such discourtesy and for his

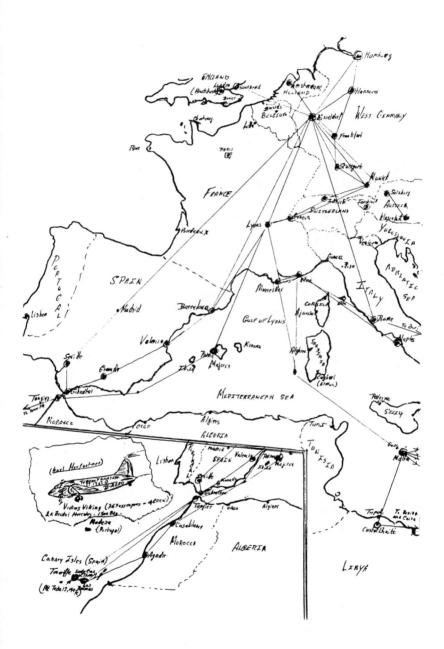

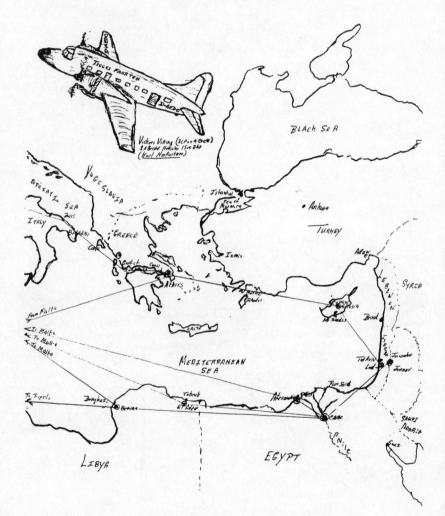

unreasonable rage. They shook hands, smiled and relaxed, and the chief accepted an invitation to a schnapps when he visited Dusseldorf in a few weeks time. Both being on duty there could be no question of a drink together that day in Stuttgart. He did turn up a week or two later, made himself known at the office, then met Jim's 'plane when it arrived just after midnight. He was introduced to Jim's lass, and the three (joined by Karl) had quite a few schnapps before a very early morning meal in a restaurant owned by a friend of Herfurtner who seemed quite used to providing meals at odd hours for his pal. So (sometimes!) friends are made. Incidentally, that fire foam did absolutely no damage to the aircraft or engines, and the flight continued on to Dusseldorf with little delay.

Back to the routing pattern. That Palma trip added Hamburg (with a different tours company doing the chartering) to the landing points a few weeks after the fire foam incident. Then soon, the company expanding rapidly, long trips at two weekly intervals began to be booked with groups of passengers spending two weeks in Israel, Egypt, Jordan, Italy and Malta, Spain and Morocco, and the Canary Islands via either Tangier or Casablanca and Agadir. On those longer flights (which took a group out to a place, returning with the previous group) a 'Reiseleiter' (tour leader) was carried which relieved the crew from any problems with difficult passengers, (and there were not just a few!). In fact the latter, not just the difficult ones, were so bullied around to make sure they got full value for money that the crews felt sorry for them. However, most of the time the tour groups seemed happy and enjoying the condensed knowledge being rammed home into them.

One the Reiseleiters was a particulary interesting man, also very fierce. It took a while but he and Jim finally found a compatability, after a few battles along the routes as to who was running the show (flight operation-wise). What he did with his tours charges was his and the tour company's business. A firm friendship eventually formed and it was then, and not until, that the story of his background was told. Before the war he had been a University professor, lecturing in the unrelated subjects of physics, history, mechanical engineering, and languages (he spoke and wrote, six – including Arabic!). He joined the Luftwaffe at the beginning of the war as an observer in Stuka dive bombers, being shot down on the Russian front, losing his right leg, and being taken a prisoner. Almost unbelievably he escaped, and found his way (on self-made crutches) back to his own lines near Stalingrad – in the winter! Since then the degree of his uncompromising temper depended firstly on how much that stump was hurting him, and secondly on the foolishness of whoever sparked it off. He had lost his wife in a bombing raid (British) but a daughter survived of whom he was inordinately fond.

Not long after Jim had returned to Britain he (the Reiseleiter) was one of two people out of 68 who escaped from a fiery aircraft crash – by jettisoning his artificial leg, which was trapped, and sliding out of the emergency window exit beside one of which he had always insisted on sitting – on whatever pretext he thought up at the time should any of his charges wish also to occupy that seat. There has been no news of him since that crash, other than he was not hurt, but Jim hopes that the luck of that remarkable man stays with him through the remainder of a happy and wholly fulfilled life – it was certainly a privilege to have known him and enjoyed his friendship.

Despite their overlong duty days, often close to 24 hours, followed by a few hours sleep then another long day/night, the crews remained happy together and enjoyed the push to get the company up and running. Jim and his future wife flew 931 hours together in the nine months and one week since she had joined the company, so they certainly had every opportunity to discover whether they could stand each other without serious differences. His job done, enough German pilots trained and ready for command (two soon became captains with Lufthansa), they left Dusseldorf to live in Britain and were married on Valentine's Day 14 February 1957.

Once again Transair re-employed him, Mr Freeman fervently hoping he had seen the final brainstorm as he put it, from Jim. He had!

22 Return to schedule – A few reminiscences – Back to Berlin – Introduction of the Viscounts

This time, 28 January 1957, Jim went back straight into command – after being checked out in accordance with the mandatory six-monthly check system introduced early in 1950 with the Airline Transport pilots licence (ATPL), to renew qualification on the Dakota aircraft and his instrument rating, an integral part of that licence. Those checks were carried out in those days on non-passenger flights, such as freight trips or local empty flights from base (still at Croydon).

Check pilots were nominated by the company and officially approved by the Air Ministry, and it was with great pleasure that Jim found Charlie Coates (the captain who had been injured in that accident in Belgium) had been promoted to training captain. When he first joined Transair in 1950 Charles, who had been with the company since its inception, had just returned to flying after having his foot repaired. They first met in the main hall at Croydon, a brash young Scot from Glasgow who had brought his wee Scottish fiancée to introduce her to his colleagues. He was short with dark curly hair, very large clear steady grey eyes with long eyelashes, small in stature, big in ability and humanity. Not at all handsome but a face full of fun and manner to match, debunking quickly and bluntly (yet without giving offence) anyone who got a bit above themselves – or showed the slightest lack of humility. His favourite slogan . . 'Amongst the quick and the dead, the unhumble are the quickest dead' . . holds very true in aviation.

As a line pilot he was exceptional. He had obtained, and kept valid, a first class navigators licence and, as the years went by, it became clear that he was a natural, and brilliant, training and check captain – a position he held with the company for the next 28 years before retiring to continue training on wide-bodied jet aircraft simulators. They and their families became close friends, the best Jim ever had, and it was a very sad day when he died from a heart attack in 1987, only a few years after retiring from actual flying at the mandatory age of 55.

Six years younger than Jim, he would have been one of the last of the third generation of pilots, and certainly had a tremendous influence on the development of the fourth, fifth and even some of the sixth generations. Being, as he certainly was, one of the best examples of the third generation, a wonderful husband and father, and a very real family friend, it seemed appropriate to Jim that this book be dedicated to him. It also seemed appropriate to include this short appreciation at this point in the book, at the stage when that friendship became a major influence in Jim's life, not least in his flying career.

Being winter when Jim rejoined the company most of the flights were freight and night newspaper ones, though early in April there was an interesting and pleasant charter to Lyons with a group of winetasters from the Society of Vintners, spending two nights and a full day there. It was a wonderful opportunity for him to catch up with Marcel and his lovely family – nine and a bit years since their friendship began during that 'Byway' trip to Australia. A new addition to the return freight loads from Hanover were the three-wheeler Heinkel Bubble cars – six at a time, which took some genius to load in a pattern which just, and only just fitted them into the Dakota's cabin. Their economy, reasonable price, side-by-side comfort, easy parking in cities, and excellence of construction had made them very popular in Britain. Then, three months to the day after they were married, he was posted back to Berlin as managing pilot – his wife going with him. This time the company was under direct charter to BEA, though Air Charter were still operating under their own contract.

The number of flights had been increased and in consequence two Dakmasters were based at Tempelhof, the second crew of two pilots rotating fortnightly by taking the early morning flight to Wahn (airport for Koln-Bonn), there changing crew with that which had brought out the newspaper flight from Croydon for them to do their two week stint in Berlin. When periodically one of the aircraft had to return to Croydon for a major check then the outgoing crew from Berlin would operate the early morning Dusseldorf flight with passengers, the seats being removed there to be fitted to the newspaper freighter (during thirty minute turn-round time) which then operated the return flight to Berlin. That change-over of seats and carpets was a job requiring considerable efficiency, despite the simple design of the seat attachment fittings, which the German ground crews everywhere took such pride in doing without delaying the scheduled departures.

At Tempelhof there was a resident engineer, a company employee from Croydon, supported by a local German one. They carried out the routine maintenance work between the major checks. Again it was a happy, trouble-free operation which continued to 30 October. Then it

266

was return to Croydon for a two week leave before starting again on the routine mail and newspaper flights, with just one charter and that to Berlin for BEA on 13 December. This coincided with the decision to use Transair throughout the winter based in Berlin – previously it had been only during the heavier traffic months May to October that BEA had needed the extra capacity, but there had been a sudden increase in passenger demand, in particular refugees from East Germany. So Jim and his wife were back there in charge of the operation until 31 October 1958.

Again the whole operation went smoothly, the two Dakotas flying even more hours than before, with Frankfurt, a new inclusion in the schedules. North-west corridor to Hamburg, central to Hanover and Dusseldorf, south-western one to Wahn and Frankfurt. There were morning and evening flights to Hamburg, Düsseldorf, and Frankfurt, with four and sometimes five a day to Hanover due to the greatly increased refugee traffic. There was a morning one to Wahn, and then a new schedule for an evening flight there which night stopped, returning early morning next day. The latter had to stay overnight to allow the crew a minimum rest period, flight and on duty time regulations having been very much tightened up. To quote from Jim's log book, which gives a good idea of the workload, the 582 flights with 682 hours by day and 215 by night (a total of 897 flight hours) in the 10½ months to 31 October, was still nevertheless able to be done within both flight and duty hour limitations for the two crews. The average time for each trip was one and a half hours, so it was quite possible (with the very quick traffic staff turn-round efforts at all stations) for the crews to fly and rest within the limits without undue strain. Although a good deal of the flying was on instruments, it was such a pleasant atmosphere of getting a good job done in conjunction with the efficient and friendly German staff (traffic, air hostesses, loaders, the lot) that it was never dull or boring and was very satisfying into the bargain.

Initially Jim and his wife took a flat right in the centre of the city, coincidentally named Düsseldorfer Strasse, near good shops and eating places, so that she did not have far to go for supplies. As she was pregnant that was a help, as most days he was away at work – also her mother and father were close by. After the baby, a girl, was born in May they moved out close to the Olympic Stadium to a half house in a small area, really a village, set in forest. The weather that spring and summer was mainly beautiful and it was an idyllic spot, yet the 'S' Bahn station was less than ten minutes walk away and the electric train ride direct to Tempelhof a mere 20 minutes so he was quickly home after work.

Unhappily her father, Willy, died in the September, young at only 57, but he had lung cancer. At least he had seen his first grandchild, and they were able to be there with her mother until, on 31 October, they returned to Britain. This time it was to Gatwick airport, recently opened after major terminal and runway works had been completed. Croydon had closed for good after 39 historic years as the birthplace of British civil aviation (except for the war years, when it was controlled by the RAF and had a Canadian (RCAF) group also stationed there).

Two weeks leave, during which they settled into a furnished rented house, keeping it warm for the couple who normally lived there who had gone to Lebanon (Beirut), where the man was on a two-year contract as ground engineer with Middle East Airlines. He was one of the engineers in Berlin during the early stages, where the familes had become friends.

Then it was back to the night mail and newspaper work until the end of November when Jim was sent off to the Vickers Aircraft Company at Brooklands for a two-week course on the new Vickers Viscount (three of which had been purchased by Transair) – the world's first prop-jet aircraft. It was all ground school (flying training would come later) and it was concentrated hard work, especially for those like Jim (now 40) whose minds had gone a bit rusty. There was a good deal of new technology to absorb – advanced hydraulic systems, electrical systems, pressurisation (allowing the aircraft to operate above 10,000 feet; to twice that height in normal cruising conditions), and very different performance parameters from the old piston-engined types.

Pilots from Airwork were on the same course, for that company already had two Viscounts (of a different mark from Transair's, though the differences were small) and had ordered two more, larger, ones. The two firms were to amalgamate, with Hunting Clan, to form British United Airways (BUA), the merger being completed later with Air Charter joining the new company, Gerry Freeman and Freddy Laker becoming joint Managing Directors. Having passed the course exams, there were two nights of freight flights on Dakotas before Jim was sent up to Derby, to the Rolls Royce factory, for a concentrated one – week course on the new turbine propeller power units, four of which were fitted to each Viscount.

Before being licenced to fly any commercial aircraft, pilots must pass a strict technical exam set, and invigilated, by the Air Registration Board (ARB). That covers construction, controls, hydraulics, electrical systems, engines and propellers, flight and take off/landing performance and restrictions, and use of the official flight manual specific to the type of aircraft.

Until now aircraft like the Dakota, Lodestar, Ensign, Anson and

Bristol 170 had been relatively simple. They were tail-wheel machines and unpressurised, their systems simple and uncomplicated. The Viscount was pressurised, had nosewheel steering for ground manoeuvre, and gas turbine engines. The electrical and hydraulic systems were very sophisticated by comparison with the older piston-engined machines, and there were new (and vastly improved) integrated flight systems though not computerised.

All that was very interesting and, once the rusty old brain cells had ceased creaking, enjoyable. The more so because the instructors at both manufacturers were superb, including the one who caused the back-to-school, prank-minded grown-up-child students daily amusement by (whenever asked the colour of various warning lights in the cockpit, which were red for immediate attention and prompt action or amber for less serious conditions) invariably answering 'reddish amber'. It was decided he must be colour blind, for there was no doubting his thorough knowledge of the subject. There was (in the illustrations of the control cabin, as the cockpit seemed now to be termed) clear indication of which light had what colour and why, so perhaps the fellows were being a bit unkind, but he took it in good part. Then it was on to flying training.

Having returned to the Dakota routes in the interim, on 3 April and 9 1959, eight hours of initial flight training was given on the Viscount – and that was it until January 1960, when training to the standard of co-pilot was given. That was followed by route operations in that capacity until 15 April (after several hours of gruelling checking out under that relentless taskmaster Charlie Coates, and by jove he was – it was a vast change from previous flying techniques, and it was hard; hard to the point almost of despair for Jim, and some others of the same ilk). 1960 saw Jim set out on his first trip in command. There had been 190 hours of check and double-check and route experience. The three and a half months as co-pilot was normal at that time in view of the very considerable change-up from the older type aircraft for pilots with years of time applying the fairly simple procedures with them, to the Viscount which cruised at twice the speed of a Dakota at twice the altitude. Those route trips had been fitted in with the normal Dakota routine, during which Jim had been upgraded and authorised to carry out six-monthly checks on other pilots in that fleet.

Apart from the ill-fated Comet Is in 1953, the Viscount was the first turbine powered aircraft in regular service anywhere in the world, that is airline service as opposed to military service. In October 1958 the first successful pure jet airliner, the Boeing 707 from the USA was introduced, flying close to the speed of sound around 30,000 feet. It was the ten years between 1952 and 1962 that saw the greatest ever impact on airline operations – significantly the era when piston engines were largely overtaken by turbine power. It was an era in which pilot thinking, attitudes, and training had to accommodate to a very marked change and become technically and operationally more professional. That is not to suggest that they had not been professional before, but that the new era demanded an upgrading as great as that of the rapid development of those very advanced machines. It was only seven years later still, March and April 1969, when France and Britain jointly introduced into the north Atlantic route the supersonic Concorde, flying at twice the speed of sound (1340 mph) and up to to 50,000 feet altitude.

To return to Jim's experiences which he believes were fairly typical of his generation of civil pilots. The reason why his Viscount training was put off for a year after the first eight hours was the effect of the company merger into BUA, and his own flipping about in and out of Transair. Seniority with pilots is, and always has been, measured by time of service with a particular company. Subject to normal competency (and no pilot lasts long in the business if he/she fails to maintain that, very high, minimum standard) promotion to new aircraft, either as captain or first officer, comes strictly in order to that seniority. It is not measured by total time in civil aviation, or by the total number of flying hours, and it is a hard and fast rule which the British Airline Pilots Association (BALPA) guards determinedly – as no doubt do most other countries' pilot associations.

There were at the time of the merger not many pilots in any of the four companies involved who were not members of the Association but, member or not, it made no difference to the strict interpretation of the rule. Jim had been back with Transair less than two and a half years, having served that time consecutively, not cumulatively – a deal less than several captains from the other three companies. Hence, and quite rightly, he had to wait his turn for promotion to the new aircraft. Had he remained for the full 10 years with Transair and not gone away twice, then his seniority would have been close to the top.

The merger itself went extraordinarily well – pilots, ground staff, ground engineers, traffic staff fitting in together at Gatwick amicably and efficiently. The operations department was greatly enlarged for to the Transair routes were added those of the other companies, plus new trooping contracts with the Navy (to Malta) and the RAF to stations in Germany now that the Viscounts were available and able to meet the Services' requirements for range, speed, and capacity – together with the economy of lower rates than could possibly have been offered using Dakotas, for instance. Air Charter brought their Whispering Giants (the four-turboprop Bristol Brittanias, famous for their extreme quietness) with seating capacity for over 100 passengers. Airwork had two Viscounts 736s, capacity 57 passengers like Transair's mark 804s (three of those), and the two Airwork mark 831s, capacity 67 passengers. To those were added the three Mark 833s from Hunting Clan, also 67 passenger capacity. The twelve Transair Dakmasters remained, though they were gradually sold off during the next two years to late 1962. The Viscounts started, during that time, to replace the Daks on the night mail and newspaper services.

The Viscounts pilots' training covered all four marks – the main differences being in the mark and powers of the Rolls Royce Dart engines and some slight differences in equipment. Extensive check lists for each type were used by the two pilots, going through every item together, for every phase of pre-take off, climb, cruise, descent, and pre-landing – also after landing and engine cut off. No problem therefore existed covering any mark differences, and the actual handling characteristics varied very little from each other so it was not necessary to have to use different techniques. They were all absolutely delightful to fly, more positive than the Dakmaster and not quite the Big Moth, but nevertheless they clearly enjoyed being in the air and were equally manoeuvrable.

Cruising altitudes varied between 15,000 and 22,000 feet, with speeds varying between 310 and 382 mph according to the aircraft mark. Approach speeds (that is on final approach) 140-145 mph, with landing (touch down) 130-135 mph. The landing weights varied, also with the mark, between 28 and 34 tons (avoirdupoids) but despite that fairly high figure compared to the Dakmaster the after-landing run was not long. The latter was largely due to a device operated by a switch, actuated by the undercarriage on touchdown (or in later marks by a lever in the cockpit), which caused the four wide-bladed propellers to twist into extremely fine pitch (called 'ground fine') which presented then almost flat 10 foot discs to the airflow, creating a strong braking effect similar to the reverse thrust action used on pure jet aircraft. It had to be a very short runway to need application of brakes before slowing enough to turn on to a taxiway, but if needed the brakes were powerful and fitted with non-skid devices.

Perhaps the most difficult thing to get used to was the nosewheel steering, operated by a small wheel to the left of the pilot (another to the right of the co-pilot who occupies the right hand seat), which was hydraulic and quite sensitive but very positive and not sloppy. Despite it being the first nosewheel steering (indeed the first aircraft fitted with a nosewheel instead of a tailwheel) he had used, it was a surprisingly short time before Jim (and the others) mastered it.

Hopefully the non-technical reader will not have become too confused with the foregoing, but it seemed right that an outline of the considerable technical changes conversion to the Viscounts involved (with which Jim and his colleagues had to come to terms and didn't themselves find at all easy either) before going on to describe the final stages of his flying career.

23 The Viscount routes – Again in Berlin; Some local 'colour' – End of the Berlin contract.

Jim started what was virtually the last five years of his flying career with a total of 13,056 hours, of which 10,636 was in command and 2420 co-pilot/navigator, and with his first flight in command of a Viscount (an 804) on 15 April 1960. It was a trooping charter with Naval personnel to Malta via Nice for refuelling, with two days off in that sunny island staying in the hills to the west of Valetta (capital) at a small hotel – the Xara Palace. The company had bought an oldish Hillman Minx car for the use of the crews, provided they topped-up the petrol tank before leaving. Public transport was scarce in Malta and virtually non-existent (other than by expensive taxi) from the tiny but historical village, in which the Xara Palace was by far the largest (and very imposing) building. Despite the varied interests of individual crew members (two pilots and two air hostesses) – wishing to rest peacefully at the hotel, go swimming, or meet friends in Valetta – there was never a squabble about who used the car, at least in Jim's experience.

That was a measure of the way the male and female crew members in the company worked as a team in harmony. It didn't seem to matter how the pilots rotated individually, or the hostesses, the harmony both on and off the job remained a wonderful feature of that company. Jim has always put that down to Gerry Freeman's consistently engendering, from top to bottom, a strongly family atmosphere. As with all families, disagreement did occur from time to time, but it was the resolution that won every time and never allowed clashes of personality on the job.

The trooping flights to Malta were regular schedules. A weekly (approved) service, as far as Benghazi ran to meet with East African Airways Viscounts which carried the passengers on to Nairobi, whilst BUA took over their passengers for the rest of the trip from Kenya to Britain. Landing to refuel (both ways) was done at Malta and the schedule was interesting in that the legs to and back from Malta (to/from Gatwick) were flown direct – no refuelling stop at Nice. Those direct flights averaged four and a half hours, too long for the standard Viscount fuel tankage. The liaison with East African Airways was one arranged with Airwork (before the merger into BUA) and their Mark 831s were provided with long range 'slipper' tanks, fitted as required, outboard of the engines – one on each outer wing. They 'slipped' on, bolted of course, and could be fitted very quickly to give a good one and a half hours extra range (some 450 statute miles) to enable the direct 1500 mile flight to be made. They were so cleverly designed that there was very little speed penalty, the extra drag of their bulk being minimal. (A similar mark of Viscount was also used in Australia, to enable direct flights to be made between Perth and Adelaide).

With the advent of spring and summer the tour trips increased – to Palma/Majorca, Basle and Toulouse/France, and Pisa/Italy. Some, but gradually fewer, Dakmaster flights were made, but there was a route addition on the newspaper flight to Düsseldorf (or rather from there) as landing on the return trip to Gatwick was made at Zuid Limberg in Holland (just north of Delft whence comes the famous pottery) which lies in the far south of the country. Textiles from there had replaced those formerly picked up in Lille, but unlike the Anson loads from there there was plenty of headroom in the Dakmasters after loading.

Alternations between Viscount and Dakmaster went on (flying-wise for Jim and others) until 22 October when he was checked out on the fourth Viscount type, the 736, which was different from the others mainly in that it was fitted with an American type automatic pressurisation system. The others had manually operated controls (through electrical connections to various switches in the control cabin – note again the upgrading from cockpit for that place up front where the pilots sit!) allowing for positive control in the event of any part of the system malfunctioning.

Not so the 736, and fortunately nothing much did go wrong, or rarely. On the odd occasion, for instance, when ice blocked the automatic opening and closing of the device which regulated the amount of compressed air flowing out of the pressurised cabin, the pilots had to keep adjusting (and very sensitive that was) the valve which normally remains closed throughout pressurised flight. If that sounds complicated – well, a full explanation of any aircraft's pressurisation system occupies several pages (including illustrations) in an instruction manual, so no need to say here other than it (the 736 automatic system) was a pest. Fortunately the two of that mark were used almost exclusively on a new BEA Berlin contract, where most of the flying was done (down the air corridors) under 10,000 feet and could, if necessary be done unpressurised, though normally a light amount was used for the better comfort of the passengers.

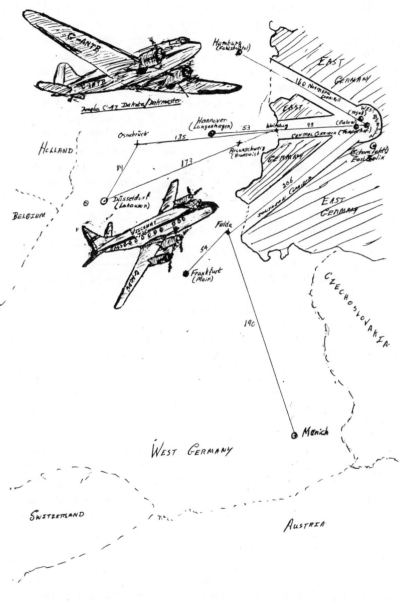

Re-positioned in Berlin 25 October 1960, as managing pilot again (this time with three children the last, a boy, only three and a half months old) they settled down in a large flat on the first floor of an old building whch stood alone (two blocks on one side and one on the other being open space where the bombing had demolished others not yet rebuilt). It was, however, one of the city's main streets quite close to the centre, and a short walk away from another along which ran a bus route direct to Tempelhof – a ride of only fifteen minutes.

There was a major shopping centre close by so trundling a two year old on foot, with the other one year old girl in a double pusher shared with the baby boy, was no great hardship and his wife's mother was around a lot of the time to help. Jim's wife was of course delighted to be back home, as was he for he had come to love the city and its goodnatured, friendly people. His German had improved considerably over the years, which facilitated making local friends, though most of those were either from her own family or the BEA traffic staff who, with visiting aircrew, made for a most acceptable social life.

The two 736s were crewed by one permanent (Jim and co-pilot) and two other crews who rotated fortnightly from Gatwick. The Viscounts, twice as fast and with almost twice the load capacity of the Daks, were able to fly many more schedules in a day, which required extra crew in order not to exceed flight time limitations (by this time those were very strict and unbendable).

The Berlin-based crew operated a regular route pattern, leaving Berlin for Hamburg at 7am up the north-west corridor – a threequarter hour flight, quick thirty minute turn-round, returning to Berlin by 9am for a leisurely and superb breakfast at Columbia House (the USAF Officers Mess/Club to which the BUA and BEA crews and their families were warmly welcomed at any time). Situated within the Tempelhof building complex, it had a view directly into the Luftbrucke Platz, named by the Berliners to commemorate the Berlin Airlift (the 'Air Bridge'). Further on was the memorial depicting a bridge at the base of which are the many plaques commemorating the names of airmen (civil and military) who died during an operation which carried even coal and petrol by air to help keep the city alive whilst under siege by the Russians. There are several publications about that incredible period which are well worth reading.

After breakfast, at 11am, they left for a one and three quarter hour trip to Munich, using the south-west corridor until out of it near Fulda (by Frankfurt), then climbing to 15,000 feet for the rest of the flight. Landing time would be just before 1pm, a full hour for lunch before leaving 2pm back to Berlin, arriving there 3.45pm. That would be the end of their duty day unless, and it happened fairly frequently, an extra flight was put on to Hanover (central corridor) due to the vastly increased number of refugees escaping to West Germany before the infamous Berlin Wall was completed by the Russians and East Germans. In that case they would not finish work until around 7.45pm, but then the next day they would not start again until the 11am departure for Munich, the early morning flight to Hamburg having to be taken by one of the other crews (whose rosters were more flexible than the permanent crew. They were only there for two weeks at a time and rest periods, in the form of days off, which could be taken on return to Gatwick.

Jim's co-pilot was an Irishman, a most amusing fellow with a fund of funny stories – and an excellent pilot, with whom it was possible in most weather conditions to share equally the take offs and landings. He would join the bus ride in the mornings a couple of stops further towards Tempelhof, his flat being in a modern building in a more newly reconstructed part of the city. He and his wife had no children. At work, and play, there was social compatability which was essential when living pretty well in each others' pockets for twelve months on end. A feature of those early morning bus rides, in particular Sundays, and observed from the upper deck, would be the number of drunks hanging on to lamp posts along the route. The time would be about 5.30am and the revellers would have been wrapped round those posts anytime between midnight and that time and they would stay there (their life support) until either sober enough to stagger home, or removed kindly by the police for a warm cell until fit to make their way home.

The main street in West Berlin is the Kurfürstendam, in some ways not unlike the Champs Elysée in Paris, for sidewalk cafés on both sides of the wide-pavemented street are numerous. They are open 24 hours a day, seven days a week, and are well patronised even in the early hours of the morning. They are enclosed to waist height (making a permanent street extension to the café, hotel, or restaurant running them) and are otherwise open in summer and those parts of spring and autumn not too cold. In winter and cold weather they are closed in with glass and overhead screening, infra-red strip heating on the walls ensuring a copy atmosphere, whilst patrons can still watch life passing by on the sidewalks and street. At night brightly lit, the length of the street, having many coloured neon signs in addition to very bright street lighting, with many of the streets leading off the main one also gay with colour.

At the top end of that wonderous street, standing at the centre of a traffic roundabout constructed round it, rises the ruined structure of the Gedächtniskirche, a church which was only partially destroyed in the bombing raids. It has been retained deliberately by the West Germans as a monument, a permanent reminder of the destruction of war, now renovated sufficiently to be safe for people to enter and climb to a viewpoint from which a lot of the city can be seen. To the east the 'Wall' which stands out like a hideous scar, the other side of which is seen the drab abodes (and still much in ruin) of East Berlin – an unhappy contrast to the mangnificently rebuilt West side with its bustling well-to-do life.

The last flight for Jim from Berlin on permanent posting was on 28 October 1961, returning to Gatwick with his family and to the new house they had bought just before leaving for Berlin the previous October. In the year he had done 890 hours flying, which covered 769 legs and checking his log book it appears that his Irish co-pilot got more than half the landings – 438 compared to his 331. And why not, he was a very good pilot and deserved all the handling practice he could get. It was probably also that Jim would have had to take on most of the marginal weather situations as a matter of principle, giving as much of the remainder as possible to his co-pilot who would, in any case, have had many full instrument approaches and landings during those.

The contract with BEA in Berlin went on another year through to October 1962, with another captain (married to yet another Berlin girl) taking over the management role and Jim joining the home-based crews on the occasional fortnightly rotation list. There were to be only two of those – June and August. BEA had found enough capacity with their own fleet not to need further chartering by the end of that October, passenger traffic (the flow of refugees in particular) having diminished somewhat. Also they were about to introduce the new pure-jet BAC 111 on that route, a machine produced to replace the Viscount and much the same size. That was to mean that operations out of Tempelhof would have to cease due to noise factor in the centre of the city, if not for performance restrictions with the jet engines. Operations were transferred to Tegel Airport (in the French sector) into which Air France had been running twin-jet Caravelles for some years.

BUA's operations from Gatwick had expanded considerably by the end of 1962, and a few regular airline schedules had been approved on top of the increased charter, tours, and trooping flights. So there was plenty of interest going on in the rapidly expanding company though Mr Freeman had left, which was an unhappy event for all the ex-Transair employees, and indeed for many from the other merged companies for he had cast his spell over many of them also. He deserved the break nevertheless, and would be very happy with his racehorses and many other, very wide, interests.

Landing and engines off –
24 The final stages –
Emigration to Australia.

In June 1962 a fifth Viscount type was added to the fleet – the mark 708. Three of them, and they were particularly interesting in that they were from the first-in-service marks (BEA had 701s) and had been operated by Air France, so fuel quantities and flows were indicated in litres instead of gallons/pounds and most of the indicator plates were in French. They also had a different type of non-skid braking system, French design and very effective once pilots got used to the semi-automatic operation. The British type, Maxaret, were fully automatic in that, no matter how hard the brake pedals were pressed, the wheels were prevented from locking by release of hydraulic pressure activated by sensors in the wheel assemblies. The French version warned the pilot that the wheels were about to lock by activating a foot-thumping device at the control pedals (a somewhat startling experience when first experienced) which left it to the pilot to release pressure himself. Once used to the smacking of the soles, the system was as effective as the British one.

Those differences from the other marks were really no problem and, once again to repeat, there was the usual check list for both pilots to use together to ensure no mistakes were made or anything forgotten. In passing it may be worth the comment (and Jim admits to this) that pilots' memories have been known to get lazy over the years, because they find it difficult without a check list. He, and some others of his colleagues, kept a small notebook on their persons to record names and facts they felt vital to remember – not just those fabled telephone numbers either!

These acquisitions, historically to note, were to replace the three Transair mark 804s which were sold to the Polish National Airline (LOT), going to Warsaw in the October of 1962. With them went a training captain (who else but Charlie Coates, as much probably for his unrivalled ability to get on with people as his undoubted technical capabilities) to train the Polish pilots accompanied by some ground engineers to familiarise their Polish counterparts. It was probably a very good deal which would more than have covered the purchase costs of the three 708s. So, G-AOXU, G-AOXV, and G-APKG changed their registrations to SP-LVA, SP-LVB, and SP-LVC respectively, the latter unfortunately being written off in an accident at Warsaw in the December of that year, after going into regular service with the airline.

Before continuing with what is, in effect, a short history of the BUA route structure in the final stages of Jim's experience, a technically non-detailed description of the main differences between piston engined aircraft and those with gas turbine power could be of interest. Most piston engines for aircraft are low revving (about half those for the average car), at something like 2700 revs per minute (rpm) at maximum take off power and around 2000 rpm when cruising. The Rolls Royce Dart-530 engines fitted to the 800 series Viscounts (similarly the Focker Friendships) spin round at 15,000 (fifteen thousand) rpm at maximum power and 14,200 rpm for climb and cruise (the 10 foot diameter propellers turning, though reduction gears, at 1/10th of those rpm). When taxiing the rpm are still high at around 12,000 rpm, which accounts for the high screaming noise outside the machine (also for pure jet aircraft, though their turbines turn around at about half the speed of the turbo-prop Darts). Inside the aircraft however there was just a subdued humming, a bit like a power house generator heard from a distance, and so very smooth, which was another marked difference from the pounding sound of piston engines.

To return to the flying scene proper, BUA and some other previously all-charter companies were gradually being allowed to operate scheduled services, at least where BOAC and BEA did not wish to go, for they had been until then the only two British airlines allowed to offer the general public regular scheduled transport. For BUA, originally operated with Vikings by Airwork, there were two routes which had in fact been licensed for some time – to Accra/Ghana in West Africa, and the one in conjunction with Sudan Airways since 1946 (in reality under charter to Sudanair) described in Part I. The west African schedule went, via Lisbon, to nightstop in Las Palmas/Canary Isles then via Bathurst and Freetown to Accra, returning the same way – a four day trip which was a welcome break from the monotony of the same day out and back to Gatwick flights which were the bulk of the current pilots' work.

The Sudan Airways trip was operated using their own Viscount 831, registered ST-AAN, with BUA crews doing the run from Gatwick to Cairo via Rome and Athens for refuelling. The stopover in Cairo was simply a minimum rest period from arrival in the early hours of the morning to departure late the same night – a good sleep in a top-rated hotel, until late afternoon, then an excellent dinner before going out again to the airport. Jim found in any case that Cairo had lost much of its appeal for him, so didn't mind much that there was no time to look around the city again.

Then an entirely new service was approved in the last quarter of 1962 – to Rotterdam twice daily (from Gatwick) morning and evening, with flight times averaging one hour 10 minutes each way. That was a fairly high pressure crew load operation, on a route with many required reporting points and in busy airways, but not all that different from any short trip in Europe – it was just that much in need of sharper reactions with less time to think than it would have been in a Dakota, to make a comparison relevant to Jim's 44-year old grey matter!

Shortly after, end of 1962, another new service was approved – to Genoa once a week each of a day and night service. The runway there was built out on reclaimed (or was it rock-filled?) land right alongside the extensive dockyards behind which the mountains at the foot of which the city lies rise near vertically to between 1500 and 3000 feet. In consequence the surface (and approach) winds along the runway were distinctly tricky at times, so the landing there was always a bit of a challenge – good, for in truth the opportunities for challenge and personal initiative were by this time beginning to run out.

That is not to say the work was beginning to get boring (in Jim's opinion the only really boring thing about flying, from the sixties onwards anyway, is being a passenger) but much of it had become routine and to an extent monotonous. He, and quite a few of his colleagues, relieved some of the monotony by giving the passengers a sort of running commentary on where they were, what was happening or about to happen (such as warning of the sudden almost cessation of sound when the Viscount's engines were throttled back for descent – that was very marked by the way) up front, and any bits of latest news concerning the places over which they passed. That was not unlike the patter he used to give joyriders, and from comments and letters sent in by passengers (even some RAF types) the practice was well received, so everyone benefited to some degree.

In the summer of 1963 a unique service was started, called the Silver Arrow, emulating the surface transport Golden Arrow train/boat/train service between London and Paris. Passengers travelled from Victoria station in London by train to Gatwick (the station there being part of the airport complex) in 45 minutes, boarded a BUA Viscount for a 35 minute flight over the Channel to Le Touquet where (newly completed) a spur line had been run to the airport allowing the aircraft to park right by the platform for passengers to continue to Paris by fast train – a journey not much over an hour. City centre to city centre time just over three and a quarter hours – much faster than any other service,

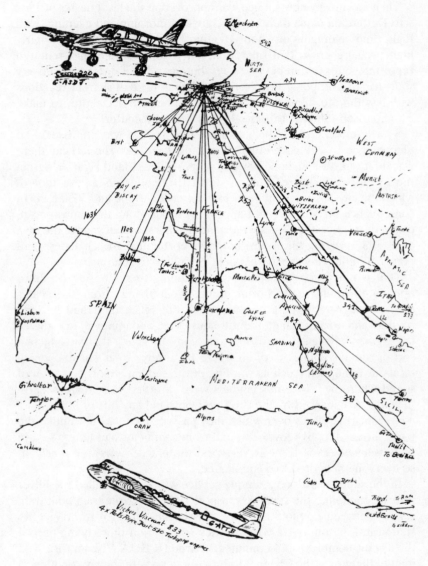

Distances in Statute Miles.

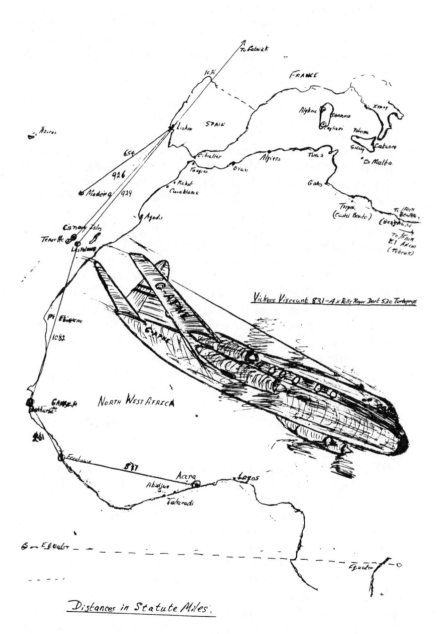

To Gatwick

FRANCE

1631

SPAIN

Lisbon

Azores

654

926

Madeira 929

Agadir

Canary Isles

Tenerife

Las Palmas

Gibraltar

Tangier

Oran

Rabat

Casablanca

Algiers

Tunis

Gabes

Tripoli
(Castel Benito)

Nîmes

Sardinia

Cagliari

Sicily

Catania

Malta

Italy

Taranto

To/from
Benina
(Benghazi)

To/from
El Adem
(Tobruk)

Vickers Viscount 831 — 4 × Rolls Royce Dart 530 Turboprops

Pt Etienne

1081

GAMBIA

Bathurst

261

Freetown

837

NORTH WEST AFRICA

Abidjan

Accra

Takoradi

Lagos

0 — Equator

Equator — 0

Distances in Statute Miles.

including customs clearances, less likelihood of weather delays as far as the flying side was concerned, and a good deal less expensive. The short flight appealed to a lot of travellers not too keen on flying, and was like old times – flown in sight of the ground and sea at low levels, not needing to exceed 3000 feet. Jim enjoyed renewal of acquaintance with his much loved Le Touquet, many of the personnel of 10 and more years previously still there.

Reference to the sketch maps will indicate the extent to which all services, tours, charters, and schedules had extended to 1963 and on to 1965. Jim has run out of instances, incidents and descriptions of which more detail would really be simply repetitive. There were a few more changes in the enormous development of BUA leading up to the introduction of their first pure jet aircraft and the phasing out of the Viscounts (so similar to that of the Dakotas) which are worth noting. The Britannia fleet became licensed to operate a scheduled service direct from Gatwick to Teneriffe in the Canaries, then BOAC relinquished their South American service to BUA, who acquired a Vickers VC10 four-jet airliner for the purpose. The route was from Gatwick to Las Palmas, over the South Atlantic to Rio de Janiero, down to Buenos Aires, then over the Andes to Lima in Peru. Both services made a profit, and were a feather in his ebullient cap for Freddy Laker (who had remained the sole managing director since Mr Freeman had left) and, maybe (just conjecture by Jim who had come to know the man fairly intimately) was the start of his planning to start his own company a few years later – Laker Airways, operating cheap-fare services in Douglas DC10 jets across the Atlantic to the USA.

Towards the end of 1964 the company had started to select crews for training on the pure-jet BAC 1-11 which was to replace the Viscount type, and this included Jim. The change in techniques and technical know-how would be small compared to that from Dakota to Viscount, and the new jet was reputed to handle very similarly to the Viscount, the main differences being the power control and the increased speeds and operational altitudes. He was excited at the prospect of finishing his career on jet aircraft, but he had started to worry about what he would do to support his family – he was soon to be 47. In eight years time he would be 55 and mandatorily retired from airline transport flying. His current salary was £3800 per year and there didn't seem to be much change after tax and mortgage payments – cost of living had increased enormously since the end of rationing in 1953 and had nearly doubled between 1958 and the present, indeed his salary in 1958 had been not much more than half the present one, yet ends had met then much better.

The Independent airlines had not been able to offer pension schemes for pilots, or any of their staff, until less than 10 years ago so benefits on retirement at 55 were relatively small. Jim's would have mounted to £982 per year at that age (as he discovered when taking a closer look) which was not indexed in any way to consumer price index though could possibly increase by as much again if negotiations between the companies and the Airline Pilots' Association bore fruit. With his three chidren in their 'teens at the time of retirement a pension (say) of £2000 per annum at very best, cost of living bound to be a deal more than now, and no job the picture certainly did not look too bright. To find any kind of work at 55 would be well nigh impossible, and in aviation the only hope would be in an operations department where very few staff are needed to service even a large number of aircraft and crews. That was a chance he decided he could not take, he was clearly at a major crossroads and a decision to stay or leave had to be made.

He made enquiries about emigrating to Australia where he felt that the future for the children would provide more opportunities than in Britain, also at the time work opportunities there for him looking quite good. There would be no hope of a flying job out there at his age now, but he had decided in any case that, unless staying with BUA, he would have to change direction completely. The Australian immigration people in Britain advised that, until he actually reached the age of 47 an application for assisted passage would be considered favourably, subject to medical checks for the whole family and satisfactory interview.

Jim and his wife talked it over for a week or more. Naturally, she in particular was very reluctant to travel so far away from her relatives in Germany, and they went deeply into every aspect about schools, work opportunities, housing and, most important, which state to live and their weather conditions. They made enquiries about selling the small home into which they had put so much thought and care – watching it built from foundations up. Planning features different from the usual basic design built-in, making a very beautiful garden, in fact doing all those things that go with pride of ownership of a first home. There was at least good news about that – the value of the house had almost doubled since they bought it in 1960 (another measure of how inflation was at the galloping stage) and a sale could be expected quite quickly.

Medicals were arranged and passed successfully, and in January 1965 an interview confirmed the family's acceptability for emigration on assisted passage of £10 each with nothing for the children then aged six, five and four. That decided it, they would go to Australia, so Jim gave notice that he would leave the company on 30 June. It was only necessary to give three months notice but, as he was due soon to start BAC 1-11 training it was obviously only right that he advise the company beforehand so that they could reorganise their programme. This they did and, as part of it, he was given a conversion training on the company's private runabout, a twin-engined Cessna 320a which the managing director and other top brass used. It was also useful for transporting spare parts quickly to wherever an aircraft may have become unserviceable, and for personnel changes to and from Gatwick or other places. It was a six-seater cruising close to 200 mph, the engines turbo charged at 350 bhp each – a very lively little machine with an excellent small field performance. He had 21 hours of sheer fun flying (between the Viscount schedules) in 18 flights from 26 February to 16 June.

The departure date from Southampton on the Sitmar Lines flagship the Fairstar was set for 14 September. A cabin on 'A' deck for the five of them was allocated with en-suite shower-cum-toilet (as in fact had most cabins on that ship) converted in Genoa from a British troopship. Coincidentally that date would be 25 years to the day Jim had sailed from Liverpool in the Duchess of Athol in 1940 for Canada, a liner then plying as a troopship.

The house was sold, completion in May just five years since they had moved in, the mortgage paid off leaving a healthy balance of nearly £3000 profit, of which £2000 (£A2500) was promptly lodged with the Savings Bank of South Australia, in the State they had decided to live and where a local building firm had sponsored them.

Jim's wife went off to Munich, then to Berlin to spend the remaining weeks with her family until he finished work on 30 June, the three children going off to board at the school they had attended by day. It was planned that he would then meet her in Berlin for a few days, return to England to make final arrangements for the shipping of their furniture, then meet her for a week in Paris. She had worked there for a year in 1950 for the Bouglione Circus (in the office – not on a trapeze!) but they had never been together in that lovely city for which both had very happy memories.

He took the BUA Silver Arrow to Paris where the tremendous increase in prices (unbelievable in the short time since he had last stayed there) caused them to cut their stay short. Nevertheless two clear days were very happily spent showing each other the places each had enjoyed so much before. She spoke almost perfect French, unusual for a German, with very little accent and he too managed the French accent well (if not the grammar – a bit like his German!). They took the Silver Arrow back to England, picked up the children from school, then travelled north to his parents' home for the rest of a beautiful summer there until the time came to sail – the children by then aged seven, six and five.

The leaving behind of all that had gone before, when it seems as the land fades away in an autumn mist such a final thing, inevitably sets the mind roaming in review. Standing together at the stern rail they were very silent, even the children, thinking their own thoughts – choking back the effects of the emotional farewells at the dockside. Jim found himself wondering how much he would miss flying, unrelated instances during 17,148 hours in the air (14,658 of them in command, 2490 as co-pilot and navigator) popping up and ranging through 29 years and hundreds of familiar faces. Suddenly, and they could not have stood there more than twenty minutes for it was getting cold as dusk fell, it was the faces that were tugging so hard at his chest – not the aeroplanes. He knew then that he would not miss the handling, only the knowing, the atmosphere, and the language and thought processes so special to aircrew. He supposed that most professions had their own special language, but he knew that it was not going to be easy to get used to not hearing his in the headset on the intercom, round the dinner table at nightstops, in pre-flight briefing and the Met office – most of all in the homes of colleagues who had become close friends over those years.

Two days later they were in the deep blue of the Mediterranean, sitting sheltered from the ship's 20 knot slipstream by the side of the freshly filled swimming pool, sipping cool drinks after having enjoyed a dip in the pool. The youngsters were splashing away, making friends (and enemies as oft the way with the very young) in the paddling pool area. It was peaceful and relaxing, a feeling of weight off the shoulders, the past slipping away and the beginnings of a new excitement stirring in Jim's heart; a feeling of satisfaction that the necessity for initiative and positive action to meet the new challenges ahead and was once again, like old times, to be set in motion.

His imagination, fired by the many stories and books he had read about Australia, its history, its outback, and its tough rough-and-ready people (their sardonic humour, their 'mateship'), was starting to bloom again. He was alive, and thinking, and active again in mind and body – a body grown too plump and soft, a mind part-addled by the constriction of rules and regulations – free again to think for itself, do for itself.

This new chapter in his life was now for real, the realisation a thrill motivating his whole being, years seeming to fall away from newly straightened shoulders. There were no more regrets – just hope, happiness, and determination to meet any new challenge head-high and head-on. And there were three weeks of perfect shipboard holiday to enjoy to the full before that new life began.

He came back to earth to find his wife smiling at him, wanting to know if he had been dreaming, as she had, about their future. They held hands, content as they watched their three happily playing offspring.

Even on board ship it seemed the airborne past was to recur, in one instance anyway. The captain made a twice-daily round of his ship, wearing white gloves which were not supposed to gather any dirt during his progress. It was a very clean vessel, the Italian crew and Chinese catering staff spotless and efficient. Once or twice during the first week he and Jim had eye contact and signs of recognition, but nothing jelled. One day, when the Captain happened not to be accompanied by another officer, Jim approached him to ask if they hadn't met before. Immediately his face broke into a big smile as he said . . .

'Now I know. It is your voice, the one I heard first on the passenger address system to advise we should be experiencing some rough weather ahead, when flying from Genoa one night six months ago. Then you came back to talk to us after we had finished bumping around. Then it was you in uniform and I in a suit, on my way from my home in Genoa after some leave, to return to this ship in Southampton'. . .

That of course led to quite a few more chats, then a visit for Jim and his wife to the bridge, and finally a call for them to go up there again to see Rottnest Island (lying off the entrance to Freemantle harbour) on the radar screen – and to say goodbye.

A final comment about airline flying from Jim, now as a passenger, is how sorry he feels for those poor souls up front on duty whilst he sits back enjoying a Scotch – always in the aisle seat if possible enabling him to catch the air hostesses' attention more quickly, without disturbing the other passengers. At least that's HIS story about choice of seat!

GLOSSARY OF AVIATION TERMS

Hallo, I'm Jim. As the explanations which follow are largely my own interpretations (may well not be found in any official manual) it seems appropriate that I accept full responsibility in person.

It is emphasised that the aeronautical terms are those used in this book (unavoidably) and certainly are not a full list. The descriptions are intended to help the general reader follow, in fairly simple terms, what Wilf's been on about in the text.

Pilots, and budding pilots, please ignore and get into your official manuals!

AAF   – Auxiliary (Royal) Air Force: (Britain).

Altitude   – Height above mean sea level as indicated by the altimeter in a cockpit CORRECTED for both DENSITY and PRESSURE of the air being flown through.

Approach   – The path followed by an aircraft intending to land. *Initial Approach* is when entering the vicinity of a landing ground (airport, airfield, aerodrome, field, or strip). *Final Approach* is when lined-up with the runway to be used for landing, and on final descent.

ASI   – Airspeed Indicator: instrument on dashboard.

ATA   – Air Transport Auxiliary: civilian wartime Aircraft Ferrying Service, internally, in Britain.

ATFERO   – Atlantic Ferry Organisation (after 1941 Atlantic Ferry Command): wartime Bomber ferry unit from Canada and the USA.

D/G   – Directional Gyro: an instrument indicating in degrees (000 – 360) the aircraft's heading – usually set for magnetic heading.

D/R   – Dead Reckoning: position calculating, based on estimates of ground speed and track made good over the ground/sea – (i.e: no positive clues from radio, radar, astro sights etc). Has been described, when practised as a necessity, as the 'Art of Intelligent Guesstimation' (using ALL of whatever known FACTS are available).

Drift   – The angle and rate at which an aircraft is affected by the upper wind speed and direction causing its (the aircraft's) directional movement over the surface to

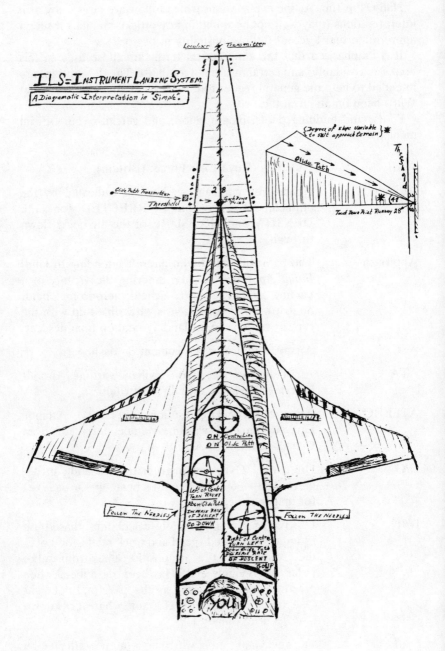

DRIFT

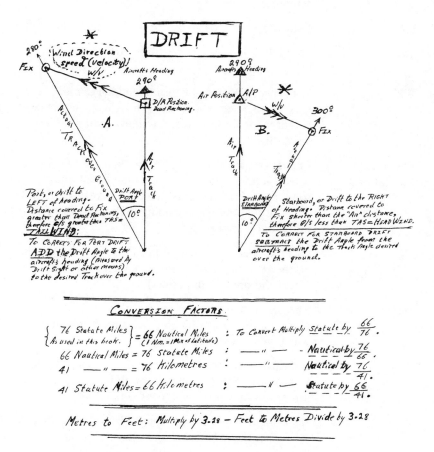

A.

280° — Wind Direction speed (velocity) W/V

FIX — Aircraft's Heading 290°

D/R Position. Dead Reckoning.

Actual Track over Ground

Air Track

Drift Angle PORT — 10°

Port, or drift to LEFT of Heading. Distance covered to Fix greater than Dead Reckoning, therefore G/s greater than TAS = TAIL WIND:
To CORRECT FOR PORT DRIFT ADD the Drift Angle to the aircraft's heading (measured by Drift Sight or other means) to the desired Track over the ground.

B.

290° Aircraft's Heading

Air Position A/P

W/V — 300° FIX

Air Track

Track

Drift Angle STARBOARD — 10°

Starboard, or Drift to the RIGHT of Heading. Distance covered to Fix shorter than the "Air" distance, therefore G/s less than TAS = HEAD WIND.
To CORRECT FOR STARBOARD DRIFT SUBTRACT the Drift Angle from the aircraft's heading to the Track Angle desired over the ground.

CONVERSION FACTORS.

76 Statute Miles (As used in this book.) = 66 Nautical Miles (1 N.m. = 1 Min. of latitude) : To Convert Multiply Statute by $\frac{66}{76}$.

66 Nautical Miles = 76 Statute Miles : — " — Nautical by $\frac{76}{66}$.

41 — " — = 76 Kilometres : — " — Nautical by $\frac{76}{41}$.

41 Statute Miles = 66 Kilometres : — " — Statute by $\frac{66}{41}$.

Metres to Feet: Multiply by 3.28 — Feet to Metres Divide by 3.28

differ from both heading and True Airspeed (TAS): *See diagram.*

ERFTS — Elementary Reserve Flying Training School: Civilian flying school training RAFVR pilots – The instructors are RAF or RAFVR qualified, trained to RAF standards.

eta — Estimated Time of Arrival: (ata – Actual Time of)

etd — Estimated Time of Departure: (atd – Actual Time of)

FIX — A positive position, by visual landmark, radio bearings, astro observation (star/sun sights using sextant/octant) – or more modern systems (Doppler/Decca/Loran/Inertial).

Flight Time Limitations — Mandatory maximum hours in flight by day/night, week, month, annually for commercial pilots (in some cases private pilots) and, PARAMOUNT, the daily hours on duty, including flight, and associated minimum rest periods.

G/S — Ground Speed: the actual speed made good over the earth. (It equals the True Airspeed (TAS) plus or minus the upper wind effect).

Height — The static height above mean sea level of a fixed object on earth (mountain, radio mast, or anything which poses a hazard to flight).

IAS — Indicated Airspeed, as shown on the Airspeed Indicator (ASI). (Corrected for altitude and temperature becomes the True Airspeed (TAS).

IFR — Instrument Flight Rules: apply whenever an aircraft is in other than clear sky, and whenever in controlled airspace regardless of weather conditions.

ILS — Instrument Landing System: *see diagram.*

RAFVR — Royal Air Force Volunteer Reserve.

RVR — Runway Visual Range: the visibility along a runway itself, as opposed to the general area visibility-landing minima are based on this factor.

TAS — True Airspeed: that shown on the Airspeed Indicator

(ASI) CORRECTED for altitude and temperature, giving the actual speed of progression through the air. (Upper wind speed and direction affects TAS to result in Ground Speed).

VFR – Visual Flight Rules: apply solely when flight is made in clear air OUTSIDE controlled airspace.